Warren Buffett
THE GOOD GUY
OF WALL STREET

Warren Buffett

THE GOOD GUY OF WALL STREET

by Andrew Kilpatrick

Ⱥimus **DONALD I. FINE, INC.** *New York*

For Pat

CONTENTS

ACKNOWLEDGMENTS

Writing a book is a journey. Along the way, in my case, there were a few cold shoulders and such comments as "deep six it," "put it aside," "please don't come for the interview," "I don't know you," and "from where?"

A few people who knew me did not grant interviews. Please don't read too much into that. Some people who had never heard of me gave interviews on the spot.

Overall, people were gracious, hospitable, helpful and encouraging.

Almost always, the more prominent a person's station in life, the easier they were to deal with. Time Warner's J. Richard Munro; Coca-Cola's Don Keough; and Miami Dolphins coach Don Shula were the standout examples.

In general, lips became tighter the closer one got to Buffett, no doubt out of respect for his much coveted privacy.

My heartfelt thanks to those who helped with this book go to:

Frances Kilpatrick, my mother, who expressed her stand with: "Please don't bother Mr. Buffett." The Securities and Exchange Commission in Washington, where folks were surprisingly helpful. My wife, Patricia Ann Burgess Terrell Kilpatrick of Birmingham, Alabama. My agent, Robin Straus, who gives agents a good name. The publisher, Donald I. Fine, president of Donald I. Fine, Inc., for taking a chance on a fellow writing his first book, and my editor, Sarah Gallick. Irving Fenster of Tulsa, Oklahoma, a Buffett admirer since the days of the Buffett Partnership, who provided a set of partnership letters. Michael Yanney of Omaha, Nebraska, who has friends whose last names are Buffett.

Most particularly of all, I would like to thank Harvey Terrell of Birmingham, who was the most reassuring of anyone along the way that I had a worthwhile project.

Enormously helpful with editing was Michael Assael, lawyer, accountant, author, linguist and investor—and thanks to his wife, Eiko.

Also: the late Robert Baker, of Chagrin Falls, Ohio, who gave the book his careful legal eye. Yves Mojonnet, of Sausalito, California. Bob Flood, of Omaha, who made the Omaha Public Library user-friendly. Marilyn Nash, of Birmingham, who can audit commas and help the hopeless become a little bit computer literate. George Eyraud, of Birmingham, who said, "You know, $100 million doesn't mean much to you and me, but it does to Warren Buffett." Jane Liss, of Columbus, Nebraska, who never missed a clip about Buffett published in Nebraska. Judy Prus, of Grosse Pointe Farms, Michigan, a woman who spells class. Tommy and Jane Johnson, of Birmingham, friends with a lakehouse, who provided the first word of encouragement. LaVerne Ramsey, of Birmingham, the Berkshire shareholder who asked Buffett the Kitty Kelley question and got: "What you see is what you get." Many photo credits go to her, although the photo of the four generations of Buffetts was supplied by Buffett's son, Howard, a former county commissioner in Omaha, and the photo of young Warren was supplied by Buffett's sister, Doris B. Bryant, of Morehead City, North Carolina.

And: Mary Jean Parson of Birmingham. Marie Stokes Jemison, of Birmingham, for early help. Gayla Watt, of Birmingham, who said it could be done in two years. Tom Hargrove, of Washington, D.C. Ed Taff, of Boston, Massachusetts, a Berkshire shareholder since the early days. Scott and Nan Shelley, of Birmingham. Paul Finebaum, Bobby Frese and Ellen Hardeman Wheeler, of Birmingham. Joanne Englebert, of Birmingham. Glory Angell, Melanie Parker, Tim Callahan, Mike Klyce, Clark Scott and Romaine Scott, William Billingsley and Gracie Kendrick, all of Birmingham, for varieties of support. Plus Nez Calhoun, who said: "He looks like Jack Benny." Bobby Vann, of Birmingham, for his reading. Wendell Givens, of Birmingham, an old pro newspaperman. Dr. Frank Kilpatrick and Robert Kilpatrick, of Madison, Wisconsin. Kay Kilpatrick, of Birmingham, for a technical assist. Peter Bradford of Nassau, New York, my old tennis partner.

My children, Jack and Anna Kilpatrick, of Birmingham, who I hope one day will write their own books that I can edit.

George Morgan, of Omaha, J.P. Morgan's distant cousin and commander-in-chief of "Buffett Wannabes." Tommy, Michael and Mark Terrell, of Birmingham, who said: "Buffett is right about Coca-Cola stock."

Ann Landers, who made my day at the Birmingham *Post-Herald* when she called.

Susan Buffett Greenberg, of Omaha.

Crawford Johnson, Claude Nielsen, Luke Cranford and Robert Lovell of Birmingham, who say, "Drink Coca-Cola." And James Abele, of Birmingham, who says, "I used to drink Pepsi. Now I drink Coca-Cola."

Finally, Berkshire Hathaway's administrative assistant, Mrs. Gladys Kaiser, who patiently endured a battery of fact-checking questions. She's a great American who brushes her teeth twice a day.

PREFACE

"I wish you well, but not too well."

This book is about legendary investor Warren Buffett, his spectacular investment vehicle, Berkshire Hathaway Inc., and the range of businesses he and Berkshire control.

These pages are a look at Buffett's business and investment as well as his driving wit and wisdom.

The work has neither Mr. Buffett's approval nor disapproval. He is contemplating a book of his own and does not plan to help others with works about him. He told me this in person the day before the annual meeting in 1990 and was most cordial about it.

Later in the year I wrote Berkshire shareholder Ann Landers a request for an interview. Apparently she forwarded my letter to Buffett, who sent me a copy of his reply to her: "Andy Kilpatrick is a decent and well-intentioned fellow, but I am not personally cooperating on the book. On the other hand, whatever my friends decide to do is up to them . . . someday I'll write my own book . . . and I don't see any sense in giving away any of the punch lines." At the bottom he added: "Andy, As you can see, I wish you well, but not *too* well. Actually everything I do is public, so I am trying to save a few things for a fresh look at some time. Warren."

I make no claim to know Buffett well, although I have watched him, mainly at Berkshire Hathaway annual meetings and related functions for nearly a decade. I have met him several times and had brief conversations, and he has responded kindly to a few letters.

I first became interested in Buffett as a result of his investment in the Washington *Post*, where my father, the late Carroll Kilpatrick, was White House correspondent from 1961 through 1975. My father and I were always amazed that one person could own such a huge piece of an enterprise such as the *Post*.

It should be noted that I am a longtime Berkshire shareholder and regard Buffett, as do so many people, as an extraordinary combination of financial genius, impeccable ethics and a wonderful sense of humor.

Although I do not fully approve of the tactic, I occasionally have injected the first person and hope the reader finds it provides useful information.

The book is generally chronological, although the chronology sometimes is broken to group together Berkshire's major, "permanent" investments, its "Sainted" businesses and the company's preferred stock holdings. Some chapters, like the man himself, simply stand alone.

1 WHO'S WARREN BUFFETT?

"I will attempt to answer any questions in the manner of a fellow who has never met a lawyer."

The financial news wires were crackling on the afternoon of August 16, 1991.

"S&P puts Salomon ratings on creditwatch: Negative."

"Salomon stock, bonds plunge on spreading scandal news."

"Salomon says Gutfreund, Strauss prepare to resign."

As Salomon's world was crashing all around, another bulletin said: "Salomon says Buffett to become interim chairman."

Who?

Omaha, Nebraska, multi-billionaire Warren Buffett is arguably the world's greatest investor. With a net worth of more than $4 billion he made from scratch, Buffett is now one of the largest stockholders in a number of America's best regarded companies. Buffett's Berkshire Hathaway Inc. has a $300 million investment in American Express, $700 million in Salomon Brothers and about *$4 billion* in The Coca-Cola Company.

Buffett's Los Angeles-based longtime partner, Charles Munger, a *magna cum laude* graduate of Harvard Law School, has said, "There were a thousand people in my Harvard Law class. I knew all the top students. There was no one as able as Warren."

Famous to an ever growing cadre of investors, Buffett has nevertheless remained largely unknown to the general public because of his private, shun-interviews, down-home lifestyle. But the bond trading scandal at Salomon, the giant securities firm, finally forced him into the limelight.

Salomon's stock plummeted after revelations that its traders had broken the law by buying up more than the legal limit of Treasury bonds at government auctions. When it was learned that top management at Salomon had known about the violations for months but had failed to report them, the matter became a full-blown scandal.

Buffett was the one person the firm, its clients, the U.S. government, regulators, investigators and investors could trust to restore Salomon's shattered reputation.

Salomon spokesman Robert Baker, who spoke with Buffett often during the crisis, said, "He's everything as advertised and more. Everytime I told him something he was waiting at the end of the sentence for me . . . and his moral compass is due North."

Within hours of being called upon to serve as Salomon's chairman, Buffett saddled up the corporate jet he has dubbed "The Indefensible," the only expensive worldly trapping he owns, and flew to Teterboro, New Jersey, from whence he made his way to downtown Manhattan and 7 World Trade Center, Salomon's one-million-square-foot headquarters.

In the midst of client defections, as he prepared to take the top position at the firm, Buffett met immediately with its managing directors and told them point-blank Salomon's reputation was on the line. Staying just within the bounds of the rules, he warned, would NOT be acceptable—the future of Salomon depended upon the firm's reputation. No reputation, no Salomon.

Buffett told them that the firm faced fines and litigation, that he would name a chief operating officer and that after an emergency board meeting Sunday, August 18, he would hold a press conference.

That was news in itself because Buffett practically never holds a press conference and rarely grants interviews.

Salomon executives were impressed enough with Buffett's first appearance before them to break into applause.

At the dramatic board meeting the following Sunday, Buffett accepted the resignations of Salomon's top executives: John Gutfreund, chairman; Thomas Strauss, president; and John Meriwether, vice chairman, the three men who admitted being aware of the unreported violations.

It would be only hours before the names of those implicated in the scandal were removed from the directory on the main floor of the headquarters building and the name of Warren E. Buffett inserted in an alphabetical listing of Salomon's top officers.

In combating the scandal, Buffett also fired two men in the bond trading department, named a new chief operating officer and put tighter internal controls in place. He would subsequently fire Salomon's law firm.

In the midst of all this chaos, Buffett managed to convince U.S. Treasury Secretary Nicholas Brady to reverse the major portion of a potentially crippling, five-hour-old ban on Salomon's highly profitable government securities trading.

This reprieve allowed Salomon to continue bidding at government bond auctions for its own account, even though it was still prohibited from placing orders for customers. In the process, Buffett drew Brady's warm praise.

Buffett, already ensconced in Gutfreund's forty-third floor office, next went out to meet with reporters. He won them over quickly by saying, "I will attempt to answer questions in the manner of a fellow who has never met a lawyer. We'll stay as long as you wish."

In the next three hours he laid it out straight, saying, "It looks to me, like in the case of the two people we fired, there were things done you and I would characterize as a coverup."

In his inimitable homespun style, Buffett described the Salomon atmosphere as "what some people might call macho and others cavalier." He added, "I don't think the same things would have happened in a monastery."

He was asked if he had read *Liar's Poker,* Michael Lewis's book about Salomon's rough-and-tumble corporate culture.

Buffett said he had. Well?

"I just don't want there to be a second edition," he replied.

The next day Buffett was off to Washington to meet with regulators and to continue his mission to save Salomon.

About a week later he was giving a fifteen-minute pep talk beamed to Salomon sales offices around the world. "I don't want anyone playing close to the lines . . . ," he counseled. "You can do very well hitting down the middle of the court."

Later he added, "If you lose money for the firm by bad decisions, I will be very understanding. If you lose reputation for the firm, I will be ruthless."

As the crisis unfolded, Buffett had to make fast decisions about how best to keep clients, how to minimize employee defections, how to reassure Salomon's creditors and the government. He decided to sell some $50 billion of Salomon's securities to finance the firm's operations to keep it competitive.

The government seemed reassured by Buffett's leadership at the firm. Investors and clients breathed a sigh of relief and Salomon's stock price, which had lost half of its value during the ordeal, steadied, then began to climb back.

For Buffett, who far prefers his quiet existence in Omaha, it was an action-packed time of racing from Nebraska to New York and Washington and living out of a suitcase.

Asked if that were a problem, Buffett quipped, "My mother's sewn my name in the underwear, so it's all okay."

2 OF PERMANENT VALUE

"I love what I do."

Imagine if back in 1956 you had invested $10,000 in a partnership founded by Warren Edward Buffett.

When that investment vehicle—Buffett Partnership Ltd.—disbanded in 1969, you could have chosen to reinvest in an ongoing business called Berkshire Hathaway that Buffett also ran.

Had you done so, your $10,000 would be worth about *$40 million* today, a 4,000-fold return in an era when the Dow Jones Industrial Average rose about six-fold.

Since 1956 Buffett has built a financial empire beyond anyone's wildest dreams. Buffett and Berkshire now control some of the world's most prominent businesses, including a seven percent stake in The Coca-Cola Company worth about $4 billion.

If your investment made you a millionaire, you may wonder what it did for Buffett. Answer: It made him a multi-billionaire.

Buffett owns about 42 percent of the stock of Berkshire, an investment company that has vast stock and bond holdings and a number of operating businesses.

Because of Buffett's huge stake in Berkshire, in many ways Buffett is Berkshire and Berkshire is certainly the creation of Buffett. He is fond of saying that "In a sense Berkshire Hathaway is a canvas, and I get to paint anything I want on that canvas. And it's the process of painting that I really enjoy, not selling the painting."

Warren Buffett is the Michelangelo of business.

"I love what I do," he told L.J. Davis in the New York *Times Magazine* (April 1, 1990). "I'm involved in a kind of intellectually interesting game that isn't too tough to win, and Berkshire Hathaway is my canvas. I don't try to jump over seven-foot bars: I look around for one-foot bars that I can step over. I work with sensational people, and I do what I want in life. Why shouldn't I? If I'm not in a position to do what I want, who the hell is?"

Berkshire's record vies with almost anything in American business. Yet Buffett—enormously famous in financial circles—was still largely unknown, until he stepped in to save Salomon. He managed one of America's largest corporations from a small office in a nondescript building in midtown Omaha, Nebraska.

Over the years, as Buffett has sat in the office reading and thinking, he has spawned billions of dollars in shareholder value, making multi-millionaires of dozens of early investors and ordinary millionaires of hundreds more.

Berkshire's stock traded at the end of 1991 at $9,050 a share, higher than any other stock on the New York Stock Exchange and sky-high above its give-away 1965 price of between $12 and $13.

Since 1965 Berkshire is up about 700-fold during a time the Dow Jones Industrial Average is up less than four-fold from about 900 to about 3,000.

By comparison General Motors stock trades at roughly the same price it did in 1965, with just one 2-for-1 split along the way in 1989. You can say that General Motors, during that time, doubled in price and paid a handsome dividend. But the return on Berkshire stock has been up about 4,000-fold for those who joined Buffett in his partnership in 1956.

So how did Buffett multiply his money 4,000 times over the past thirty-five years?

Said simply, he compounded the invested money at a shooting star pace. But how he achieved his remarkable results—through his trademark value-oriented, marathon distance investing—is even more remarkable.

Buffett Partnership, in its thirteen years, never had a down year, despite some threatening bear markets. Instead, it forged a 29.5 percent compound annual rate of return. And Berkshire's own annual increase in stock price, about 25 percent a year, has exceeded its annual return on book value of better than 23 percent.

Although Berkshire stock has had several years in which it ended lower than it began, Buffett has *never ever* had a down year for return on stockholders' equity, a unique record that defies anything in the business world.

Along the way Buffett created an enterprise of permanent value, enormous permanent value.

He essentially did it making a few large, wildly successful decisions. More than half his net worth is attributable to less than a dozen investment decisions. "We own fewer stocks today at $7 billion than we did when the total portfolio was $20 million," he announced at the 1991 annual meeting.

He made most of these investments at distressed times and bargain prices. He held on for the long term, through good times and bad, for a far sunnier day. "Time is the friend of the wonderful business, the enemy of the mediocre," he said in Berkshire's 1989 annual report.

When it comes to investing, Buffett is a marathon man. Beyond the dollars Buffett has accumulated, beyond the worth of the businesses and the stocks and bonds Berkshire owns, there is an even greater value.

The permanent value he has created is a statement—a statement about how to do things right, how to do them ethically, sensibly, simply and inexpensively.

There is, for example, no waste.

In some years, Buffett, who would get no objection from Berkshire shareholders were he to pay himself $10 million a year, lowers his salary several hundred dollars. Usually he keeps his salary at the current rate of $100,000 a year, making him one of the lowest paid

Fortune 500 chief executives in the country and also making him easily the best price-to-value money manager on the planet.

Buffett has never been interested in building any monuments to himself at shareholder expense. There is no Buffett Tower, no Buffett Plaza, Airport or Boulevard.

There is no touting of Berkshire's shares. If anything, Buffett downplays the historic runup of their worth and often tells shareholders next year's return on book value probably won't be as good as last year's.

There is no company logo for Berkshire Hathaway, now one of the largest and most financially powerful firms in the United States.

There are no cosmetic stock splits creating ten one-dollar bills instead of one ten-dollar bill.

Despite Berkshire's extraordinary success, it is largely ignored by Wall Street to this day. Few analysts follow it and stockbrokers almost never mention it to investors. It is rarely written up as a stock to buy. In many major Blue Chip corporate lists, it is not even mentioned.

Berkshire itself makes no effort to be known. You have to discover it for yourself.

There are no photos—color or black-and-white—no bar charts, no graphs in the company's annual report—famous among its fans, but unknown to others. The annual report is the company's only real communication to anyone, and nothing else in the business world quite matches it. What it lacks in gloss, it makes up for in value.

There are instead humor, common sense, insights into the business world and human nature and high praise for the managers of the disparate group of businesses Berkshire owns.

Buffett's literary pyrotechnics in the reports offer commentary on Berkshire's huge interests in some of the world's major corporations, including Coca-Cola Co., Capital Cities/ABC Inc., and the Gillette Co., and a 1991 purchase of a stake in Guinness PLC, the London-based liquor giant, all spiced with wit and wisdom about the human condition.

And the Berkshire annual meeting is also unlike any other. More than 1,500 shareholders from all over the country, even the world, make a pilgrimage to investment mecca in Omaha each year. There Buffett dispenses with company business in five to ten minutes, then fields a question and answer period that can last for hours.

Buffett, who is normally self-effacing and steers to an un-flamboyant, low key style most of the time, describes his principles as "simple, old and few."

"If principles are dated, they're not principles," he told the annual meeting in 1988.

Buffett's unique ability is to separate what is actually the case from what most people think is the case. "Traditional wisdom can be long on tradition and short on wisdom," he likes to say.

The practical manifestation of Buffett's ability in the stock market is to buy a good business when it's out of favor with the rest of the market. Buffett wants to buy a great business—or in his words, a "wonderful" business, at a time when its price is temporarily depressed due to some unwarranted stigma, fear or misunderstanding about the company.

"Great investment opportunities come around when excellent companies are surrounded by unusual circumstances that cause the stock to be misappraised," he has said (Fortune, December 19, 1988). American Express, Wells Fargo and Gillette are among the stocks of stellar companies he acquired when they temporarily faltered.

He has always insisted on rock bottom operating costs, plenty of cash on hand and "little or no debt."

Always tight-fisted about expenses, Buffett allows himself few personal luxuries, although he did dip into his $4 billion net worth to add a handball court to his modest house.

In his garage he stores the cases of his beloved Cherry Coke. He buys the Cokes—fifty twelve-packs at a time, getting a good discount and making fewer trips to the store that way. Even so, it's not too long before he has to go back for a refill because he says he drinks about five servings of Coke a day, to the delight of Coke and Berkshire shareholders everywhere.

For most of his life, Buffett has worked out of a small office on the fourteenth floor at the Kiewit Plaza office building a mile and a half from both his home and downtown. Operating from the rather small, spartan office he's dryly dubbed "World Headquarters," Buffett is the nerve center of a financial empire whose reach and influence flows across the land and beyond.

Buffett is a beacon of simplicity and sanity—and probably a genius. Rationality and common sense, actually uncommon sense, are his guiding lights.

His own three-word job description is simply: "I allocate capital." His more wordy explanation is: "My job is to figure out which businesses to invest in, with whom, and at what price."

Buffett is quite content to be holed up in the heartland of America —a locale for steaks and cornstalks and peace and quiet. "I think it's a saner existence here," he told L.J. Davis of the New York *Times Magazine* (April 1, 1990). "I used to feel when I worked back in New York that there were more stimuli just hitting me all the time, and if you've got the normal amount of adrenaline, you start responding to them. It may lead to crazy behavior after a while. It's much easier to think here."

It's a quiet life.

"We read. That's about it," says Buffett, with typical understatement. He regularly devours Barron's, the *Wall Street Journal,* Fortune, Business Week, Forbes, the Washington *Post* and the Omaha *World-Herald,* as well as myriad trade magazines and corporate annual reports.

Mainly, Buffett buys privately owned businesses outright or shares in publicly owned businesses on the stock market. But what Buffett does not do is as important as what he does. He does no program trading (although Berkshire investee Salomon does), he makes no quick bets on a company's upcoming quarterly earnings, he mouths no threats and will not participate in hostile takeovers, and he does not try to force things with debt, loud talk or wild shots.

The secret to making money, in his view, is not to take on risks, but to avoid them. "We've done better by avoiding dragons rather than by slaying them," Buffett said at the Berkshire annual meeting in 1991.

The investment shots he talks about making are layups, of putting money in places he's sure about and holding on through good times and bad. Buffett says, "Our favorite holding period is forever."

On the question of ethics and integrity, there is no question.

Operating far from the madding crowd of Wall Street, Buffett's net worth of $4.2 billion makes him America's eighth richest person, according to *Forbes* magazine, which in October 1991 ranked him behind Metromedia's John Kluge with $5.9 billion, Microsoft Corp.'s William Gates with $4.8 billion and five members of the Sam Walton family of Wal-Mart fame with $4.4 billion each.

That $4.2 billion net worth figure must be balanced against Buffett's debts.

Buffett's entire debt is $70,000! He's clearly living beneath his means.

Let's get the numbers down. He has at least $4,200,000,000 in assets and owes $70,000 on a second home mortgage. "Margin of safety?"

Speaking to Salomon clients on September 13, 1991, about his distaste for debt, Buffett said, "You're looking at a fellow who owes $70,000 on a second home in Laguna and I've got that because of the low rate . . . and that's all I've owed for I don't know how many years."

"If you're smart, you don't need debt. If you're dumb, it's poisonous," Buffett said.

There was a time in the late 1980s when, in the words of Buffett's longtime friend, Michael Yanney, chairman of America First Capital Associates in Omaha, "Greed on Wall Street exceeded its intellect."

What was Buffett doing in that era of frenzy? He was running businesses such as World Book, See's Candy and the Buffalo *News* and buying Coca-Cola stock, quietly piling high honest, well-earned wealth.

But beyond his wealth, Buffett is the most influential investment mind in the land.

And he has even provided two sure-fire rules for all who seek riches:

Rule No. 1. Never lose money.

Rule No. 2. Never forget Rule No. 1.

With his slightly Jack Benny-like appearance and manner, he remains a modest and dryly witty man. Once a Berkshire shareholder, knowing of Buffett's love for bridge, sent him an Omar Sharif bridge tape. Buffett thanked the shareholder in a note saying, "If I listen to it long enough, will I be as handsome as Omar Sharif?"

In describing Berkshire's acquisition policy, he once told shareholders, "It's very scientific. We just sit around and wait for the phone to ring. Sometimes it's a wrong number."

And when he shuffles off this mortal coil to investor's heaven, he has promised to keep in touch with us. He once told author Adam Smith that, looking into the future, "I see myself running Berkshire as long as I live and working on seances afterward."

The mystique of Warren Buffett is so out of this world he just may do that.

3 "FIREBALL"

"My high school career was not particularly illustrious—I was more interested in the pinball machines than in the classroom."

Warren Buffett was born in Omaha on August 30, 1930, into a family prominent for six generations in the city's political and business endeavors.

The first Buffett into Nebraska opened a grocery store in 1869.

Warren Buffett's mother, Leila (Stahl) Buffett, eighty-eight, a lively woman with an easy, humorous manner, walked into the Berkshire annual meeting in 1992 and said, "I'm still here." His father was Howard Homan Buffett, a stockbroker who founded Buffett-Falk & Company in 1931. He was conservative enough to sell diamonds to his clients as an inflation hedge.

Later Howard Buffett served in Congress from 1942 to 1948 and from 1950 to 1952 and died in 1964 of cancer at the age of sixty. He was known as a forceful writer and astute observer of politics and commerce who called things as he saw them.

Mrs. Buffett, twice widowed, took back the Buffett name after the death of her second husband, Roy Ralph, because she had been married to Congressman Buffett twenty-seven years.

Warren Buffett's parents, who also had two daughters—Doris

Bryant, now of Morehead City, North Carolina, and Roberta Bialek, now of Carmel, California—met while they worked on the college newspaper at the University of Nebraska.

Buffett's father edited the *Daily Nebraskan*, where his mother, who had set type in her family's printshop and report for her father's newspaper, the *Cuming County Democrat*, came calling for a job. Genetics gave Warren Buffett a lifelong love of the newspaper industry, in which he has been everything from delivery boy to Pulitzer Prize winner to mass media owner.

But even before his delivery boy days, one of young Buffett's favorite toys was a metal money changer he strapped around his waist. "He loved it," recalls his older sister, Doris Bryant, who describes young Warren as "a typical younger brother." He was fascinated by the process of making change and keeping track of the money. Mathematical calculations, particularly when they concerned money, absorbed him from his very earliest days.

"As a child he was so cautious he walked with his knees bent so he wouldn't have too far to fall . . . but as an adult he was capable of grand gestures . . . It (buying $1 billion of Coca-Cola stock) was a broad stroke," Mrs. Bryant said.

Leila Buffett recalls her son's first appreciation of free enterprise occurring when young Warren was six years old. The escapade was fitting for a man who would one day own billions of dollars of Coca-Cola stock.

"We were at Lake Okoboji in Iowa. Warren paid twenty-five cents for a six-pack of Coke and sold it for five cents a bottle. Warren always had a fascination for numbers in connection with earning money," Mrs. Buffett has said.

By the time Buffett was ten, his favorite soft drink was Pepsi. He later explained why to Berkshire shareholder Paul Cassidy of North Andover, Massachusetts. "I originally started on the Pepsi because at the time (1940) Pepsi came in twelve-ounce bottles and Coke came in six-ounce bottles, and the price was the same. That was a pretty powerful argument."

"While most youngsters were content to get sodas out of machines and never gave things a further thought, Buffett was retrieving the discarded bottle caps from soda pop machines, sorting and counting them to find out which soda brand was really selling," said Irving Fenster of Tulsa, Oklahoma, who has known him since they were young men and who became one of Buffett's earliest investors.

"No boy will ever succeed as a man who does not in his youth begin to save," said Theodore Roosevelt. Well, Buffett always saved from the beginning and he always easily tracked the numbers in his head.

Dubbed "Fireball" by his father because of his boundless energy, the precocious youngster was popular, witty and industrious, but even at Rosehill Elementary School he was known more as an "egghead" than as an athlete. It was there that he briefly picked up a nickname, "Bathless Buffett," from a character in the "Lil' Abner" comic strip that was popular at the time. That's not to say he didn't get along well with his peers. He did, striking a balance between basketball and business.

"He wanted to be around the guys and he would play basketball with them and then while the others were still playing, he'd be over reading the *Wall Street Journal*. The others would just say, 'That's Warren,' " says Kathryn Haskell Smith, recalling a story her late sister, Carolyn Haskell Hallquist, told her.

It was Carolyn whom Buffett often dropped in to see when the Buffett and Haskell families lived a few blocks from one another in the Country Club section of Omaha. Some evenings the teenage pair struck up a duet with Buffett on the ukulele and Carolyn on the piano.

Kathryn Smith, wife of Homer Smith, a football coach who oversees UCLA's offense, knew the Buffett family as a result of a friendship that her father, John Haskell, and Buffett's father formed back in their days at the University of Nebraska. For years Haskell's stockbroker was Howard Buffett.

"He [Warren Buffett] would come over to our house sometimes and talk finances with my father . . . My father agreed with Warren's father that you should buy good stocks and keep them for a very long time . . . He was always so quick and witty . . . He was a great guy, lots of fun, but it was obvious he was way ahead of us in brains," she said.

Wherever Buffett went, he could always keep his companions in stitches with his jokes, some on the raunchy side. But what occupied Buffett's mind all along were things financial.

"I was aware he wanted to make money. He was very industrious and was always trying to get money to buy stocks but no one ever dreamed it would come to this," Mrs. Smith said.

It was somewhat of a surprise to Buffett's father, a devout Presbyterian who had little interest in amassing money, to find that his son, whom he hoped would one day join the clergy, was so spellbound by the power of the dollar.

Buffett's father, widely regarded for his staunch integrity and conservative views, was the first member of the John Birch Society in Nebraska, attracted to the controversial organization because of its fierce opposition to Communism.

"Mainly he had a fear of creeping socialism," recalls Mrs. Bryant. "And he worried about inflation. He was ahead of his time about inflation and wrote about it and was advising his clients to hedge against it in 1932," she said. "He encouraged people to buy art and jewelry."

The Buffetts come from a long line of staunch Republicans but all the Buffetts have independent streaks. Warren Buffett grew up and became a Democrat in the 1960s, largely persuaded Democrats had a better approach to civil rights matters. Susie Buffett has told Forbes (October 21, 1991), "It caused great commotion" in the family.

Warren Buffett's son, Howard, inherited his father's maverick streak. Howard, a Republican, served on the Douglas County Commission, where he was known as a friend to the disadvantaged and an advocate of ethanol. He later took a job at Archer-Daniels-Midland.

Congressman Buffett was such an upright fiscal conservative he once returned to the U.S. Treasury his share of a congressional annual pay raise from $10,000 to $12,500. Warren Buffett was thirty-three-years-old when his father died.

"They were the best of friends," Leila Buffett says of her son and husband. "When he died, Warren cried for days."

Buffett remains close to his mother. At the height of the Salomon scandal he flew home from New York to be with her when she was honored as Woman of the Year by the Nebraska Chapter of the Arthritis Foundation. "She's been woman of the year for the last eighty-seven years," said Buffett.

When "Fireball" Buffett was just eight years old, he began reading books about the stock market, some left around the house by his father. Before his teens he was working at Harris, Upham & Company, a NYSE firm in the same building as Buffett-Falk. His job: marking stock prices on a blackboard.

Even while at tan-bricked Rosehill Elementary School, just two miles from his current home, Buffett charted the rise and fall of stock prices. "I was fascinated with anything to do with numbers and money," he told Linda Grant in the Los Angeles *Times* on April 7, 1991. At the grand age of eleven, Buffett began buying stocks in a small way and found his opinions about them were better than others'.

Buffett, ever the student, took in the early stock investment lessons well—do not be guided by what people say and don't tell fellow investors what you are doing at the time you do it. That hallmark idea never left Buffett, who in 1965 was writing to members in his Buffett Partnership, "We derive no comfort because important people, vocal people, or great numbers of people agree with us. Nor do we derive comfort if they don't. A public opinion poll is no substitute for thought."

Buffett said when you find a situation you understand, where the facts are ascertainable and clear, then act, whether the action is conventional or unconventional and whether others agree or disagree. When you are dead sure of something and are armed with all the facts, everyone else's advice is only confusing and time-consuming. When most everyone was dismissing the newspaper business as unappealing in the 1970s, Buffett spotted their monopoly-like franchises and bought one media stock after another.

From his early days Buffett rarely showed his hand until he had to. "I prefer the iceberg approach toward investment disclosure," he wrote his partners in his July 22, 1966, letter. The practice would take on far greater significance later when Wall Street would try to guess what he was doing. Only rarely did his moves in the market leak out. To this day Buffett tries to keep his investments secret until publication of the next Berkshire quarterly report and sometimes until the annual report is issued in March.

Music had long been part of Buffett's life. At the age of eleven, he sang "America the Beautiful" with his sisters as part of a radio campaign for his father for Congress. Maybe it helped—in any case, Howard Buffett was elected to the first of four terms.

The Buffett family moved to Fredericksburg, Virginia, in January, 1943, and Buffett, the uprooted twelve-year-old, was immediately unhappy about it. He returned to Omaha to live with his grandfather, grocer Ernest Buffett, and his Aunt Alice for four months. Each night his grandfather would dictate a few pages from his memoir, *How to Run a Grocery Store and a Few Things I Have Learned about Fishing.* Buffett likes to joke that his grandfather's longwinded literary style had an unfortunate impact on his own.

Of his six week stay in Fredericksburg, as he told L.J. Davis in the New York *Times Magazine,* April 1, 1990, "I was miserably homesick. I told my parents I couldn't breathe. I told them not to worry about it, to get themselves a good night's sleep, and I'd just stand up all night."

The Buffett family came home for the recess of Congress in the summer of 1943, and then the entire family moved to Washington that fall to 49th Street near Massachusetts Avenue.

At the age of thirteen, Buffett ran away from his Washington home briefly, and headed for Hershey, Pennsylvania, enchanted with the idea of touring the Hershey chocolate plant and getting a free candy bar. But he didn't tour the plant and didn't buy the company. Buffett told this story to Atlanta *Constitution* business writer Melissa Turner, who asked him if he might bite into Hershey stock. His reply, "I've driven a car all my life, but I haven't bought any car companies."

"He ran away with a friend, Roger Bell. I think they were picked up by the police," Mrs. Bryant said.

Still, Buffett often mentions the attributes of Hershey when he gets going on the concept of "consumer franchises." A valuable consumer franchise exists, he says, when people prefer a certain name brand so much they would pay extra for it, or walk an extra block or even across town because they have to have it. In Hershey's case, just because some chocolate bar is five cents cheaper, you're still likely to go with the Hershey name.

When Buffett was thirteen, he began paying taxes on an income of $1,000 he earned from two newspaper routes, and to this day he has his tax returns dating back to his early business ventures.

Buffett rejoined the family in Washington and attended nearby Alice Deal High School, where his grades were poor. They improved only when his father threatened to take away his cherished paper routes.

Still unhappy and rebellious and looking for his place in the world, Buffett undertook a series of financial ventures, including retrieving lost golf balls at a suburban country club.

But his main entrepreneurial thrust was as an energetic newspaperboy. Buffett at one point delivered 500 newspapers on five paper routes, mainly to apartment houses.

"Thinking he could better use the time it took to collect from his customers, he developed an effective scheme for selling magazine subscriptions. He would tear the stickers with the expiration date from discarded magazines, file them, and at the right time ask the customer for a renewal," Robert Dorr wrote in a May 29, 1966, story for the Omaha *World Herald.*

Buffett was an enterprising paperboy for both the Washington *Post* and the Washington *Times-Herald.* At the age of eleven, Buffett also published a racetrack tip sheet, *Stable-Boy Selections,* about handicapping and betting on horse races.

"He was always fascinated by the stock market," recalls Mrs. Bryant. "I never had any doubt. I never knew it would amount to this but even back then everyone recognized he knew about the stock market."

Even when Buffett started his partnership in his bedroom, it did not create a stir in the family. "We took it for granted he knew what he was doing," Mrs. Bryant said.

As a youngster, according to stories told by his longtime friend Carol Loomis, Buffett virtually memorized a book called *A Thousand Ways to Make $1,000,* fantasizing in particular about penny weighing machines. He pictured himself starting with a single machine, pyramiding his take into thousands more.

The Loomis connection began in the mid-1960s when Loomis' husband, John, later a money manager with the First Manhattan Co. in New York, went to Omaha to discuss business with Buffett and reported back to his wife, "I think I just met the smartest man in the country."

Carol Loomis has been a journalist with Fortune magazine since 1954 and serves on its board of editors. Over the years she has interviewed Buffett frequently. In one such interview, Buffett recalled that as a boy in church he calculated the life span of the composers of hymns, checking to see if their religious calling rewarded them with extra longevity. His conclusion: no extra allotted time, here on earth anyway, for their good deeds.

Perhaps that was the reason Buffett became an agnostic.

At the age of fifteen, while at Woodrow Wilson High School in Washington, D.C., Buffett and a friend bought a 1934 Rolls-Royce for $350 and rented it out for thirty-five dollars a day. Occasionally Buffett would get in his Rolls-Royce and, like some big shot, brandish a cigar and read the *Wall Street Journal.*

That same year, he and another student bought a used pinball machine for twenty-five dollars, fixed it up and installed it in a barbershop on busy Wisconsin Avenue. After the first day of operation, the youngsters returned to find four dollars. Buffett has said, "I figured I had discovered the wheel."

As other barbers asked for the machines, the Wilson Coin-Operated Machine Company expanded to seven machines and was hauling in fifty dollars a week. "I hadn't dreamed life could be so good," Buffett is quoted by John Train, author of *The Midas Touch.*

He was also pulling in about $175 a month from paper routes, according to Adam Smith in *Supermoney.*

While still in high school, Buffett was able to save enough to buy a $1,200 unimproved forty-acre farm in northeastern Nebraska, which his father had bought a few years earlier. Young Buffett paid cash.

I once wrote Buffett that my mother, Frances Kilpatrick, taught at Woodrow Wilson High School, the same school he attended.

Buffett replied, ". . . I went to Woodrow Wilson in 1945–1947. I don't remember a Mrs. Kilpatrick, so she must have been teaching one of the harder courses at the time. My high school career was not particularly illustrious—I was more interested in the pinball machines than in the classroom. Best regards. Sincerely, Warren E. Buffett."

Buffett picked up speed as a student and by the time he graduated from Woodrow Wilson at sixteen he had amassed a sum of about $6,000, largely from his paper routes. Although he could have, he did not pay for college. His parents did, letting young Buffett keep his money for investing.

By December 31, 1950, he had amassed $9,000 just before taking Ben Graham's course at the Columbia School of Business. He had about $9,800 when he graduated from Columbia in June, 1951.

At the urging of his father—and it took some doing to convince young Buffett to go to college instead of going on with his business pursuits—young Buffett headed for the Wharton School of Business at the University of Pennsylvania in 1947. "I didn't feel I was learning that much," he has said of his Wharton experience, so in 1949, in his junior year, he transferred to the University of Nebraska, where he earned a B.S. degree in 1950, graduating at nineteen.

That summer Buffett applied to Harvard Business School.

He took a train to Chicago, where a Harvard alumnus interviewed him. Years later Buffett told Carol Loomis that all the Harvard representative saw was "a scrawny nineteen-year-old who looked sixteen and had the social poise of a twelve-year-old." When the interview was over, so were Buffett's prospects at Harvard. "The interview in Chicago took about ten minutes and they threw me back in the water," Buffett has said.

The rejection stung, but he says it turned out for the best because he soon realized that the greatest business professor of all was teaching at Columbia's business school. Buffett applied there and was immediately accepted.

When he was a senior at the University of Nebraska early in 1950, Buffett had read Benjamin Graham's newly published book, *The Intelligent Investor,* which preached "value investing"—finding companies that are undervalued in the stock market, that is, companies whose intrinsic values are substantially greater than the value the stock market assigns to the enterprise. A value investor tries to buy stocks for substantially less than what the underlying business is worth in the real business world. He wants to buy stocks selling at a discount to what is sometimes called the "transactional value" of the business. Graham urged the investor to keep a "Margin of Safety" by being sure the business he is buying is worth substantially more than what he has to pay for it in the securities markets. Popularity, fads and all the rest had no place in a value investor's decision—only price and value.

Buffett would become the world's greatest practitioner of value investing.

Buffett has told Omaha *World-Herald* reporter Robert Dorr that reading the *The Intelligent Investor* was an epiphany. "I read the first edition of this book early in 1950, when I was nineteen. I thought then that it was by far the best book about investing ever written. I still think it is" (March 24, 1985). "I don't want to sound like a religious fanatic or anything, but it really did get me," Buffett told L.J. Davis in an interview in the New York *Times Magazine* of April 1, 1990.

Buffett has always recommended the book as required reading for any successful investor. He has said chapter 8 about investor attitudes and stock market fluctuations, and chapter 20 about "Margin of Safety," is the most important investment advice ever written—that the true investor takes advantage of stock prices when they become silly in either direction, and he buys at bargain prices compared to real worth.

Buffett also recommends the early books by investment guru Philip Fisher as well as *The Money Masters* by John Train.

Buffett earned a master's in economics at Columbia Business

School in 1951. His academic record was one of the highest ever recorded there. It is said that at the time Graham was teaching young Buffett at Columbia he felt that Buffett would become the greatest financial mind of his time. Buffett made an A+ under Ben Graham, according to both Jim Rogers, who teaches finance at Columbia, and John Burton, former dean of the Columbia University Graduate School of Business. Buffett says he did *not* make *the* highest grade ever. "He was gifted in math, but his ability to perceive economic value is his genius," Burton has said of Buffett.

Bill Ruane, a Harvard Business School graduate who became interested in the teachings of Columbia's Ben Graham and David Dodd, took one of Graham's courses and thus became a classmate of Buffett's in 1951. Today Ruane is the chief of the Ruane, Cunniff & Co. investment management firm, runs the Sequoia Fund (which has large investments in Berkshire and Freddie Mac stocks) and also is a director of The Washington Post Co. and GEICO Corp. Ruane, who has said the only difference between him and Buffett is about $4 billion and 100 IQ points, has said a kind of intellectual electricity coursed between Graham and Buffett and that the rest of the class was a rapt audience. "Sparks were flying," recalls Ruane. "You could tell then he [Buffett] was someone who was very unusual."

After the school year was over, Buffett offered to work for Graham's investment company, Graham-Newman & Co., for free "but Ben," Buffett has said, "made his customary calculation of price to value and said no." So Buffett returned to Omaha to work in his father's brokerage firm from 1951 to 1954.

During that time he taught a course in investing at the University of Omaha's adult education program. One evening he found only four students in attendance and dismissed them, saying he was sorry there wasn't enough interest to warrant holding the course. Eventually his class got off the ground. Omaha *World-Herald*'s Robert Dorr has written that class members, whose average age was in the forties, snickered slightly when they first saw young Buffett. Dorr says that Buffett has admitted, "I was skinnier then and looked like I could get into a basketball game as a high school student." When Buffett began speaking, however, the snickering stopped. "After two minutes he had the class in his hands," said a former student.

As always, Buffett was investing and not every venture worked out. "I guess my worst decision was that I went into a service station when I was twenty or twenty-one. And I lost twenty percent of my net worth. So that service station cost me about $800 million now, I guess," he said at the Berkshire annual meeting in 1992. "It's very satisfying when Berkshire goes down because the cost of that service station mistake declines."

On April 19, 1952, he married Susan Thompson, a petite brunette with a winning smile, the popular daughter of Dr. William Thompson, a psychology professor and dean of the School of Arts and Sciences at the University of Omaha. Susie, as she is known to everyone, had been attending Northwestern University, where she roomed with Buffett's sister, Roberta.

Mrs. Buffett, always interested in music, took up music in earnest in the mid-1970s after her children were grown. For a time she sang at Omaha's French Café and has been quoted by Associated Press (Sept. 25, 1977) writer Kiley Armstrong as saying, "I sing to keep my soul alive."

And music, Buffett has said, helped in winning his wife's hand. During their college days Buffett won Susie's attention by playing the ukulele with her father, a mandolin player. "It was obvious I was not Number One with her," Buffett told Kiley Armstrong. "But he became very pro-me. It was two against one." Howard Buffett agrees. "That's true. My father really did court her through her father."

Warren and Susie Buffett would have three children: Susan, born on July 30, 1953; Howard Graham, born December 16, 1954; and Peter, born May 4, 1958.

"My dad was so involved in his work, which is his fun," said daughter Susan Buffett Greenberg. "My mother had a very different life . . . We have such great parents. They were very affectionate. They still have strong relations. Once the kids were raised, my mother didn't want to sit home," she said. By the middle of 1977, Susie Buffett had moved to San Francisco to pursue her musical career and indulge her love of travel. Some time after that, Astrid Menks, a vivacious former hostess at the French Cafe, and Buffett began to live together.

"Astrid was not around until after my mother left for San Francisco," said Susan.

Buffett, Astrid and Susie are all on friendly terms today. Astrid Menks has been a Berkshire shareholder for many years, and Susie Buffett was named to Berkshire's board in 1991. Warren and Susie see each other about once a month and she travels with him on most non-business trips."

Of the separation Buffett has said, "It works well this way. She sort of roams; she's a free spirit." (Forbes, October 21, 1991)

Howard Buffett says, "If the comment 'behind every good man there is a good woman' has any truth to it, then you absolutely must give my mother credit for a good share of my dad's success. She is the most understanding and kind person I have ever known, and her support throughout his career has been very important to him."

Susan Buffett Greenberg says her mother was long active in racial and women's causes in Omaha but in recent years has devoted a lot of time to helping Susan through a difficult pregnancy, helping her son, Howard, campaign for the county commission and helping her sister face a lengthy battle with cancer.

Warren, Susie and Astrid showed up at a party held for shareholders at Borsheim's the day before the annual meeting in 1990 and all were cordial to one another. Astrid Menks and Buffett are close.

But all that came later. In the early years of his marriage to Susie, Buffett was still trying to get a job with the man he admired second only to his father: Ben Graham.

"I wanted to work for Ben Graham," he often tells graduating MBA students, "but he didn't hire me immediately. I offered to go to work for him for nothing, too, so it's even worse than it sounds. So I started trying to be useful to him in various ways. I did a number of studies I dreamed up. I tried to suggest ideas. If I wanted to be starting quarterback on the Washington Redskins, I'd try to get them to watch me throw a few passes."

Graham finally hired Buffett in 1954 and he stayed at Graham-

Newman for two years until Graham wound up the business and retired in 1956. (Graham died in 1976.)

Irving Kahn, now in his late eighties, head of Kahn Brothers & Company, Inc. of New York, who worked for Graham for twenty-seven years as an assistant at Columbia and at Graham-Newman, recalls young Buffett as Graham's prized protégé. "He was much the same as he is now but he was a brash, cocky young guy . . . He was always busy on his own. He has tremendous energy. He could wear you out talking to you," Kahn said.

"He was very ambitious about making money," continued Kahn, adding that Buffett had an extraordinary understanding about how business worked. Kahn said Buffett's father knew Ben Graham and that both, seared by the experience of the Depression, sought ways to restore old values and to come up with ways that would insure price stability.

"Warren's father was at the forefront of the Depression in Omaha and for farmers he had a deep feeling that the system had broken down . . . It was a widespread farmbelt feeling. He was also in the securities business. Coming out of the Depression, he met Ben Graham in Washington, who was a sort of Renaissance man. They talked a lot about tying price stability to commodities and what could be done for lesser developed countries."

During his years with Graham-Newman, young family man Buffett commuted by train from his White Plains home in Westchester County. "It didn't seem like much of a life," he told Linda Grant of the Los Angeles *Times*, April 7, 1991. "People kept coming up to me all the time, whispering into my ear about some wonderful business. I was getting excited all the time. I was a wonderful customer for the brokerages. Trouble was, everyone else was, too."

He decided to strike out on his own and never again had a boss. At the age of twenty-five, Buffett returned to settle in Omaha, 1,100 miles from Wall Street.

The man who would become known as the Wizard of Omaha was on his way.

4 BUFFETT PARTNERSHIP, LTD.

"My activity has not been burdened by second-guessing, discussing non-sequiturs, or hand holding. You have let me play the game without telling me what club to use, how to grip it, or how much better the other players were doing."

Nothing more clearly portrays who Buffett is than how he started his partnership. Operating alone from the upstairs bedroom and sun porch of his $32,000 home, sometimes keeping notes on the back of envelopes and keeping very much his own counsel, he forged one of the most successful investment vehicles ever.

At twenty-five Buffett had been married four years and had two small children. He was fresh off a brilliant academic career and a two-year stint on Wall Street. His personal fortune stood at $140,000.

"I thought it was enough to retire on . . . I had no master plan," Buffett told L.J. Davis of the New York *Times Magazine.*

But, approached frequently for investment advice, he pooled $105,000 from friends and relatives and founded Buffett Associates, Ltd. in 1956, telling investors, "I'll run it like I run my own money, and I'll take part of the losses and part of the profits. And I won't tell you what I'm doing."

He recalled in a 1990 interview that "I told them 'What I'll do is form a partnership where I'll manage the portfolio and have my money in there with you. I'll guarantee you a six percent return, and I get twenty-five percent of all profits after that. And I won't tell you what we own because that's distracting. All I want to do is hand in a scorecard when I come off the golf course. I don't want you following me around and watching me shank a three-iron on this hole and leave a putt short on the next one." *(Fortune/Investors Guide,* 1990)

Organized May 5, 1956, Buffett Associates, Ltd. had seven limited partners—four family members and three close friends—who contributed $105,000 but had no voting power, no say in the running of things.

For the history books, and according to a certificate of limited partnership filing at the Douglas County Courthouse in Omaha, the following limited partners were the real Lotto winners of 1956:

Charles E. Peterson, Jr.	$ 5,000	(Buffett friend in Omaha)
Elizabeth B. Peterson	$25,000	(the mother of Charles, Omaha)
Doris B. Wood	$ 5,000	(Buffett's sister)
Truman S. Wood	$ 5,000	(Buffett's brother-in-law)
Daniel J. Monen, Jr.	$ 5,000	(Buffett friend who was an attorney in Omaha)
William H. Thompson	$25,000	(Buffett's father-in-law)
Alice R. Buffett	$35,000	(Buffett's aunt)

General Partner Warren Buffett, listed as residing at 5202 Underwood Avenue, chipped in $100 and so the partnership actually began with $105,100. He would add more and more of his own money later. As manager young Buffett received 25 percent of the profits above six percent annually, with deficiencies carried forward.

That summer of 1956, Homer Dodge, a physics professor from Vermont who heard of the wunderkind from his friend Ben Graham, arrived in Omaha seeking Buffett and became the first outside partner. According to the *Fortune/1990 Investors Guide,* Dodge had driven 1,500 miles in hopes of persuading twenty-five-year-old Buffett to manage his family's savings.

"Homer told me, 'I'd like you to handle my money,'" Buffett recalled in the same *Fortune* piece. "I said, 'The only thing I'm doing is a partnership with my family.' He said, 'Well, I'd like one with you.' So I set one up with Homer, his wife, children and grandchildren."

Dodge invested $100,000 for his family in Buffett Associates, and when Dodge died in 1983, the sum had multiplied into tens of millions of dollars. Dodge's son Norton has said, "My father saw immediately that Warren was brilliant at financial analysis. But it was more than that."

After the Homer Dodge visit, it wasn't too long before a fellow named Laurence Tisch, later to become chairman of Loews and CBS, sent Buffett a check for $300,000 and a note saying "Include me in." Tisch, no slouch as an investor—one of the handful of the best in the country—would later describe Buffett as "the greatest investor of his generation."

Not everyone was so impressed. Author John Train recalled in *The Money Masters* that "At that very early stage he had no office at all, and ran things from a tiny sitting-room off his bedroom—no secretary, no calculator. When I found that the holdings could not be revealed, I decided not to sign up."

Buffett's neighbor, Donald Keough, then a Butternut Coffee salesman, was also dubious. "I had five small kids and left for work each day," Keough recalled for a profile of Buffett by Bernice Kanner in New York magazine, dated April 22, 1985. "Buffett had three and stayed home. He had this marvelous hobby, model trains, and my kids used to troop over there and play with them. One day, Warren popped over and asked if I'd thought about how I was going to educate these kids . . . I told him I planned to work hard and see what happened. Warren said if I gave him $5,000 he'd probably do better [for me]. My wife and I talked it over, but we figured we didn't know what this guy even did for a living—how could we give him $5,000? We've been kicking ourselves ever since. I mean, if we had given him the dough, we could have owned a college by now."

Fortunately for Keough, he became president of the Coca-Cola company.

By January 1, 1957, combined assets were $303,726.

To talk to Buffett face to face during the first years, "You went in the back door of his home, walked through the kitchen, the living room and went up the stairs to the bedroom," the Omaha *World-Herald* quoted one partner in a May 5, 1986 story. "If you were impressed with show and image, Warren was not your man. He always dressed like he got his clothes out of a grab bag."

By the time Buffett was thirty-one in 1961, he was a millionaire.

He had begun teaching an investment course since 1956 and would continue to do so until 1965. "I had lot better ideas back then than I do now," he has told Adam Smith, the pen name of George J.W. Goodman, host of television's "Money World" show.

As time passed, some original partners added money and new partners came on board. One of these was William O'Connor, now a vice president of Mutual of Omaha, who was working for IBM when he met Buffett.

"I invited him to our investment club," O'Connor recalls. "Like most of us he was about our age of about twenty-four, but unlike us he was so profound when it came to business and finance. He was so well received, we invited him back the next year and each time he played a little penny-ante poker and he left some small sums. He would say it was against his better judgment, but said 'I'll call.' "

O'Connor took Buffett's ten-week investment course at the University of Omaha. During breaks Buffett and the students would drink Pepsi and Buffett would share his investment thoughts. "He rarely gave us specific advice, but he gave you a lot to think about. He left his students well grounded in the principles of compounding," said O'Connor.

It was O'Connor who convinced Buffett, by now well on his way to being a millionaire, to acquire a $295 IBM typewriter for the partnership in December 1958. "He was always saying he didn't need it," recalls O'Connor. "It was an IBM Standard Model electric typewriter. He bought the standard model rather than the more costly executive model."

Over the years, O'Connor would sell Buffett additional office equipment. "Perhaps what got the most use," he speculates, "was the dictating machine I sold his wife, Susie, who used it for her correspondence with sixty or seventy minority children she helped with college and moral support."

O'Connor has continued to add to his Buffett holdings, occasionally selling off some for family needs. "My wife, Jean, questioned my judgment" about putting so much with Buffett, but O'Connor told her that if she knew what he knew about Buffett, she'd understand. O'Connor's faith paid off and he became one of Omaha's many Buffett millionaires.

"Warren really is a very uncomplicated person. He's a super nice guy who just keeps things simple," O'Connor said, adding that "he is truly a remarkable person. His technical knowledge and his humor are unique. It's truly entertaining to be associated with him . . . He has an insatiable thirst for knowledge. He reads from all sources and he has a photographic memory that helps him recall and reconstruct things in an orderly, logical fashion . . . He plays a little tennis and golf, but I really think he'd rather read—and play bridge —than anything."

Later there were other partnerships, amendments to the original partnership really, and at year end 1961 he merged ten of his partnerships.

In 1957, the partnership recorded a gain of $31,615.97—a 10.4 percent increase. A modest gain on the face of it, but significant when compared to the Dow Jones Industrial Average, which slumped 8.4 percent that year.

That comparison would remain about typical of the partnership until it was dissolved at the end of 1969.

The partnership never failed to beat the Dow. It never had a down year. On average, from 1957 through 1962, while the Dow grew 8.3 percent a year, the partnership grew 26 percent a year.

The partnership was reorganized on January 1, 1962, changed its name to Buffett Partnership, Ltd., moved out of Buffett's upstairs bedroom and the adjoining sun porch to offices at 810 Kiewit Plaza, and hired its first employees.

Net assets of the partnership, compiled by Buffett while still under his own roof at home, were $7,178,500!

In November 1962, the partnership, which along the way had
invested in strange windmill makers and anthracite producers, began buying shares of a New Bedford, Massachusetts, textile mill,
Berkshire Hathaway. Buffett bought his first shares of Berkshire
Hathaway at a price of $7.60 and kept buying it between seven and
eight dollars a share. The company was suffering from a prolonged
slide and Buffett bought its unimpressive operations for the prover-
bial song. By 1965 he gained financial control and became a director.

From the very beginning, Buffett knew his mission was to compound his cash at a hefty, steady clip. In 1963 Buffett wrote his
partners the following lessons about the "Joys of Compounding": "I
have it from unreliable sources that the cost of the voyage Isabella
originally underwrote for Columbus was approximately $30,000
. . . Without attempting to evaluate the psychic income derived
from finding a new hemisphere, it must be pointed out that even had
squatter's rights prevailed, the whole deal was not exactly another
IBM. Figured very roughly, the $30,000 invested at four percent
compounded annually would have amounted to something like
$2,000,000,000,000,000 (that's two trillion, for those of you who are not
government statisticians) by 1962." He adds, "Such fanciful geomet-
ric progressions illustrate the value of either living a long time, or
compounding your money at a decent rate."

In the same letter Buffett told partners he had moved from an
office off his bedroom "to one a bit (quite a bit) more conventional.
Surprising as it may seem, the return to a time clock has not been
unpleasant. As a matter of fact, I enjoy not keeping track of everything on the backs of envelopes."

In 1965 Buffett was telling partners, "If our record is better than
that of these [market averages], we consider it a good year whether
we are plus or minus. If we do poorer, we deserve the tomatoes."

Between 1962 and 1969, with assets of $104,429,431 at the end of
that period, Buffett was really loading on manpower. He added Bill
Scott, who now manages Berkshire's bond portfolio at headquarters.

From 1963 to 1969 rent soared from $3,947 to $5,823. Dues and subscriptions skyrocketed from $900 to $994. "At least the situation hasn't gotten completely out of control," Buffett commented dryly in his January 22, 1969, letter to his partners.

Along the way, a Dun and Bradstreet report dated November 13, 1963, described the partnership as follows: "Volume steady. Condition sound . . . Due to the nature of this business subject is not a general seeker of mercantile credit however maintains a prompt pay record locally." As for its finances, the report found that at the start of 1963, the partnership had a worth of $9.4 million, "consisting of cash resources, income producing securities and other investments. A sound condition continues. Cash averages a low to moderate six figure amount in two local depository [sic] with a high six figure amount owing secured and relations satisfactory . . . Employs one. Location: Rents office space on eighth floor of multi-story brick office building located [in an] outlying business district. Premises orderly."

At the time of the Dun and Bradstreet report there were more than ninety limited partners.

At this point Buffett made one of his celebrated great decisions: to invest big in American Express.

In late 1963 a scandal broke when an American Express subsidiary that issued warehouse receipts mistakenly certified the existence of huge quantities of salad oil. When the salad oil turned out not to exist, the subsidiary found itself possibly liable for hundreds of millions of dollars worth of claims. The resulting crisis could have left American Express with a negative net worth.

"A great investment opportunity occurs when a marvelous business encounters a one-time huge, but solvable problem," Buffett has said many times.

Buffett, the ultimate advocate of a franchise business, liked the American Express charge card and travelers check businesses and concluded their strength would carry the company through the salad oil-less days.

Buffett knew American Express possessed a huge cash "float" generated by the travelers check business. So he wanted to make sure the underlying business was not hurt by the cloud hanging over

American Express. In Ross's Steak House in Omaha—one of his favorite eating places—and in other establishments, Buffett stood behind the cashier and peeked into the cash register to see whether people were still using the American Express card.

They were, and Buffett, believing the credit card and travel services parts of American Express empire remained intact, invested 40 percent of the net worth of the Buffett Partnership, or roughly $13 million, in American Express stock that had collapsed to $35 a share from a high of more than $62.

In doing so he violated one of his rules: never put more than 25 percent of the partnership money in one investment. But he wrote a new rule: buy great companies when they temporarily stumble.

In the next two years American Express stock tripled and the Buffett Partnership reportedly sold out with a $20 million profit. Apparently his partnership made even more, because Buffett told the Omaha *World-Herald* (August 2, 1991) he held the stock for four years, although published reports indicated he sold out after two years.

A Dun and Bradstreet report of December 9, 1964, found the worth of the enterprise was more than $18,000,000.

In his January 18, 1964, letter to the limited partners, Buffett reports the partnership began the year with assets of $17,454,900. "Susie [Mrs. Buffett] and I have an investment of $2,393,900 in the Partnership. For the first time, I had to withdraw funds in addition to monthly payments, but it was a choice of this or disappointing the Internal Revenue Service."

Two years later he writes, "Susie and I have an investment of $6,849,936, which should keep me from slipping away to the movies in the afternoon."

At this time Buffett keeps telling of three main investment categories the partnership is engaged in:

"Generals"—Undervalued stocks generally to be held for a long
  time.
"Workouts"—Securities with a timetable, arbitrage situations arising from sell-outs, mergers, reorganizations and the like.

"Controls"—Owning such a sizeable block that the partnership gains control of the business.

In the midst of all this Buffett is saying, "We like good management—we like a decent industry—we like a certain amount of 'ferment' in a previously dormant management or stockholder group. But we demand value."

One undervalued investment that started as a "general" in 1956 was Dempster Mill Manufacturing Co., a farm equipment maker. Buffett reported that the stock was selling at $18 a share with about $72 in book value. Buffett continued buying the stock in small quantities for five years. By mid-1961 the partnership owned more than 70 percent of the company.

Things didn't go particularly well for Dempster Mill and that's when Buffett called in Harry Bottle, an early investor, to run things. Two years later the business was sold. Because Dempster Mill was the largest employer in Beatrice, the city helped finance the acquisition of Buffett's stake, and the company became First Beatrice Corp. Bottle still pops up at times to turn around some operating problem for Buffett.

By 1965, the partnership's net assets had grown to $26 million from $105,100 ten years earlier.

Buffett celebrated by adding 227 1/4 square feet of space at headquarters in the spring of 1965, about the size of an ordinary room.

The January 20, 1966, letter to his limited partners began: "Our War on Poverty was successful in 1965. Specifically, we were $12,304,060 less poor at the end of the year."

For the year 1965, when the Dow was up 14.2 percent, the Buffett Partnership had orbited the world. A 47.2 percent return! That was about the time Buffett started saying, "Democracy is great but not in investment decisions."

Buffett had told partners his goal was to beat the Dow by 10 percentage points. From 1957 through 1965, the Dow rose 11.4 percent, on average. The partnership returns were 29.8 percent a year. Goal achieved and surpassed.

"I now feel that we are much closer to the point where increased size may prove disadvantageous," he said in 1965 and repeated almost every year afterward. He's been saying it for at least a quarter of a century. Yet the partnership kept growing and the returns kept coming in at more than 20 percent per year on average.

In a July 12, 1966, letter to partners, Buffett assured Buffett Partners that "if we start deciding, based on our guesses or emotions, whether we will . . . participate in a business where we . . . have some long run edge, we're in trouble. We will not sell our interests in businesses when they are attractively priced just because some astrologer thinks the quotations may go lower."

Later that summer he was telling the partnership that "I am not in the business of predicting general stock market or business fluctuations. If you think I can do this, or think it is essential to an investment program, you should not be in the partnership."—Buffett Partnership letter, July 22, 1966.

The partnership continued its astounding success in 1966. In his January 25, 1967, letter he wrote: "The Partnership had its tenth anniversary during 1966. The celebration was appropriate—an all-time record (both past and future) was established for our performance margin relative to the Dow. Our advantage was 36 points which resulted from a plus 20.4 percent for the Partnership and a minus 15.6 percent for the Dow."

But in the same letter he assured his partners that "these conditions will not cause me to attempt investment decisions outside my sphere of understanding (I don't go for the 'If you can't lick 'em, join 'em' philosophy—my own leaning is toward 'If you can't join 'em, lick 'em')."

That October Buffett wrote to partners saying he was worried about excesses in the market. "I do believe certain conditions that now exist are likely to make activity in markets more difficult for us in the immediate future." Nevertheless, his January 24, 1968, letter began: "By most standards, we had a good year in 1967. Our overall performance was plus 35.9 percent compared to plus 19.0 percent for the Dow, thus surpassing our previous objective of performance ten points superior to the Dow. Our overall gain was $19,384,250 which, even under accelerating inflation, will buy a lot of Pepsi [Buffett's drink of choice in those days]. And due to the sale of some long-standing large positions in marketable securities, we had realized taxable income of $27,376,667, which has nothing to do with 1967 performance but should give you all a feeling of vigorous participation in The Great Society on April 15."

In this same letter he reported that through the partnership's two controlled companies, Diversified Retailing and Berkshire Hathaway, two other companies had been acquired—Associated Cotton Shops, later named Associated Retail Stores, and National Indemnity (along with National Fire & Marine, an affiliated company). Associated was bought by Diversified Retailing and National Indemnity was purchased by Berkshire Hathaway.

In his July 11, 1968, letter, Buffett is still clearly worried about a speculative blowoff for the market. "I make no effort to predict the course of general business or the stock market. Period. However, currently, there are practices snow-balling in the security markets and business world which, while devoid of short-term predictive value, bother me as to possible long term consequences . . . Spectacular amounts of money are being made by those participating (whether as originators, top employees, professional advisors, investment bankers, stock speculators, etc.) in the chain-letter type stock-promotion vogue."

Even so, by January 22, 1969, he is reporting the partnership results were up an unbelievable 58.8 percent. The Dow rose 7.7 percent that year.

From 1957 through 1968, the Dow's annual compound growth rate was 9.1 percent; Buffett Partnership's was up 31.6 percent.

But Buffett was not happy. "A hyperactive stock market is the pickpocket of enterprise," he said then, and many times since.

"The investment management business, which I used to severely chastise in this section for excessive lethargy, has now swung in many quarters to acute hypertension," he wrote to his partners. He even quoted an unnamed investment manager who had assured him that "the complexities of national and international economics make money management a full-time job. A good money manager cannot maintain a study of securities on a week-by-week or even a day-by-day basis. Securities must be studied in a minute-by-minute program."

"Wow!" said Buffett. "This sort of stuff makes me feel guilty when I go out for a Pepsi."

By May 29, 1969, he was writing, "About eighteen months ago I wrote to you regarding changed environmental and personal factors causing me to modify our future performance objectives." He said the investing environment was becoming more negative and frustrating and, further, "I know I don't want to be totally occupied with outpacing an investment rabbit all my life. The only way to slow down is to stop."

When he stopped at the end of 1969, the partnership had rung up a 29.5 percent annual compound return while the Dow had a 7.4 percent annual return! An investor who put in $10,000 in 1956 had almost $300,000.

Buffett liquidated the Buffett Partnership in 1969, giving the partners a range of options: an investor could maintain a proportional interest in Diversified Retailing Co. or in Berkshire Hathaway, or the investor could take cash.

He also offered to help former partners make bond investments. He even recommended another money manager, his old friend from Columbia Business School, Bill Ruane, who established the Sequoia Fund on July 15, 1970, to serve limited partners when Buffett Partnership closed.

At that time the market was well into a long tailspin that would culminate in the collapse of 1973–74.

Buffett's caution about market conditions and his timing in getting out were right on the money.

In a final letter to partners, dated February 18, 1970, Buffett wrote: "I am out of step with present conditions. When the game is no longer played your way, it is only human to say the new approach is all wrong, bound to lead to trouble, and so on . . . On one point, however, I am clear. I will not abandon a previous approach whose logic I understand (although I find it difficult to apply) even though it may mean foregoing large, and apparently easy, profits to embrace an approach which I don't fully understand, have not practiced successfully, and which possibly could lead to substantial permanent loss of capital."

Buffett also thanked his partners—numbering about ninety by then—for giving him a free hand. "My activity has not been burdened by second-guessing, discussing non sequiturs, or hand holding. You have let me play the game without telling me what club to use, how to grip it, or how much better the other players were doing.

"I've appreciated this, and the results you have achieved have significantly reflected your attitudes and behavior. If you don't feel this is the case, you underestimate the importance of personal encouragement and empathy in maximizing human effort and achievement."

"Herein lies the management genius of Buffett," says Berkshire stockholder Michael Assael.

"But Buffett's genius goes deeper," says Assael. "It now revolves around three elements, and the interplay among them.

"1. Finance. Buffett understands 'return on investment' better than anyone. He knows how to get the most bang for Berkshire's buck.

"2. Economics. He's sensitive to the economic landscape and uses the economic environment to Berkshire's advantage.

"3. Management and the ability to motivate people. Buffett is touched by the importance of human sensitivity, encouragement and empathy in maximizing human achievement.

"Combining these elements makes Buffett unique. He views the investment world in a multi-dimensional way, much as Einstein viewed the solar system, and Freud the human brain. The results of his genius speak for themselves."

Buffett became chairman of Berkshire Hathaway upon the liquidation of the Buffett Partnership.

When the partnership closed, it had grown to about $105 million and Buffett's own stake was worth about $25 million, much of which he quietly invested in Berkshire Hathaway. His interest, managerial and financial, had increased in Berkshire, which in 1969 had bought the Illinois National Bank and Trust of Rockford, Illinois.

The departing limited partners were allowed either to go off on their own or Buffett bought them some municipal bonds with their money and referred them to Bill Ruane, his old colleague at Columbia and later at the Graham-Newman firm.

Ruane has run the Sequoia Fund, a highly successful mutual fund that often invests in the same companies as Berkshire Hathaway does, such as the Washington *Post,* GEICO, and Capital Cities/ABC.

Three years after the Buffett Partnership was disbanded, the market suffered the collapse of 1973–74.

5 APPEARANCE AND STYLE

"I'll be in Omaha as long as I live."

Warren Buffett is a genial, pleasant looking, rather muscular man with large horn-rimmed glasses.

Admirers salute Buffett's "almost photographic memory," recall that he "used to read encyclopedias," marvel that "his mind is encyclopedic, [he] has tremendous concentration," and of course note that "he has no peer in security analysis."

Ask them to cite a flaw and you get something like: "He needs help turning on the radio," or "Can barely start a car," or "Wouldn't notice a new rug in his living room." There's some question whether he knows how to use a fax machine. His son Howard says "My dad couldn't run a lawnmower, but he once told me it takes a lifetime to build a reputation and five minutes to ruin it."

Slightly above average in height at five feet, eleven inches tall and medium build at 190 pounds, he possesses a sort of everyman's body (that just happens to have an extraordinarily fine-tuned mind) and could easily pass for a clerk, an accountant, a banker, the next guy in line at the supermarket, maybe a bartender. In fact, Buffett once made a nonspeaking, cameo appearance in 1988 as a bartender in an ABC-TV soap opera, "Loving."

In 1991 Buffett and his friend, Capital Cities/ABC chairman

Thomas Murphy, made a four minute appearance on ABC's soap opera "All My Children." Playing themselves, they were beseeched by femme fatale Erica Kane, played by actress Susan Lucci. She asked the financiers for advice about her cosmetics company. Buffett's recommendation: go public. For their advice, Ms. Kane gave Buffett and Murphy big hugs and Buffett said, "Murph, Erica Kane gives a whole new meaning to the word 'takeover.'"

Buffett would later joke "If we run against the test pattern on the other two networks, I expect to do very well," and he followed up with flowers to the show's producer and a note saying he wanted to renegotiate his contract.

"He looks like an old college professor," says Omaha stockbroker Cliff Hayes, who for years executed some of the stock trades—including The Washington *Post* Co. and GEICO Corp.—that were to make Buffett a billionaire. "He's often just in casual clothes."

Buffett kids about his own appearance, once telling Salomon clients participating in a conference by speaker phone that they were in a "preferred position" because they could hear him but not see him.

Buffett looks like the absent-minded professor—tousled hair, rumpled clothes and all. It is when he opens his mouth that people snap to attention because of the crystal clarity, penetration and facile summary which he can articulate about a complex problem.

Patricia Bauer, the West Coast editor for Channels magazine, reported that Buffett showed up for a November, 1986 interview at Omaha's Red Lion Inn in khakis and a jacket and tie. "I dressed up for you," he said, smiling sheepishly.

"He's not a clotheshorse. He buys on need," says an employee at Parsow's, where Buffett sometimes buys his clothes.

Although the *Wall Street Journal* once reported he wears $1,500 Italian suits, that is certainly the exception and not the rule with Buffett.

As his daughter told the Omaha *World-Herald* on February 12, 1992, "My mother was in town one day and said, 'Let's get him a new suit.' We were so sick of looking at those clothes that he's had for thirty years. So we bought him a camel-hair blazer and a blue blazer, just to get some new ones. And he had me return them. He said, 'I have a camel-hair blazer and a blue blazer,' and he was serious. I sent them back. Finally I went out, unbeknownst to him, and picked out a suit. I didn't even look at the price tag. I looked for something that would be comfortable and conservative-looking. He won't wear anything that isn't extremely conservative. And he tried it on. It was comfortable. He didn't even look at the price tag. The suit was very boring and conservative, and he bought a few of them. Now he's getting criticized, and it makes me furious because I'm the one to blame for that."

A cowlick and unruly thatch of thinning hair stands atop a round, open, owlish face that somehow says "I am from the Midwest," and which often has an eager, quizzical look. His head is somewhat egg-shaped, dotted with hazel eyes that need the help of thick bifocals. His forehead is high; his ears Lyndon Johnson-like.

His gait is a loping affair. In his eagerness to get where he's going, he seems to overstep slightly what would be a normal stride. The resulting somewhat ungainly appearance is that of a man trying to step across a room in one less stride than normal.

His smile wrinkles are deep and his impish grin comes easily. His face is usually animated, but can become positively grim at the bridge table. When his mouth opens, rapid speech comes in a Mid-western twang delivered from a reservoir of total intellectual honesty. He has a fast, dry wit and in both appearance and style, and in his sunny disposition, he comes across as somewhat of a mix between Jack Benny and Will Rogers.

He has great energy and zest for life.

His manner is that of a great teacher searching restlessly and conscientiously for the truth, trying with all his heart to pass on to others what he's discovered about coping in an imperfect world, which happens to contain an imperfect stock market, whatever others may say about its efficiency. Buffett teaches that the true investor waits as long as it takes for the misappraised stock price, the one that offers great value, then when it's "two inches above the navel," you swing for the fences.

Perhaps more than a teacher, the core of his being is that of a student. The essential reason for his success is his common sense, his own genius, and his extraordinarily intense study of his area of greatest interest—business.

Seriousness of study has done nothing to hamper a great sense of fun and sophisticated sense of humor, whether it be needling himself, Wall Street, or human conduct in general.

A large worry line runs straight down his forehead just to the left of its center. One would guess it's the result of years of reading the *Wall Street Journal*, Value Line and Moody's sheets as well as hundreds of trade publications and annual reports. He also reads the mainline business magazines and has a subscription to Outstanding Investor Digest, joking that reading it is a good way to keep up with what Munger is doing. He has said he owns 100 shares of about 200 companies, because he's an annual report nut who wants the reports mailed directly to him and not through the slow bureaucracy of brokerage firm mailings. And he tells shareholders to do the same, to have at least one Berkshire share registered in your own name. That way you can get the reports in a timely fashion.

His "aw shucks" attitude is genuine and his manner is open and straightforward. Most often it is described as folksy, corn-fed and homespun.

Once, the pilot for Peter Kiewit & Sons, Inc., who flies the Berkshire plane, called Buffett's office to inquire if he needed lunch reservations. Buffett's administrative assistant, Gladys Kaiser, said not to bother, that Buffett wouldn't need a thing. "He arrived with his mother and a picnic lunch," says Omaha stockbroker George Morgan.

For lunch Buffett often has popcorn, potato chips and Cherry Coke. The menu has not impressed his doctors, but they declare him healthy.

Warren Buffett's easy manner and down-home ways do not exclude him from being the highly sophisticated man he is. Occasionally he does put on a black tie, as he did to escort Katharine Graham to her seventieth birthday party. He has had dinner with Ronald and Nancy Reagan and been seated at dinner parties next to both Barbara Bush and Jane Muskie. He has even popped up at fancy watering holes in the Bahamas and he showed up at the 1988 Winter Olympics in Calgary, where Agnes Nixon, creator of "All My Children," talked him into his first soap opera appearance.

Scheduled to team with Martina Navratilova in a celebrity tennis match against Pam Shriver and former Dallas Cowboys quarterback Danny White, he assured interviewers that "the majority of my training for this event is to learn how to say 'yours' in Czechoslovakian." (Omaha *World-Herald*, January 21, 1992)

And despite his kidding about how little he knows about technology, particularly computers, he has spent hours at a time swapping stories with Microsoft Corp. founder William Gates. Buffett is no hayseed.

Still, funny things do happen to Buffett. One Sunday in the mid-1980's, Buffett found himself unable to pay a small bill. "He was in his grubbies having a malt and chips or something, and I realized there was some problem in paying the bill," recalls Virginia Lee Pratt, a retired schoolteacher in Omaha who is a long-time bridge playing friend of Buffett's mother.

"I said, Warren, could I help and he said, 'this is pretty embarrassing'."

The bill at Goodrich Dairy was $3.49 but Buffett had given his children his small bills and had only a $100 bill on him that the small shop couldn't change.

Pratt stepped in and paid the bill.

"He sent a check the next day with a letter asking if, since he had established credit, could he up his line of credit to five dollars," she said.

Mrs. Pratt was so honored to have a check signed by Buffett that she didn't cash it and wrote him that he should check his books because he'd be off by $3.49.

"At our next bridge game, his mother brought me $3.50 in cash," Pratt said.

Buffett is conscientious about paying his bills, but he also wants full value when he's on the receiving end, even to the point of taking advantage of coupons.

Once Buffett presented a coupon for $3.95 off his dinner at the

French Cafe. "I want this to show up on the check," waiter Chris Nisi recalls him saying. "When the bill came, he checked it over and found it was there. He had kidded about it all along. He was half kidding but he was half serious, too."

In his early days he served on some civic boards, furthering the cause of Planned Parenthood or the local Boys Club, but he has so many demands on his time, he doesn't do a lot in the way of civic or charity work, and there is some grumbling about that in Omaha. He has certainly made substantial contributions to the local United Way, education generally and a little to AIDS education. He has committed most of his giving to reproductive freedom (pro-choice). And his civic and charity efforts are hardly finished. After all, he is leaving his fortune to the Buffett Foundation and thus to society.

Buffett does his own taxes, saying they actually are quite simple.

Some have described him as almost reclusive. Neighbors rarely see him. He is not a yard hound and doesn't tend it himself. Instead he spends time indoors reading or attending board meetings related to Berkshire's far-flung empire.

He's quite gregarious around friends. He hoards a good portion of his time for reading and studying. Some people have described him as shy and yet he can talk up a storm and dominate conversations at will. And if he is shy, it does not mean he doesn't have confidence in his own abilities. He has said, after all, he knew even as a youngster that he would be rich.

In person, Buffett is totally unpretentious, though well aware he is something of a folk hero and that Wall Street—and others in the room—are watching him. "I watch my every move and I'm not that impressed," he quips.

Who's Who in America carries just a brief mention, describing him as a "corporate executive," which is about the equivalent of saying Michael Jordan plays basketball.

Herbert Sklenar, president of Birmingham's Vulcan Materials Co., the nation's foremost producer of crushed stone, grew up on a farm near Omaha, attended Benson High School and is among those who see Buffett at class reunions (although Buffett never actually attended Benson, having left for Washington when his father was elected to Congress).

"He [Buffett] was the second person I ran into at the reunion in 1988," Sklenar recalls. During the reunion attendees were asked to update their lives and Sklenar said he was with a company "that makes big stones into little stones." Buffett got up before the group and offered a little witty investment advice.

Sklenar, who went to Harvard and has hefty experience on the financial side of corporations, admits he'd want to think twice about any possible business proposition with Buffett. "He's just so darn smart," Sklenar said.

Buffett's style is to tackle problems his intellectual brilliance can solve, but to steer clear of problems it cannot. He has often said he is trying to step over one-foot obstacles, not jump over seven-footers. He strives to make things as easy as possible by seeking common sense, efficient ways of doing things, of making the layups he talks about, not wild shots from half court. He works hard at the possible and avoids the impossible.

One of his great messages is to avoid trouble. In the stock market, that means staying away from permanent capital loss. "Anything can happen in stock markets," he warns, "and you ought to conduct your affairs so that if the most extraordinary events happen, that you're still around to play the next day."—Buffett on Adam Smith's "Money World" show, June 20, 1988.

Buffett is generally early to bed and early to rise.

He watches television about seven hours a week, keeping abreast mainly of news and sports. He is a statistics nut and his recall of basketball trivia is nearly encyclopedic.

An occasional trace of ego slips through. L.J. Davis wrote in the April 1, 1990 edition of the New York *Times Magazine* that Buffett has no calculators, no Quotrons, and no computers in his office. "I am a computer," Buffett told him flatly.

Buffett and a staff of ten operate out of a five-room suite (dubbed by him as "World Headquarters") on the fourteenth floor of pale green Kiewit Plaza, in the shadow of the far more imposing home office of Mutual of Omaha. "World Headquarters" has been described as "linoleum floors and throw rugs." Over the years it has been upgraded to industrial carpet and cypress green plastic-weave wallpaper, but it is far from the opulence of most corporate offices. On the door is a sign saying "No admittance except by appointment."

Russ Fletcher, now with Torchmark, did have an appointment one Saturday morning in the mid-1980s when he dropped in to see Berkshire vice president Mike Goldberg. "I walked in and he [Buffett] was behind his secretary's desk opening the mail," Fletcher recalls. "He was dressed in blue jeans and a turtleneck. . . . He said 'hi' and we exchanged pleasantries . . . He's very unassuming."

When he's not opening the mail, Buffett runs Berkshire's empire from a rather small desk near the corner of the 325-square-foot office he calls "the Pleasure Palace." Berkshire's entire "World Headquarters" is 3,775 square feet—leased. Buffett reads and stays in constant phone contact with his managers, friends and brokers, and sends a steady stream of short, witty notes in the mail.

Rare visitors are greeted by a small porcelain plaque given to him by his wife. The inscription reads, "A fool and his money are soon invited everywhere."

Mementos of stock market history abound. Scattered about are miniature sculptures of bulls and bears. On the walls are stock quotations from the stock market crash of 1929, a portrait of Buffett's father and a photo of Ben Graham. Also on the office wall is a Pulitzer Prize for the exposé of Boys Town by his now defunct Omaha *Sun* newspapers.

In *The Money Masters,* John Train noted the presence of an antique Thomas Edison stock ticker tape given to Buffett by a friend, and several editions of Graham and Dodd's *Security Analysis.*

Buffett's desk, though strewn with copies of the *Wall Street Journal,* the Omaha *World-Herald* and business magazines, is neither clear nor messy. "It's in between," says Dr. Ronald W. Roskens, former president of the University of Nebraska, who has occasionally called on Buffett at his office about civic or charitable missions. "It's what makes sense . . . He's trying to keep things simple." At times, the desk sports notepads that read, "In case of nuclear war, disregard this message."

He has other notepads as well. Buffett once sent me a photo of myself with Coca-Cola's Don Keough at the Berkshire annual meeting in 1991. It came with a little Post-it note saying he thought I'd enjoy the photo. What was unusual about the note was the inscription at the bottom which read:

> "An absolutely brilliant memo"—*NY Times*
> "Clear . . . concise . . . to the point"—*Fortune*
> "Masterful use of the language"—*Atlantic.*

At his office, there are few visitors—maybe two or three people a week will get a short audience—and they never include stockbrokers or analysts.

But he has an extraordinarily wide range of friends with whom he stays in contact by phone and letter. He occasionally lectures at schools like Columbia, Stanford, Harvard, Notre Dame or Creighton, but he almost never goes on television and only occasionally grants an interview.

Buffett's aversion to interviews was documented in a four-page story in Money magazine by Gary Belsky, who told about not being able to get an interview with Buffett after his administrative assistant, Mrs. Kaiser, turned down his request.

Even after Belsky flew to Omaha, Belsky got the same answer when he called Mrs. Kaiser from the lobby of Kiewit Plaza. He reported that the guard who heard the phone conversation said: "You took that better than most."

BELSKY: Most? Do people drop by like this a lot?
GUARD: About once a day.
BELSKY: Does she ever let them up?
GUARD: Sometimes.
BELSKY: Do you think she'll let me up?
GUARD: No. (Money magazine, August 1991)

The story was reported in the Omaha *World-Herald* under the headline "Buffett Ignores Money," which would certainly be news.

With few visitors, Buffett hunkers down over his work, often snacking at his desk. The storeroom is filled with staples of Buffett's phoneside lunches—Hawaiian potato chips, Cherry Cokes and See's Candy, all of which accompany the hamburgers he often has for lunch.

Not all calls to Buffett are about billion dollar deals. "Sometimes it's a wrong number," he jokes. And sometimes it's a request for an annual report. Recalls Dr. Wallace Gaye, a Berkshire shareholder who lives in Durham, New Hampshire: "I called Berkshire in 1988 because I didn't get my annual report. I cannot prove this in a court of law, but I'm 99 percent sure I got him . . . He had a clipped, fast voice. He said 'that's awful' that I didn't get the report. I started to ask if he was Warren Buffett, but I just couldn't . . . He was fast. He said something like he'd fix it. Two days later I got the report."

People who have known him for years say they have never seen him angry.

His reply to things that are okay with him is usually "Yeah, sure." If something displeases him, his reply can be, "We don't need any of that."

He works very hard and long hours. "He's thinking about three things at a time. He's thinking about it [Berkshire] twenty-four hours a day," says an employee of a Berkshire subsidiary.

Buffett's administrative assistant, Gladys Kaiser, has been with him since December 1967, when she walked in as a "temporary" Kelly Girl. Buffett expects her to remain on the job forever. He told Fortune magazine on April 11, 1988, that "things just wouldn't quite work around here without her . . . I wish her immortality. If Gladys can't have it, I'm not sure I want it either."

Another of the handful of people working close to Buffett at "World Headquarters" is Michael A. Goldberg, forty-four, an intense, hard-driving man who heads Berkshire's far-flung nationwide insurance operations. "He's so damn smart and quick that people who are around him all the time feel a constant mental pressure trying to keep up. You'd need a strong ego to survive in headquarters," Goldberg has told Buffett's friend and chronicler, Carol Loomis of Fortune magazine.

Goldberg, who was already a top executive with the Pacific Stock Exchange when he came to Berkshire as a young man, told Loomis, "I've had a chance to see someone who can't be believed. The negative is: How do you ever think much of your abilities after being around Warren Buffett?" Goldberg later told Linda Grant for a Los Angeles *Times* story, April 7, 1991, that: "Warren Buffett is a person who, the closer he gets, the more extraordinary he gets. If you tell people about him, the way he is, they just think you were bamboozled."

Buffett's one acknowledgment of modern technology is a bank of two telephones that can connect him with brokerage firms when the need arises. Actually, he's also installed a fax machine, but the number is unlisted.

His health has always been good, although he suffers somewhat from a back problem that has forced him to cut back on tennis. He has played golf off and on for years and has about a twenty handicap. Those who have played with him describe his game as so-so, but they say he is very competitive, improving as the round goes and most likely to come through in the clutch, say, when things are tied up on the eighteenth. His style in golf is to save his two mulligans for the last two holes, says one golfing partner.

Over the years a slight paunch has developed in his middle. He admits his diet and exercise habits are not all they should be. At the height of the Salomon crisis, Buffett called his friend James Burke, the former chairman of Johnson & Johnson. Buffett said he was having trouble sleeping and asked Burke for help. When Burke said he ran three to five miles a day during Johnson & Johnson's Tylenol crisis, Buffett hesitated and then said, "Any other suggestions?" (*Wall Street Journal*, November 14, 1991)

His home is the same three-story, five-bedroom frame house he bought in 1958 for $32,000, located in a middle class Dundee section several blocks from where he was born and near where his wife was born. It is about twenty blocks from Kiewit Plaza, where he runs Berkshire.

Over the years he has furnished the home largely with items from Omaha's Nebraska Furniture Mart, which Berkshire bought in 1983. His home is full of books, including the works of Bertrand Russell, from which Buffett can quote long passages. From his house, Buffett can nose down to the Pleasure Palace in less than five minutes. Another several minutes and he's in downtown Omaha.

One of his main guideposts is that it's a lot easier to stay out of trouble now than to get out of trouble later. Along with keeping things simple, he wants to keep distractions to a minimum and to be consistent. If you can live close to the office, do. If the restaurant serves a hamburger or steak you like, why search out a diner across town?

One Wall Streeter, Marshall Weinberg, a stockbroker with Gruntal & Co., has recalled going to the old Reuben's restaurant in New York for a meal with Buffett. "He had an exceptional ham-and-cheese sandwich. A few days later, we were going out again. He said, 'Let's go back to that restaurant.' I said, 'But we were just there.' 'Precisely. Why take the risk with another place? We know exactly what we're going to get.' "

One of Buffett's tenets is don't run all around without a good reason. You can do most of what you need to do right where you are. "I'll be in Omaha as long as I live," Buffett has told Berkshire shareholders.

Another lesson is do things yourself. He drove himself to the Berkshire annual meeting in 1989, parking his car around back of the Joslyn Art Museum. Just as he was about to get back in the car after the meeting, a Berkshire shareholder came up to him with a very thick pile of papers and asked him if he would look at them. He said he would and she asked if she should mail them to him.

"Oh, no. I'll just take them and read them back at the office." He took the pile, got in his 1983 dark blue Cadillac and, no doubt, drove back to the office and read the papers.

It was not until 1991 that Buffett actually bought himself a new car, a Lincoln Town Car, four-door sedan. "I think he's getting a little mellower," said Omaha stockbroker George Morgan of the purchase.

In addition to tennis and golf, Buffett's hobbies include handball, but his particular passion is for bridge—on occasion with a deck of cards that say on the top of each card, "Make checks payable to Warren Buffett." Bridge, he is fond of saying, is better than a cocktail party. "I always say I wouldn't mind going to jail if I had three cellmates who played bridge," he says. "Any young person who doesn't take up bridge is making a real mistake," he told the New York *Times* on May 20, 1990.

Buffett's bridge partners have included ageless comedian George Burns, who played Buffett (and Munger and others) at a table reserved for Burns at the Hillcrest Country Club in Los Angeles under a sign that reads, "No Cigar Smoking if Under 65." Burns, an excellent player, beat Buffett.

Instead of drinking and dancing at some big city disco, he takes an interest in his family, gets some exercise and has been a lifelong model train buff.

When he is in New York, he often stays at Katharine Graham's apartment and plays bridge with John and Carol Loomis and George Gillespie III. Gillespie, a close friend, is a partner in the Cravath, Swaine & Moore law firm and a large shareholder in The Washington Post Co. He is known for his support in fighting muscular dystrophy. The foursome pass the evening playing bridge and eating peanuts, ice cream and deli sandwiches. It's their idea of a big night in the Big Apple.

6 BERKSHIRE HATHAWAY INC.

"We learned a lot of lessons, but I wish we had learned them somewhere else."

In 1929, several textile operations with a lot of common ownership were joined together with Berkshire Cotton Manufacturing Co. (incorporated in 1889) and renamed Berkshire Fine Spinning Associates. The resulting operation was a textile giant that once spun a quarter of the nation's fine cotton.

In the 1930s its many mills used about one percent of the electric output in the New England states. However, the company was not a money maker and preferred dividends were omitted in late 1930 and for the next six years. World War II and the immediate postwar years, however, brought profits.

In 1955, Hathaway Manufacturing Co., a New Bedford, Massachusetts, manufacturer of both synthetic and cotton textiles, was merged into Berkshire Fine Spinning Associates and the name was changed to Berkshire Hathaway Inc., the company that would soon become Buffett's investment vehicle.

Even though the company has no relation to the Hathaway shirts made famous by its ads featuring a man with a patch over his eye, Buffett has said when he first bought Berkshire Hathaway, "I must have had seven calls in Omaha asking if I had to wear an eye patch."

Once, Barron's editor Alan Abelson described Berkshire this way in his column: "Warren Buffett, for recent emigres from Minsk and Pinsk, is the investor who runs a funny company called Berkshire Hathaway, which everyone thinks makes shirts but really makes money."

Back in 1948 the combined Berkshire Hathaway companies had after-tax earnings of almost $18 million and employed 10,000 people at a dozen large mills throughout New England.

The merged companies had 1955 sales of $595 million, which produced a loss of $10 million. That year, Berkshire Hathaway's stockholders' equity was $55,448,000.

During the next nine years, Berkshire Hathaway's stockholders' equity fell to $22,139,000. But as late as 1961 its managers were still calling it a strong company with a bright future. In a 1961 address to the Newcomen Society, a group dedicated to promoting free enterprise, Berkshire Hathaway president Seabury Stanton said, "Today, Berkshire Hathaway is the largest textile manufacturer of cotton and synthetic fabrics in New England. A total of about a million spindles and approximately 12,000 looms each year produce 225,000,000 yards of fabrics, consisting of fancy colored dress goods, handkerchief, fabrics, lawns, voiles, dimities, combed and carded sateens, rayon linings, dacron marquisette curtain fabrics and dacron cotton blends. The total employment numbers approximately 5,800 people. All seven plants operate on a three-shift basis and Berkshire Hathaway does an average annual business of better than sixty million dollars."

But business kept declining in the early 1960s. Buffett began buying shares of Berkshire Hathaway in 1962, picking them up for $7 and $8 a share for his Buffett Partnership, Ltd. Still the business downturn continued and Berkshire's balance sheet on October 3, 1964, showed stockholders' equity of $22 million and assets of $27,887,000.

Buffett kept up the buying and by 1968 the partnership had a 70 percent controlling interest in the company. Buffett's total stake in Berkshire was acquired for about $14 million. (Forbes, October 21, 1991)

Berkshire chairman, Malcolm G. Chace, Jr., paved the way for Buffett to buy a key block of stock from Chace's relatives, allowing him to gain the controlling interest. Chace's immediate family held on to its Berkshire stock and became superwealthy.

Buffett became chairman of the board of Berkshire Hathaway in 1970. He would keep the textile business until 1985, although it was never very prosperous. He finally sold it for almost nothing, getting only scrap value for the equipment. It turned out to be one of the few business quagmires into which Buffett sank money.

Buffett would explain at the Berkshire annual meeting in 1991 that the textile business was essentially a commodity business and, despite the fact that a huge number of men's suits had Hathaway linings in World War II, it all eventually came to mean nothing when a foreign business could produce the linings more cheaply. "I knew it was a tough business . . . I was either more arrogant or innocent then. We learned a lot of lessons, but I wish we could have learned them somewhere else," he said.

Today the old red Berkshire buildings in New Bedford are about worthless. But under the management of Bill Betts, who leases parts of them as office space and for warehouse storage, they provide Berkshire a small stream of income that is shipped off to Buffett to invest.

Although the textile business, which was once described by Berkshire Hathaway vice chairman Charles Munger as "a small, doomed New England textile enterprise," didn't last, the name Berkshire Hathaway did. "He named the company after his biggest mistake," says stockbroker George Morgan.

Even Buffett, in looking back over what he said were the mistakes of the first twenty-five years, has said his first mistake was buying Berkshire at all. Even though he recognized it as an unpromising business, he bought it because the price looked cheap.

But he used Berkshire's cash inflow to buy other business for Berkshire.

In 1965 Buffett Partnership informed Berkshire it held 500,975 shares, or about 49 percent of the outstanding stock of the company. Buffett's Partnership had become Berkshire's largest shareholder.

And Buffett Partnership kept right on buying. By January 1967, it owned 59.5 percent and as of April 1, 1968, it owned almost 70 percent of Berkshire, according to documents filed with the Securities and Exchange Commission.

Meanwhile Berkshire was making its own acquisitions, launching into the insurance business with a tender offer for National Indemnity Co. on February 23, 1967.

And in early 1969 Berkshire bought 97 percent of The Illinois National Bank and Trust Co., and at about the same time it bought all the stock of Sun Newspapers, Inc. and Blacker Printer, Inc., which were Berkshire's first entry into the publishing business.

Sun Newspapers published five weekly newspapers in Omaha with a circulation of about 50,000. The related printing businesses were run under the management of Stanford Lipsey, soon to become a close friend of Buffett.

In 1970 Buffett Partnership ceased to be a stockholder and parent of Berkshire and distributed, pro rata to its partners, 691,441 Berkshire shares. After the liquidation, Buffett quietly stepped in to buy Berkshire shares for himself.

By the time Buffett was forty years old, he controlled Berkshire.

Today it is a far-reaching investment holding company that holds seven percent of the stock of Coca-Cola, 18 percent of the stock of Capital Cities/ABC, more than 48 percent of the stock of GEICO and about 11 percent of the stock of Gillette stock, as well as other large stock, bond and cash holdings.

It also has nine diverse operating businesses and a large insurance business.

Berkshire fits no real category—in corporate listings it variously gets lumped in with insurance, candy, media, diversified, nonbank financial, investment, miscellaneous or conglomerate firms. Berkshire is a hybrid that is all of the above.

Although Berkshire's stock market value makes it about the 60th largest public company in the United States, and about the 150th largest in the world, practically no analyst follows it. To find out about the company, you have to make your own effort.

Perhaps several times a year the company will issue one-sentence announcements of a new investment. And about the only way to get a picture of how Berkshire stands is to ask the company for an annual report.

Beyond its plain looks—its largely hidden-from-view chairman, its tiny headquarters in Omaha at Kiewit Plaza, its plain-bound annual report, its largely no-comment policy—lies a world of beautiful businesses.

They're not sexy businesses—the products are ordinary items like uniforms, shoes, vacuum cleaners—but they are profitable. Some of the businesses earn a return on equity of 20 percent.

Well, have a seat. Warren Buffett's mundane businesses in some years return an astronomical 50 percent return on equity alone and in 1989 reached an astounding 67 percent return based on historical returns, a figure almost no one in the business world has ever heard about or seen! Most businessmen talk happily in terms of a 15 to 20 percent return on equity.

The dry businesses that supply these heavenly numbers are: The Buffalo *News*, a newspaper in upstate New York; Fechheimer, a uniform company based in Cincinnati; Scott Fetzer Manufacturing Group, of Chicago, which has a variety of manufacturing businesses; World Book, also of Chicago, the encyclopedia maker; Kirby, a vacuum cleaner maker based in Cleveland, Ohio; Nebraska Furniture Mart, a large furniture store in Omaha; and See's Candies, a San Francisco, California, candy maker with 225 stores, mainly in the West, serving chocoholics of all ages; and H.H. Brown Shoe Company, Inc., of Greenwich, Connecticut.

Berkshire also owns Borsheim's, a jewelry store in Omaha, which might not sound like much, until you find it may have more sales than any other single jewelry store in the country, with the exception of Tiffany & Co.'s New York store.

Further, Berkshire's Wesco Financial Corp., of Pasadena, California, in some ways a sort of baby Berkshire, in turn owns a handful of businesses, mainly the Mutual Savings and Loan Association. Wesco also has an insurance business, a steel business, some land in California, about 7.2 million shares of Federal Home Loan Mortgage

Corp. stock and many of the same investments as Berkshire, such as Coca-Cola stock.

In addition to these operating businesses, there is the separate insurance business. It is the property and casualty insurance business—Berkshire's largest operating business—that is the vehicle through which Buffett usually makes his securities investments such as his $1 billion purchase of Coca-Cola stock. Berkshire's insurance operations consist of twelve rather small companies led by National Indemnity Co. of Omaha.

Berkshire—listed on the New York Stock Exchange under the symbol BRK and as BerkHa in newspaper listings—has about 22,000 employees, as well as about 30,000 mostly part-time workers who sell World Books.

Buffett's 479,242 shares (41.8 percent) of Berkshire's 1,146,441 shares is by far the largest ownership position. Buffett's wife, Susie, owns 36,994 shares (3.2 percent) of the stock. Her voting and investment power is shared with her husband.

Most top officers have a substantial portion of their net worth in Berkshire. Buffett's description is apt when he tells people, "We eat our own cooking."

According to Standard & Poor's, only seven percent of the stock (about 78,000 shares) is held by institutions (104). That leaves some 93 percent of the stock in the hands of Buffett and about 15,000 shareholders. Many of those individuals own ten shares or less. Some consider it an honor to own even one share.

On the other hand, Buffett, his wife, and Berkshire vice chairman Charles T. Munger own almost 50 percent of the company.

Munger and Buffett's friend Sandy Gottesman, who heads the First Manhattan investment firm in New York, and Dr. William Angle of Omaha are among the major shareholders. Malcolm Chace, a private investor in his late eighties, a former chairman of Berkshire, is a large stockholder whose cost basis on some of his Berkshire shares is said to be twenty-five cents. Chace and his son, Malcolm G. Chace III, who replaced his father on the Berkshire board in 1992, are the largest Berkshire shareholders after the Buffett family.

Berkshire, managed by Buffett and just a handful of people, operates in such a lean manner it is almost a parody of other corporations. Munger has said that one time in its early days Berkshire was subpoenaed for its staffing papers in connection with one of its acquisitions. "There were no papers. There was no staff," Munger said at Berkshire's annual meeting in 1991.

In keeping with its lean corporate structure, carefully devised by Buffett, there are only six directors on the board. Furthermore, the board has no standing committees and gets little in the way of outside advice. Berkshire's board includes Buffett himself; his wife, Susan T. Buffett; Munger; Malcolm G. Chace, III; J. Verne McKenzie, Berkshire's chief financial officer; and Walter Scott, Jr., chairman and chief executive of Peter Kiewit Sons, Inc., a privately held construction firm based in Omaha, whose record is so good that Buffett has said he won't recount it for fear of making Berkshire shareholders restive.

Munger is the chairman of Wesco and vice chairman of Berkshire. Buffett is chairman of the board, chief executive officer, and Berkshire's heart and soul.

7 BERKSHIRE HATHAWAY INSURANCE GROUP AND GEICO CORP.

"If you want to be loved, it's clearly better to sell high-priced corn flakes than low-priced auto insurance."

Some of Warren Buffett's most lucrative if not glamorous investments have been in the insurance business. Berkshire Hathaway's largest business is property and casualty insurance and Berkshire also owns a major interest in GEICO Corp., which sells auto and home insurance through the mail and by telephone.

Normally, Berkshire Hathaway writes insurance for commercial vehicles and workmen's compensation through a dozen insurance companies nationwide. But Berkshire has insured carnivals, free-throw contests, basketball and hockey games. Buffett says Berkshire may be the largest writer of super-catastrophe ("super-cat") business in the world. It writes such business as $10 million policies against earthquakes and coverage other insurance companies buy to protect themselves against a major catastrophe.

The firm got its risk-taking philosophy from Jack Ringwalt, who died in 1984. Ringwalt founded National Indemnity in 1940 for two Omaha cab companies that couldn't get insurance. In 1967 Buffett bought the company, which still did much commercial vehicle business.

Ringwalt wrote his own memoirs and, according to the Omaha

World-Herald story, Ringwalt said Buffett was about twenty years old when the two met. Buffett was trying to raise $100,000 to start an investment pool. Ringwalt said he offered to invest $10,000. Buffett, however, said he would accept nothing less than $50,000. "I remarked, 'If you think I am going to let a punk kid like you handle $50,000 of my money, you are even nuttier than I thought,'" Ringwalt wrote. Ringwalt took back his offer of the $10,000. "If I had put in $50,000 at the time he so desired, I could have taken out $2 million after taxes twenty years later. I did pretty well with National Indemnity Co., but not that well."

Although it covers risks, insurance itself can be a risky business, as even Buffett's sometimes up and down insurance record can attest. Insurance companies always have a huge potential for liabilities should claims come due. And that potential problem includes Berkshire. "The property-casualty insurance industry is not only subnormally profitable, it is subnormally popular," Buffett wrote in Berkshire's 1988 annual report.

Occasionally, Buffett has misjudged the insurance business, known for its boom-and-bust cycles, and has been the first to admit it. Overall, his predictions about industry trends have been remarkable, often predicting years ahead how things would turn out.

In 1988, he said a tough cycle, which started in 1986, would probably last about another four years. He got those four years right. He also predicted that, at some point, Berkshire would be ready to write some big insurance business while much of the rest of the industry was in trouble.

The appeal of the insurance business is that premiums come in up front—cash in the form of other people's money arriving at the office every day. You take those premiums and invest the money and the money grows. Essentially, the insurance businesses provide "float" that can be invested. They provide Berkshire with cheap financing. "We have about $1.5 billion at a cost of $20 or $30 million. That's attractive to us," Buffett said at the annual meeting in 1990. By 1992 the float was more than $2 billion.

Berkshire usually writes "long tail" insurance policies most likely to be paid off in the distant future. Clearly, it's good to have the policyholder's money for as long as possible, but Buffett also has warned that long tail policies are tricky because, by the time comes to pay policyholders, inflation and regulations may have raised costs so much, there are no profits left.

Another factor that has hurt the insurance business is court-award judgments far in excess of what was contemplated at the time the policies were written.

Insurance is an important business, especially in Nebraska, where the business has received favorable treatment by state lawmakers.

Starting in March 1967, when Berkshire made a tender offer for National Indemnity and National Fire and Marine Insurance, Buffett bought the dozen insurance businesses Berkshire now owns.

Berkshire entered insurance for diversity and for increased profits.

National Indemnity, which as late as five or six years ago was still using old IBM card sorters, occupies a six-story, 35,000-square-foot building in Omaha and owns an adjoining 9,600-square-foot building, not far from Berkshire's headquarters.

In addition to National Indemnity, Berkshire's lead insurance company, Berkshire also owns:

- Columbia Insurance Company, Omaha, Nebraska
- Cypress Insurance Company, Pasadena, California
- National Liability and Fire Insurance Company, Chicago, Illinois
- National Fire and Marine Insurance Company, Omaha, Nebraska
- Redwood Fire and Casualty Insurance Company, Omaha, Nebraska
- Continental Divide Insurance Company, Englewood, Colorado
- Cornhusker Casualty Company, Omaha, Nebraska
- Kansas Fire and Casualty Company, Overland Park, Kansas
- National Indemnity Company of Florida, St. Petersburg, Florida
- National Indemnity Company of Mid America, St. Paul, Minnesota

- Wesco-Financial Insurance Company, a subsidiary of Wesco, Omaha, Nebraska.

The underwriting activities of these businesses include the handling of almost all forms of property and casualty insurance, through agents, in the District of Columbia and in all fifty states except Hawaii.

The sale of auto insurance accounts for about half of the business. The businesses also sell trucking insurance, workers compensation, homeowners, fire, and even insurance policies for those who serve as officers and directors of companies.

For many years Berkshire wrote insurance for taxicabs in Omaha, but it no longer handles that business. Berkshire doesn't have life or health insurance businesses.

Berkshire affiliate, See's Candies, buys its workers compensation insurance at minimum rates through the Berkshire Hathaway Insurance Group.

The insurance group also writes insurance for farm owners, business owners, garage owners, as well as insurance for luxury cars, marine accidents, earthquakes, cargo damage, and burglaries, as well as personal and commercial package policies.

The Berkshire insurance companies also do a hefty reinsurance business, taking on the insurance risk and reward of insurance written by other companies. Reinsurance involves insuring other insurance companies. Reinsurance exists so no one company will get hit with the total cost of something like an earthquake, which might bankrupt a primary insurance company with thousands of policyholders. Reinsurers repackage and then parcel out the really big risks, spreading the risk around as well as taking some of it themselves. To be in reinsurance means one better be able confidently to take on a possible big loss. Berkshire is just that sort of company and its unusual financial strength is a good marketing tool for seeking both insurance and reinsurance business.

The Berkshire folks will write the policies and charge a stiff price for them, but if there is a major catastrophe, Berkshire does have a large risk. "When a major quake occurs in an urban area or a winter storm rages across Europe, light a candle for us," Buffett wrote in Berkshire's 1990 annual report.

For a four year period expiring August 31, 1989, Berkshire had a contract with Fireman's Fund for a seven percent quota share of that company's business. That contract was not renewed.

Buffett apparently would like to expand the insurance business. In 1985 he joined with American Express's Sanford Weill and some senior Fireman's Fund executives in a plan to buy Fireman's Fund from American Express. But the plan, organized by Weill, was rejected by American Express.

Insurance is a tricky business and Buffett has said he is not all that enamored of it. He is, however, in love with the float his far-flung insurance operations provide.

Berkshire's insurance companies own many of the investments Buffett makes, investments which provide such enormous financial strength that it is clear Berkshire can pay policyholders. Carrying far more assets than normally required by the insurance regulators, all twelve of the companies carry an A+ (superior) rating from A.M. Best & Co., the highest rating offered by the insurance rating firm.

A.M. Best's insurance reports leave little doubt about how they regard Berkshire's insurance operations: "The Berkshire Hathaway, Inc. Group is currently within the top 100 insurance groups based on net premiums written. In 1989, total assets were $7.9 billion with policyholder surplus of $6.0 billion . . . Consolidated underwriting commitments of the Berkshire Hathaway Insurance Group remain very conservative in relation to net resources available to meet contingencies . . . Surplus which has advanced annually by at least 25 percent in each of the last five years and a total of 364 percent for the period (1984–89) is over 18 times current writings . . . Cash and other liquid assets greatly exceed reported statement liabilities."

In the early days Buffett himself oversaw the insurance business but he has long since turned it over to Berkshire vice president Mike Goldberg. Ask Goldberg how business is and and he answers, "Lousy." End of conversation.

Because the insurance group is not publicly listed, as are some of the companies in which Berkshire has invested, it's tough to tell exactly what the insurance business is worth. In a 1990 *Barron's* piece about Berkshire being overvalued, no mention was made of Berkshire's insurance businesses, thereby assigning them no worth. But they are of course worth a great deal. Some Berkshire shareholders say the value of the insurance businesses is well above $1 billion.

Always looking for that edge, Buffett early on took a fancy to GEICO Corp., which sells auto and home insurance through the mail and by telephone. Since GEICO doesn't have to pay commissions to agents, but sells directly to consumers, it can undercut its competition.

Buffett's interest was sparked when Ben Graham, his guru at Columbia Business School, served on the company's board. Buffett, only twenty-one at the time, invested $10,000—a whopping two-thirds of his net worth—in it. A year later he sold at a 50 percent profit.

Today, in a tricky industry, GEICO is almost half owned by Berkshire, and is a standout.

The nation's seventh largest insurer of private passenger vehicles, GEICO relies on efficient direct marketing. And it offers a twenty-four-hour, seven-days-a-week telephone line for customers to call in.

Although most property and casualty companies usually lose money in some years on their underwriting, GEICO's losses are considerably below industry average. And only once in the past fourteen years has it failed to make an underwriting profit. That means that almost every year GEICO is generating huge amounts of money to invest without having to pay anything for it—essentially an interest-free loan.

Insurers generally overcome their underwriting losses by making profits from their investments, and here GEICO is well known for savvy investments. It is willing to invest more heavily in the stock markets than most insurance companies, usually outdistancing stock performance averages because of the stock picking abilities of its vice chairman, Lou Simpson.

Back in his college days, Buffett visited GEICO's office one Saturday and found it closed. He knocked on the door until a janitor appeared. Buffett asked if anyone was at work. It turned out that Lorimar A. Davidson was there, a man who was later to become chairman. (John Train, *The Midas Touch*)

Buffett has said, "I was very fortunate many years ago that GEICO's Lorimar Davidson, who didn't know me at the time, spent four to five hours with me one Saturday afternoon explaining GEICO's advantages."

Buffett bought a small amount of the stock.

Eventually he tried the idea out on stockbrokers, but Buffett could not convince them of the promise of the business that sold directly to customers, short-circuiting agents, and thereby making a 20 percent profit on its underwriting activities, compared to the normal rate of about five percent.

The entire company at that time had a market value of $7 million. Today, it's worth more than $3 billion.

But in 1976, because of a miscalculation of its claims and under-pricing, GEICO was closing in on bankruptcy. Buffett believed that GEICO's competitive advantages were still intact. Further, he had great confidence in a newly-named chief executive, John J. Byrne. So, in 1976, Buffett bought 1,294,308 shares of GEICO at an average price of $3.18. During the following five years, Buffett invested $45.7 million of Berkshire's money in GEICO. By December 1980, he had acquired 7,200,000 shares, or one-third of the company, at an average price of $1.31 per share (adjusted for the 5-1 stock split in 1992).

Buffett and Byrne became close friends and GEICO became a cornerstone of Berkshire's growth. Today Berkshire's stake of more than 48 percent of GEICO stock is worth about $1.5 billion.

During its brush with bankruptcy, GEICO needed the help of an investment banker. Salomon Brothers and its partner, John Gutfreund, offered a hand with the turnaround. "Charlie and I like, admire, and trust John. We first got to know him in 1976 when he played a key role in GEICO's escape from near bankruptcy," Buffett wrote in Berkshire's 1987 annual report. (The recent scandal at Salomon may have forced Buffett to revise his opinion of Gutfreund.)

Buffett has described his thinking on the GEICO purchase this way (*Investing in Equity Markets*):

"It wasn't necessarily bankrupt but it was heading there. It was 1976. It had a great business franchise which had not been destroyed by a lot of errors that had been made in terms of exploiting that franchise. And it had a manager . . . I felt he had the ability to get through an extraordinarily tough period there and to re-establish the value of that franchise. They still were a low-cost operator. They made all kinds of mistakes. They still didn't know their costs because they didn't know what their loss reserves should be and they got captivated by growth: they did all kinds of things wrong but they still had the franchise.

"It was similar to American Express in late 1963 when the salad oil scandal hit it. It did not hurt the franchise of the travelers check or the credit card. It could have ruined the balance sheet of American Express, but the answer of course was that American Express with no net worth was worth a tremendous amount of money.

"And GEICO with no net worth was worth a tremendous amount of money too, except it might get closed up the next day because it had no net worth, but I was satisfied that the net worth would be there. The truth is, a lot of insurance companies for the ownership of it would have put up the net worth. We would have put it up. But they were trying to save it for the shareholders, which is what they should have done. It had a very valuable franchise. Take away all the net worth. Let's just say that GEICO paid out a $500 million dividend right now which would eliminate the net worth of GEICO, would it still have a lot of value? Of course, it would have a lot of value. You'd have to do something, you'd have to be part of another entity that kept insurance regulators happy, but the franchise value is the big value in something like that . . ."

GEICO was founded in 1936 in Texas by Leo Goodwin, who had been working as an accountant in an insurance company in San Antonio, Texas. (GEICO annual report of 1985, which contains history of the company's first fifty years.) By studying accident statistics, Goodwin learned that federal, state and municipal employees had fewer accidents than the general population. He also learned that the largest overhead expense for most casualty insurance companies was the cost of advertising and selling. Goodwin saw that if you could cut out the middle man and insure better-than-average drivers, you could sell a thirty-dollar car insurance policy at a large savings of six or seven dollars.

Today, GEICO advertises through such media as CNN, but it still keeps advertising costs low.

In 1936, at the age of fifty, Goodwin chartered Government Employees Insurance Company in Fort Worth to sell car insurance to government workers and military employees, and it eventually grew from that niche into a nationwide writer of automobile and homeowners coverage. In the early days Goodwin sought out Fort Worth banker Cleaves Rhea, who believed in his idea. Rhea agreed to invest $75,000 if Goodwin could put up $25,000 to capitalize the fledgling company. When it was chartered on September 1, 1936, Goodwin received 25 percent of the stock and Rhea 75 percent.

In the difficult early years Rhea and his wife, Lillian, worked twelve hours a day, 365 days a year for a combined monthly salary of $250. Goodwin devoted Saturday afternoons and Sundays to writing personal responses to customers' inquiries or complaints.

The Goodwins targeted government employees as safe drivers with steady incomes. There were more of them in Washington, D.C., so the company was moved there and rechartered on November 30, 1937.

In the fall of 1941, a severe hailstorm damaged thousands of cars in the Washington, D.C., area. Goodwin arranged with repair shops to work twenty-four hours a day exclusively for GEICO policyholders. Anticipating glass shortages, Goodwin had truckloads of glass shipped to Washington, D.C. GEICO's policyholders had their cars repaired in days, while policyholders with other companies waited weeks.

The new company's underwriting losses declined each year until a $5,000 underwriting gain was achieved in 1940, with a $15,000 net income. This was the first of thirty-five consecutive profitable years.

In 1948 the Rhea family sold its 75 percent stock holding to the Graham-Newman Corp. and a small group of private investors. The value of the company was about $3 million. Later that year, when the stock was split into 175,000 shares, Graham-Newman distributed its stock to its shareholders and the company became publicly owned, trading over-the-counter at $20 a share.

In 1949 GEICO passed the $1 million profit mark and began to expand its operations. In 1952 it broadened its insurance eligibility to include all state, county and municipal employees, thus gaining a much larger group of prospects. More than 41,000 new policyholders bought GEICO insurance that year. Written premiums increased by more than 50 percent to $15.2 million.

GEICO President Leo Goodwin retired in 1958 at age seventy-one and became Founder Chairman. He had seen his novel concept —with its operating principles of selling direct and marketing to preferred-risk customers—grow from $104,000 in written premiums to $36.2 million in 1957. From a handful of employees and policyholders, the company had grown to 985 employees and 485,443 policies nationwide.

Investors had fared well, too. If one had bought 100 shares of stock in 1948 for $2,000, he would, at Goodwin's retirement ten years later, have seen his investment grow to a value of $95,000.

But by 1975 GEICO was in financial trouble, at the brink of bankruptcy. In the prior two years, the insurance business had changed drastically. No-fault insurance had been introduced and public clamor over skyrocketing insurance rates had resulted in states requiring prior approval of rates, issuing tough insurance regulations and mandating rate reductions.

In May 1976, the board of directors elected John Byrne as chairman, president and chief executive officer. Byrne took three drastic steps to turn the company around.

> First, Operation Bootstrap—This included rate increases, vigorous cost controls and a reunderwriting of the entire book of business.
> Second, Reinsurance—Byrne convinced twenty-seven GEICO competitors that providing reinsurance relief was in their best interest.

Third, New Capital—The investment banking firm of Salomon Brothers agreed to underwrite a $76 million stock offering, increasing common stock to an equivalent of 34.3 million shares.

Operating profit returned in 1977 with a three-cents-a-share dividend declared late that year.

GEICO had created "sister companies" in 1949, and in 1977 GEICO began to buy back stock of those sister companies.

Considering the diverse businesses, it was apparent a holding company was needed and in 1979 GEICO Corp. was formed. Then, through a series of purchases and tender offers, the company steadily reduced shares outstanding.

From a GEICO dividend of three cents a share in 1977, GEICO's dividend rose to $2.00 in 1990.

The company, headed by chairman William B. Snyder and vice chairman Lou Simpson, in addition to being one of the largest private passenger insurers, also writes homeowners' and life insurance and engages in financial services.

And the company succeeds by using tight cost controls and being choosy about whom it will insure. The emphasis at GEICO is on stellar driving records, and if anything goes wrong with that record, Snyder has said, "We can be fairly unforgiving."

GEICO has kept its underwriting ratios below 100 for all but one year in the past decade, meaning that GEICO takes in more in premiums than it pays out in claims. That sets it apart from most other property-casualty companies, which pay out more in claims than they take in in premiums and rely on investments alone for profits. In general, the industry is substantially dependent on investment income for profits.

In the recent insurance industry-wide slump, GEICO has been beefing up advertising and lowering rates in regions where competitors are hurting. The strategy has resulted in slightly increased market share.

Along the way GEICO has made various investments of its own. A main one is a 34 percent ownership of AVEMCO Corp., an aviation and marine industry insurer. GEICO officials serve on its board.

GEICO has about 6,000 employees, almost all of whom are on the underwriting side, along with just a handful of people under Simpson who make up the investing team. It has more than 3,000 shareholders.

Riggs National Bank of Washington, D.C. holds about nine percent of GEICO stock in a fiduciary capacity, but Berkshire is by far the largest shareholder. GEICO has long been listed by Buffett as a permanent holding.

And so it has been surprising that rumors were circulating in 1990 that Buffett may want to sell part or all of his stake. Or perhaps it was not so surprising, since insurance companies were doing so poorly and analysts were marking down their earnings estimates.

The cloud that looms over GEICO, and other insurance companies, is rate reform and additional regulation. Under California's Proposition 103, GEICO may be required to return to policyholders premiums that have been deemed excessive by the California Department of Insurance.

The company has been adding to reserves for such a contingency as well as withdrawing from doing business in the state, a blow, since it did so much business in the state with huge distances to drive, making cars a particularly important part of life. Of course, GEICO also worries that California's insurance revolt will spread to other states.

The insurance industry has many worries. "GEICO could benefit from the unhappiness," Buffett said at the Berkshire annual meeting in 1990. As other companies run into real trouble, GEICO's strong franchise has enabled the company to increase its business.

Buffett has not sold his stake in GEICO, and what may be more likely is that Buffett will one day wind up being the owner of a greater percentage of GEICO. That's because if GEICO keeps buying back its own stock, long a hallmark of its way of business, Berkshire would ultimately become the majority owner with more than 50 percent of the stock.

In 1991, when Berkshire already owned 48 percent of the stock, the stake was duly noted by Snyder at GEICO's annual meeting, held at a regional office in Dallas. Buffett himself showed up for the meeting, taking a seat in the back row. At the meeting more than 90 percent of the stock was represented in the room. With Buffett in the room, about half the stock is present and accounted for. Snyder, conducting the meeting and spotting Buffett in the back of the room, said, "Warren Buffett is here [applause]. Together Warren Buffett and I own 48 percent of the company."

Actually, Snyder owns well over one percent of GEICO's stock himself.

The prospect of being controlled by Berkshire doesn't seem to bother Snyder, who says, "Warren Buffett is such an enlightened owner that we frankly wouldn't be distressed. We thought about this back when he had thirty-five, thirty-seven percent of the stock and we see no problem. Nothing will change." Snyder has said Buffett exercises no control over the company.

Vice Chairman Lou Simpson echoes the sentiment, "Absolutely nothing changes." Except, of course, that Buffett is on the verge of being the majority owner of GEICO.

Berkshire owns 34,250,00 shares of GEICO.

Former GEICO chairman, David Lloyd Kreeger, a big stockholder who was part of the group that purchased 75 percent of GEICO in 1947, died on November 18, 1990, and rumors began to float—in the midst of a strong third quarter report that showed excellent underwriting results and better news about the insurance environment in California—that the company was possibly for sale.

The rumors came and went, but the company was not sold. GEICO only became stronger and Berkshire's stake in it steadily increased.

GEICO now has about a $755 million stock portfolio and more than $2 billion bond portfolio consisting of tax exempt municipal bonds and Treasury securities. At the end of the 1990s, the GEICO equity portfolio held just eleven positions, positions that included American Express and Federal Home Loan Mortgage Corp., both stocks of interest to Berkshire. Unlike many insurance firms, GEICO has no exposure to real estate and little to junk bonds.

By April 1991, GEICO had bought Tucker, Georgia-based Southern Heritage Insurance Co. for about $17.5 million. It serves Georgia, Alabama, and Virginia and plans expansions to other states. On the heels of that acquisition, GEICO acquired Merastar Insurance Co., of Chattanooga, Tennessee, a property and casualty subsidiary of The NWNL Companies, for about $27 million.

The timing of the transactions could not have been better, as they came when a number of other insurers were withdrawing from the business. As Buffett said in the 1988 Berkshire Annual Report: "If you want to be loved, it's clearly better to sell high-priced corn flakes than low-priced auto insurance." (New York *Times*, March 28, 1989)

GEICO was strong enough to pick up some of the pieces. And it certainly has the ability on the investment side to do something wise with the investable money. After all, its investment folks are occasionally in touch with Warren Buffett.

8 THE OMAHA *SUN* AND THE PULITZER PRIZE

"I told our editor to get a copy of the Boys Town filing."

Buffett's lifelong interest in media properties has always gone far beyond cash flows. He is genuinely interested in media businesses, claims top journalists as friends and has said that if business had not been his calling, journalism might have been. He has a reporter's instinct for the story and his search for undervalued businesses combines a canny business sense and a reporter's detective skills.

Buffett made his first newspaper purchase in 1969 when Berkshire Hathaway bought the Sun Newspapers, neighborhood weeklies in Omaha.

Buffett's role in his many media properties has been almost exclusively devoted to the business side, but he had a very definite impact on the editorial side of things when he played a key role in helping disclose the scandal at Boys Town in Omaha.

Back in 1917, Father Edward J. Flanagan, a lanky Irish Catholic priest, paid ninety dollars to rent a drafty Victorian house to shelter five homeless boys. The home expanded greatly but it also became a financial powerhouse. It helped some children, but it could have helped more with the huge stock portfolio it began accumulating from fundraising.

In 1972, as Buffett recalled for then-*Wall Street Journal* reporter

Jonathan Laing in a March 31, 1977, story, "I knew of an IRS regulation that required charitable foundations to publicly disclose their assets for the first time, so I told our editor to get a copy of the Boys Town filing. I'd heard a lot of rumors during my fund days about Boys Town large stockholdings, but even I was staggered when we found that the home, which was constantly pleading poverty and caring for less than 700 kids, has accumulated assets of more than $200 million."

The subsequent stories in the *Sun* newspapers won a Pulitzer Prize in May 1973, for special local reporting.

Today Boys Town is a well regarded institution helping thousands of youngsters.

"Let's face it," Buffett told Laing, "newspapers are a lot more interesting business than, say, making couplers for rail cars. While I don't get involved in the editorial operations of the papers I own, I really enjoy being a part of institutions that help shape society."

9 THE WASHINGTON POST CO.

"There are some businesses that have very large moats around them."

With his investment in The Washington Post Co., Warren Buffett would demonstrate one of his greatest investment ideas: the concept of the monopoly as a toll bridge. According to Buffett, when a monopoly exists, customers can cross only that "toll bridge." There's no other place to go. A monopoly newspaper like the *Post* is the perfect toll bridge. If you want to advertise in print, there's no other place to get your message across. It's the only game in town.

As he explained in *Investing in Equity Markets*, "There are some businesses that have very large moats around them and they have crocodiles and sharks and piranhas swimming around them. Those are the kind of businesses you want. You want some business that, going back to my day, Johnny Weissmuller in a suit of armor could not make it across the moat. There are businesses like that . . . The trick is to find the ones that haven't been identified by someone else. What you want is a disguised television station or newspaper."

The reason you would like a monopoly television station or newspaper is because most other businesses have to go through that business to advertise.

That amounts to what Buffett calls a "royalty on the other guy's gross sales"—a payment that almost every business in town must make. If you have the only newspaper or television in town, you have to get a good percentage of the advertising business. It becomes a "toll bridge."

Nowhere was this more brilliantly illustrated than in Buffett's experience with the Washington *Post*—although it hardly looked promising at the time.

Founded in 1877, the Washington *Post* had gone through three owners and was bankrupt when financier Eugene Meyer bought it at auction for $825,000 in 1933, during the depths of the Depression. Meyer devoted a fortune to making the morning paper viable, but it lost money consistently for almost a decade, ringing up its first meager profits during the war years 1942–45.

By 1946, Meyer's daughter Katharine had married the brilliant, charismatic Philip Graham. The relationship between Meyer and Graham was very close and, when President Harry Truman tapped Meyer to become the first president of the World Bank, Meyer handed leadership of the paper to his son-in-law. Graham quickly set out to make the *Post* a journalistic and financial success.

The turning point for the *Post* came in 1954 when it bought the *Times-Herald* for $8.5 million and became the sole morning paper in the nation's capital. The purchase doubled circulation and sent ad revenue jumping.

Philip Graham was bursting with ideas, pushing the *Post* into television in a big way, buying Newsweek in 1961 and an interest in Bowater Mersey Paper Co., Ltd., the firm that supplied most of the paper's newsprint. Unfortunately, Graham also suffered from manic-depressive illness and committed suicide on August 3, 1963, at the age of forty-eight.

The fate of the *Post* fell immediately to Katharine Graham, but her interest in journalism or business was limited at the time. Her main credentials were that her father had owned the paper and her husband had run it.

"When my husband died, I had three choices," she has said. "I could sell it. I could find somebody to run it. Or I could go to work. And that was no choice at all. I went to work." She went on to add:

"It was simply inconceivable to me to dismantle all that my father and my husband had built with so much labor and love."

Once, asked if she wasn't terrified, she replied, "Congealed." Nevertheless, she built the *Post* into one of the best newspapers in the country, one known for investigative reporting, stylish prose and profitability.

Her first major change at the *Post* was to name Benjamin Bradlee managing editor. Bradlee, who would later occasionally play tennis with Warren Buffett, energized a highly talented and competitive newsroom, and a decade later he was one of the heroes of the 1971 publication of the Pentagon Papers.

That same year The Washington Post Co. went public. The Class B common stock came on the market at $6.50 a share, adjusted for subsequent stock splits.

In 1973 there were about 14 million shares of Post stock outstanding, of which 2.7 million Class A controlling shares were owned by Katharine Graham.

At the beginning of the 1973–74 stock market slump, the price dropped to $4 a share. That's when Buffett bought his $10.6 million of Post stock, a 12 percent stake of the Class B stock or about 10 percent of the total stock, making Berkshire the largest Post shareholder outside of the Graham family.

At the time revenues of The Washington Post Co. and its subsidiaries were about $200 million. The subsidiaries included the Washington *Post* newspaper, Newsweek, the Times-Herald Company, four television stations and a paper company that provided most of its newsprint.

The *Post* was worth four times that amount—since one rule of thumb is that good newspapers may sell for about two and a half times annual revenues. Buffett has said he bought Post stock at a good price because people just weren't enthusiastic about the world at that time.

After Buffett's purchases, the stock price fell from $10 million in 1973 to $8 million in late 1974. The price of Post stock did not move solidly ahead of Buffett's purchase price until 1976.

Since then the stock has steadily forged ahead and today Buffett's original investment of about $10 million is worth about $350 million.

But in the very beginning, Buffett was not a welcome guest. Among those concerned was Andre Meyer, a family friend (but no relation to Eugene Meyer). In *Financier*, his biography of Andre Meyer, Cary Reich reports that "he was irate when one of the country's most successful private investors, Warren Buffett, took a substantial position in Post shares. As someone who had done that sort of thing himself, Meyer was naturally suspicious of Buffett's motives."

Graham told Reich that "Andre kept warning me about Warren Buffett. He regarded all people who bought into companies uninvited as threats. But I checked Warren out rather carefully and decided that we were quite lucky, in that he was a very hands-off and honorable man."

After his investment, Buffett wrote to Mrs. Graham and told her he was no threat to her position and he fully understood she controlled the company through her ownership of the company's Class A stock.

One thing that may have broken the ice was that Buffett was able to remind her he had worked for the *Post* as a paperboy twenty-five years before. Buffett and Mrs. Graham were first in touch in 1971 when Buffett asked her to help him in buying The New Yorker magazine, an offer she declined. They arranged to meet in person for the first time in 1973, after Buffett's purchase of Post stock, at the office of the Los Angeles *Times*. Reassured by that encounter, she asked him to come to dinner in Washington and take a look at the Post. A strong friendship was born.

In 1974 Buffett was named to the Post board and, appropriately, chaired its finance committee.

One of Buffett's first moves was to recommend that the Post buy back its own stock. Few companies in the 1970s were doing that. Between 1975 and 1992, the Post bought back about 43 percent of itself. Average cost: $60 a share. So it bought back more than 40 percent of its business at roughly a quarter of its present value.

The Washington *Post*'s coverage of the Watergate scandal, particularly by Bob Woodward and Carl Bernstein, brought the paper a Pulitzer Prize in 1973, but two years later it would be deeply affected by a crippling strike.

Post labor unions had resisted the introduction of new technologies at the paper, and relations between labor and management were already strained when negotiations for a new pressmen's contract deadlocked. The strike's ugliest moment came with the trashing of the pressrooms, a blow to the finances and pride of the newspaper. On October 1, 1975, during the night pressrun, several pressmen jumped a night foreman, beat and threatened to kill him. During the next twenty minutes a number of others sabotaged the *Post*'s nine presses. Nevertheless, the *Post* lost just one day's publication before it found six small newspapers within 200 miles of the *Post* willing to print the paper.

Mrs. Graham was uneasy about the risk of holding out, particularly in view of the competition from Washington's afternoon paper, the *Star*, but Buffett encouraged her.

As many as 200 employees slept on cots in the *Post* building, doing their regular jobs during the day and then donning coveralls for production jobs that night. On occasion Buffett joined Mrs. Graham and other *Post* executives at the plant, taking the places of striking workers.

The strike collapsed on February 16, 1976, after the mailers union voted to accept a new contract.

All through the bear markets, the Watergate scandal, and the strike, Buffett never sold one share of Post stock.

For his patience, he was well rewarded.

In 1981 the *Star* folded, making the *Post* essentially a monopoly newspaper in the nation's capital.

For Buffett and Berkshire shareholders, the 1980s would be boom times as Buffett rode the tiger of his greatest idea: that monopoly newspapers are "toll-bridges."

Buffett served on the Post board until 1986, when he resigned because Berkshire committed $512 million to help Capital Cities Communications buy ABC. Buffett went on the board of the resulting company, media giant Capital Cities/ABC.

Federal Communications Commission rules prohibit an individual from serving simultaneously as a director of a company that owns a television network (Capital Cities/ABC) and of one that owns cable television systems (The Washington Post Co.). A similar prohibition applies to overlaps of television signals from stations owned by different companies, such as Capital Cities' New York station and the Post's Hartford, Connecticut, station. The overlap was another reason Buffett was prohibited from serving on both boards at the same time.

If Mrs. Graham ever had reservations about Buffett or his intentions, they have long since vanished. She told the *Wall Street Journal,* in a September 30, 1987, article, "Our board was just devastated by his departure. They really miss him."

They remain close friends and today she only sings his praises. "He has wisdom, human sensitivity and, above all, humor. I think it's a unique combination," Mrs. Graham told Adam Smith, host of "Money World," in a show about Berkshire's April 30, 1990, annual meeting.

Buffett jokes, not very convincingly, about his lack of influence at the Post since he left the board, but it's apparent he remains a trusted friend to Katharine Graham. Her son, Donald Graham, now the president and chief executive officer of the Post, has said of Buffett: "In finance, he is the smartest guy I know. I don't know who is second."

It was the Post investment—a 40-fold return Buffett classic—that firmly established Buffett's reputation as a master investor.

Today the *Post* is the dominant paper in one of the world's major cities. Daily circulation of the *Post* is more than 800,000 and Sunday circulation is approaching 1.2 million.

In recent years, the *Post* has begun to surpass its bigger archrival, the New York *Times,* in profitability and stock market value. In addition to the *Post* newspaper, which accounts for about half of the Post empire's profits, the company continues to own *Newsweek,* the national news weekly which, with 3.3 million subscribers, has long run second in circulation to its main competitor, Time magazine.

The Post also owns four television stations: WDIV/TV4 in Detroit,

WPLG/TV10 in Miami, WFSB/TV3 in Hartford and WJXT/TV4 in Jacksonville.

It owns one other newspaper, *The Herald,* in Everett, Washington, which in 1991 switched from an afternoon to a morning paper to take advantage of reader preference for a morning newspaper.

Also, it owns a large cable television franchise it bought from Capital Cities/ABC-TV in 1986 for $350 million when the franchise had about 360,000 subscribers. The Post's cable business, which has grown through acquisitions and new subscribers to more than 451,000 subscribers at the end of 1991, is vastly more profitable than when it was acquired.

The *Post* has a 49 percent interest in a Nova Scotia paper mill belonging to Bowater Mersey Paper Co. Ltd., which supplies two-thirds of the *Post*'s newsprint.

Further, the Post owns the Stanley H. Kaplan Educational Center, purchased in 1984. Its some 150 tutoring centers and 600 satellite locations prepare students for licensing exams and admissions tests. Kaplan now serves some foreign markets such as Panama City, Panama, and Seoul, Korea.

The Post owns 28 percent of Cowles Media Company, which publishes the Minneapolis *Star and Tribune* and other properties.

The Post, which has about 6,000 employees, also owns Legi-Slate Inc., a computerized tracking service covering congressional and regulatory actions. It owns one-half, with The New York *Times* owning the other one-half, of the *International Tribune* newspaper that is published in Paris and printed in eight cities and which circulates both *Post* and New York *Times* stories in 164 countries.

In March 1992, the *Post* acquired an 80 percent stake in Gaithersburg Gazette Inc., the parent firm of Gazette Newspapers, which has eleven weekly newspapers in Montgomery, Frederick and Carroll counties in Maryland. The weeklies have a combined circulation of more than 180,000.

Berkshire owns about a 15 percent share of the Post, up from the original 10 percent of the company it bought in 1973. Over the years, with the Post buying back a portion of its own stock, Buffett's ownership percentage has been boosted.

But in 1990 the recession caught up with the Post, and Mrs. Graham was forced to write in the 1990 annual report that financial results were "very disappointing." Donald Graham later called 1991 a terrible year.

Mrs. Graham attended the Berkshire annual meeting in 1990, sitting in one of the front rows of the theater where Buffett was holding court.

When a question arose in the session following the annual meeting about the future of the *Post,* Buffett said it might have some short term problems but would be fine in the long run. He then asked Mrs. Graham for her comment about prospects for the *Post* and she said, "Ditto." The well-publicized nationwide recession in advertising has outlasted Buffett's expectations, but the Post remains a mighty enterprise.

The *Post* and Buffett have treated one another well.

Buffett is often invited to dinners at Mrs. Graham's home, an invitation reserved for the high and mighty. Buffett usually passes up the gourmet meal and has a hamburger, fries and sundae. "He has a limited palate," says Mrs. Graham. (*USA Today,* September 18, 1991)

The Buffett-Graham friendship goes beyond dinner. Buffett occasionally has written an article for the paper, and when he first testified before Congress in connection with the Salomon scandal, Katharine Graham had a front row seat.

Buffett was surrounded by reporters and photographers throughout his testimony, and as he left the hearing room, they pursued him. But he eluded them and slipped into a limousine that took him to the Washington *Post,* where he met with the editorial board.

Buffett and the *Post* know all about scoops.

10 CAPITAL CITIES/ABC, INC.

"I literally do not work with anyone I don't like."

Buffett's great interest in media stocks culminated with the announcement in 1985 that Capital Cities Communications would buy giant American Broadcast Companies, Inc., with Buffett owning almost 20 percent of the new media powerhouse.

On March 18, 1985, Buffett agreed to invest $517.5 million in cash to buy three million shares of Capital Cities at $172.50. That facilitated the $3.5 billion merger in January 1986 of what became Capital Cities/ABC, Inc.

Buffett's part of the deal was wrapped up in the mid-afternoon of March 13, 1985. Two hours later Buffett was engrossed in a six-hour bridge game with three New York friends, putting the deal out of his mind. "I don't think about anything else when I play bridge," he told Omaha *World-Herald*'s Robert Dorr.

Buffett's investment came about after his longtime friend, Capital Cities chairman Tom Murphy, sought advice about piecing together the acquisition of ABC. Buffett has always had high regard for Murphy, and has said, "I think he is the top manager in the U.S." (Fortune, April 15, 1985) Murphy has returned the compliment and has said of Buffett, "If I were around him all the time, I'd have a huge inferiority complex . . . He's one of the greatest friends. He will try and do anything he can to help you. Without him, I wouldn't have been able to buy ABC." *(USA Today,* September 18, 1991)

Buffett once told Patricia Bauer, West Coast editor for *Channels* magazine in November, 1986, "I love being associated with Murph. I literally do not work with anyone I don't like. I'm fortunate to be able to spend the rest of my life working with people that I like and admire. And here's Murph up at the top of that list with a terribly interesting business."

But does Buffett plan to shape opinion or tell ABC what programs to air? No, he told Bauer, "I'm not the right guy to ask about those things." He said it again at the Berkshire annual meeting in 1991: "I'm a director of Cap Cities/ABC, but they don't ask me for my suggestions on shows. That's not my end of the game."

At a Berkshire annual meeting (1987) Buffett was asked if he thought there was too much sex on television. "I don't see anything wrong with sex on television, but there ought to be a few shows where the gal says no."

Buffett and Murphy met in the late 1960s when a former Harvard Business School classmate of Murphy's seated them together at a lunch in New York.

Murphy was so taken with Buffett that he invited him to be on the board of Capital Cities/ABC. Buffett declined but the two became fast friends.

In 1985, at seventy-nine, Leonard Goldenson, who had founded ABC in 1953, and given the world "Charlie's Angels," "The Dating Game," "Monday Night Football," instant replay, and the miniseries, decided that Murphy and his number two man, Daniel Burke, whom he had long admired, would be the right people to run his company and keep it in one piece.

In his foreword to Goldenson's 1991 autobiography, *Beating the Odds,* Buffett paid tribute to Goldenson and gave a brief recollection about the Capital Cities purchase of ABC. He observed that "Business management can be viewed as a three-act play—the dream, the execution, and the passing of the baton. Leonard Goldenson will be remembered as a master of all three." Of the purchase, Buffett said one day in Washington he got a call from Murphy who said, "Pal, you're not going to believe this. I've just bought ABC. You've got to come and tell me how I'm going to pay for it." Buffett did just that. He told Murphy he needed "a nine-hundred-pound gorilla" investor to keep raiders at bay; then Buffett kicked in $517 million.

Buffett said he had not envisioned a role for himself until Murphy brought it up, adding, "We made a deal in about thirty seconds." Buffett became that nine-hundred-pound gorilla, the King Kong of Capital Cities.

But there was still a problem. There was an FCC "cross owner-ship" rule forbidding one company from owning a television station and a newspaper in the same town. Buffett told Murphy he didn't want to sell the Buffalo *News*, which meant Capital Cities had to sell a television station in Buffalo. Buffett said in the Goldenson book he told Murphy he was committed to the Buffalo *News:* "I promised the people there that I would never sell it. I told them, when they wrote my obituary it would say, 'He owns the Buffalo *News.*'"

Actually, it's more likely Buffett's obituary will say he was the gorilla investor in Capital Cities/ABC.

"This deal popped up three weeks ago. Four weeks ago I had no idea it was about to happen," Buffett told New York *Times* reporter Vartanig G. Vartan on March 20, 1985. "I was up there on a Thurs-day morning on April 2, 1989," Buffett told Atlanta *Constitution* business writer Melissa Turner, "I said, 'How many shares do you want me to buy?' He said, 'What do you say?' I said, 'How's three million?' He said, 'Fine.' I said, 'What price should I pay?' He said, 'What do you think?' I said, '$172.50.' He said, 'Done.'"

Buffett has said the acquisition almost fell through as a result of wrangling over the final price.

Joseph Flom, ABC's merger lawyer, and First Boston merger ex-pert Bruce Wasserstein, continually pushed for more for ABC share-holders. According to Murphy, it was Buffett, who, along with Was-serstein, came up with a kicker for the deal for ABC shareholders. The agreement called for each ABC shareholder to get $118 cash for each of his shares, plus a warrant to buy one-tenth of a share of Capital Cities stock for two and a half years after the acquisition. Capital Cities valued the warrants at $3 and would redeem them at that price for ninety days after the merger. But the real worth of the warrants is that they gave ABC shareholders a right to buy some Capital Cities shares at $250. If the merger worked out well and the price rose above that, warrant holders would be well rewarded. They were.

Buffett became a director of Capital Cities/ABC. He also agreed to vote with management for eleven years as long as either Tom Murphy or Daniel Burke was in charge. "With them [Murphy and Burke] in place, the first-class managers with whom we have aligned ourselves can focus their efforts entirely upon running the business and maximizing long-term values for owners. Certainly this is much better than having those managers distracted by 'revolving-door capitalists' hoping to put the company 'in play.' (Of course, some managers place their own interests above those of the company and its owners and deserve to be shaken up—but in making investments we try to steer clear of this type.)" Warren Buffett, Berkshire's 1986 annual report.

In the same annual report Buffett addressed another matter in his usual self-deprecating style: "Of course some of you probably wonder why we are now buying Capital Cities at $172.50 per share given that this author, in a characteristic burst of brilliance, sold Berkshire's holdings in the same company at $43 per share in 1978–80," he wrote. "Anticipating your question, I spent a lot of time working on a snappy answer that would reconcile these acts. A little more time, please."

Capital Cities has been a good investment, despite a long struggle to turn the ABC network around. Today, as a result of the 1986 merger, Capital Cities owns ABC Television Network, seven ABC Radio Networks serving 2,200 affiliates, radio's largest advertising medium, eight television stations, twenty-one radio stations, and 80 percent of the highly successful ESPN sports cable channel; it also publishes newspapers, trade journals, shopping guides, business publications, books and records, provides research services and distributes information from data bases.

The other 20 percent of ESPN, which was owned by RJR Nabisco, was sold in 1990 to Hearst Corp.

ESPN, through its twenty-four-hour-a-day sports cable television programming service, reaches 60 percent of U.S. households—more than any other cable network. It has been highly successful.

Capital Cities/ABC owns 38 percent of The Arts and Entertainment Network, a cable programming service devoted to cultural and entertainment programming, one-third of Lifetime, a cable programming service devoted to women's lifestyle and health programming, as well as half of Tele-Munchen GmbH, a Munich, Germany-based television and theatrical production/distribution company with interests in cinemas, a Munich radio station and a German cable television program service.

But Murphy and Burke are the first to say the Big Three networks have had a lot of trouble in the past decade trying to retain their hold on the television audience as overall network audiences continue to decline. The prime time audience share of the three major networks has declined from about 95 percent in 1970 to about 60 percent today.

Still, ABC has made real efforts to fight for viewers. "Good Morning America" was the top-rated early morning program for the year. Roone Arledge's "World News Tonight" with Peter Jennings finished 1989 as the nation's number-one-rated early evening news program for the first time since ABC began broadcasting the evening news in 1953, and in 1990 it was the most-watched evening news broadcast.

Ted Koppel's "Nightline," and "20/20" with Hugh Downs and Barbara Walters, have been successful shows.

In 1989 ABC News premiered "PrimeTime Live," hosted by Sam Donaldson and Diane Sawyer.

In sports, ABC's "Monday Night Football," hosted by the announcing trio of Howard Cosell, Frank Gifford and Dandy Don Meredith, was in its heyday the most popular prime-time program among men. "Wide World of Sports" was the most popular anthology series.

On Tuesday night, "Roseanne," starring Roseanne Barr, was 1989's top rated show among all households. In recent years, ABC turned heavily to comedy and came up with another big hit, "America's Funniest Home Videos."

In early 1990, ABC Sports entered into a new four-year agreement with the National Football League to telecast "Monday Night Football."

The division also has rights for CFA college football for five years and a new NFL spring football league for two years, both starting in 1991.

The company's eight television stations, located in New York, Los Angeles, Chicago, Philadelphia, San Francisco, Houston, Durham-Raleigh and Fresno, reach more than 24 percent of all homes with television in the country (federal rules permit the ownership of up to twelve television stations by a single entity but no more than 25 percent of total viewership).

The ABC Radio Networks serve more than 2,200 affiliates nationwide. The networks feature a variety of programming, including respected radio commentator Paul Harvey. The company's twenty-one radio stations (eleven AM and ten FM) reach more than 25 percent of the United States.

The company's publishing unit owns Fairchild Publications, publisher of such magazines as Women's Wear Daily.

Capital Cities/ABC also owns the Chilton Company, the largest of the ABC publishing operations, and Word, Inc., a book and recorded-music publisher serving the inspirational market. It publishes *Institutional Investor* and a number of newspapers and trade, business, real estate and agricultural publications.

The company even has investments in such Broadway plays as *Cats, Phantom of the Opera, Amadeus* and *Dreamgirls*—investments with a view toward the potential of pay-per-view. (New York *Times Magazine,* July 28, 1991)

Back in 1989, the company adopted a shareholder rights plan, a common practice by businesses in light of the 1980s takeover craze. The plan becomes operative in certain events involving the acquisition of more than 20 percent of the company's common stock by anyone not approved by the board. But in Berkshire Hathaway's case, the plan is not activated until a 30 percent ownership point is reached.

As with all stocks, Capital Cities/ABC has had its ups and downs, but one of its worst days came on July 24, 1990. That's when its earnings for the second quarter came in below expectations, with word from Burke that the third quarter could even come in below the year ago quarter. The stock immediately plunged from $588.50 to $533, down $55.50 from the previous day's close.

In 1990, after hitting a high of $633 just after Burke took over, the stock fell 23 percent to $488. "The joke around here is, we had a 3-for-2 stock split but we didn't send out any certificates," Burke was quoted in a Financial World story of April 2, 1991.

The great franchises of Capital Cities/ABC were coming under increasing attack from competitors. As Buffett said at the Berkshire annual meeting in 1987, "The networks used to own people's eyeballs, and they don't anymore. The people at Cap Cities are sensational managers, but they may have to be."

The early 1990s turned out to be tough for Capital Cities, Berkshire and almost everyone else.

Still, for the Super Bowl, aired January 27, 1991, ABC was getting $800,000 for a thirty-second commercial that would reach 100 million Americans.

As a sidenote, Capital Cities held talks with Time, Inc. officials when negotiations for the merger of Time and Warner Communications had temporarily stalled. "Yes, we talked to Buffett," says former Time Chairman J. Richard Munro, who describes Buffett as one of the most unassuming people he's ever met. He said nothing came of the talks with Buffett, who has been an on and off Time investor. Apparently, there were several meetings about a possible business combination with Capital Cities but network-cable cross-ownership rules were a stumbling block. Time's leaders also balked because Capital Cities/ABC's Murphy was pushing for an acquisition of Time. (New York *Times*, August 13, 1989)

Stay tuned. Buffett is.

11 BUFFETT'S AD IN THE *WALL STREET JOURNAL* OF NOVEMBER 17, 1986

"If you run an ad for chihuahuas, you get a lot of collie replies."

We want to buy businesses worth $100 million or more before December 31, 1986.

If you own such a business, there's a vital reason why you should consider selling.

In 44 days the tax you must pay on the sale of your business may soar to 521/2 percent.

All of us know about the change in the Federal capital gains tax rate from 20 percent to 28 percent. In most cases, effective state tax rates on capital gains will also materially increase.

A second tax consideration is less well known, but in many cases looms far more important. Effective January 1, the General Utilities doctrine is repealed. This change can produce the equivalent of a 521/2 percent Federal capital gains tax on the sale of a business. Ask your lawyer, accountant or investment banker how it will affect your situation.

The change in the General Utilities doctrine will not apply to transactions completed by December 31. Other things being equal, you will net dramatically more money if you close a sale by that date than if you delay.

Berkshire Hathaway will have no problem in completing a transaction by the December 31 deadline. We have the money, and we can act with extraordinary speed. Most of the purchases we have made have been agreed to after one meeting with the owners. If you phone us with a general description of your business and tell us the sort of transaction you are seeking, we can immediately tell you whether we have an interest. And if we do, we will proceed instantly.

Here's what we are looking for:

1. Large purchases (at least $10 million of after-tax earnings, and preferably much more).

2. Demonstrated consistent earning power (future projections are of little interest to us, nor are "turn-around" situations).

3. Businesses earning good returns on equity while employing little or no debt.

4. Management in place (we can't supply it).

5. Simple businesses (if there's lots of technology, we won't understand it).

6. An offering price (we don't want to waste our time or that of the seller by talking, even preliminarily, about a transaction when price is unknown).

These criteria are firm so we would appreciate hearing only from owners whose businesses fully meet them.

We invite potential sellers to check us out by contacting anyone with whom we have done business in the past. You'll find we are unusual: we buy to keep (no periodic "restructuring" convulsions); we leave subsidiary managements alone to operate in the future as they have in the past; and our own ownership and management structure is predictable for decades to come.

If you are interested, call me at 402-346-1400. Or, if you like, first call Mrs. Kaiser at the same number to request express delivery of Berkshire Hathaway's current annual report. Your inquiry will be totally confidential; we use no staff, and we don't need to discuss your company with consultants, investment bankers, commercial bankers, etc. You will deal only with Charles Munger, Vice Chairman of Berkshire, and with me.

If you have any possible interest, call promptly. Otherwise a 20 percent tax will become 28 percent to 52 1/2 percent.

Warren E. Buffett

Although nothing came of the $47,000 ad, Buffett personally took at least 100 telephone calls. (Omaha *World-Herald,* January 1987)

One caller was a native of Pakistan who wanted to sell him a newsstand in New York for $185,000. That one didn't meet Buffett's test on size.

Another caller from Jackson, Mississippi, wanted to sell her antebellum mansion. Buffett turned that one down politely, but quickly. (Omaha *World-Herald,* December 3, 1986)

Other callers offered farms or small-town businesses.

"If you run an ad for a chihuahua, you get a lot of collie replies," and "We're looking for 747s, not model airplanes," he has often said.

Buffett said the ad worked in the sense that the next time people would be more aware of what Berkshire wanted and would be more likely to think of Berkshire.

Also in 1986 Berkshire ran a different ad, published three times in Business Insurance magazine, titled "Berkshire Hathaway wants to see property/casualty risks where the premium is $1 million or more."

As a result of the ads, which cost a total of $20,000, Berkshire's insurance subsidiaries generated new business that produced more than $100 million a year in premiums.

12 DIVERSIFIED RETAILING COMPANY, INC.

"If they need my help to manage the enterprise, we're probably both in trouble."

Warren Buffett has likened the hunt for acquisitions to "bagging rare and fast moving elephants." Way back in time and space, long before Buffett was making billion dollar investments, he was fishing in far smaller investment streams, bringing those smaller streams together into a river of income.

Toward the end of 1978, Diversified Retailing Company, Inc. was merged into Berkshire Hathaway.

Buffett, long the largest shareholder of Berkshire, had been chief executive officer of Diversified since 1966 and was also by this time the majority stockholder in Diversified, holding 56 percent of Diversified's stock.

All along Buffett was gradually buying up both Berkshire and Diversified stock. By 1976, Buffett, then chairman of both Berkshire and Diversified, owned about 36 percent of Berkshire and 56 percent of Diversified.

At the time, Berkshire's principal executive offices were located at 97 Cove Street in New Bedford, Massachusetts, and those of Diversified at 1300 Mercantile Bank & Trust Building, 2 Hopkins Plaza in Baltimore, Maryland.

Diversified, a holding company incorporated in Maryland in 1966, was the parent firm of Associated Retail Stores, Inc.'s more than eighty-store chain, and also owned a substantial amount of Berkshire stock as well as stock in Blue Chip Stamps.

Associated, based in New York, was acquired by Diversified in 1967. Its eighty-five stores operated stores in eleven states under such names as York, Amy, Goodwin's Gaytime, Fashion Outlet, Madison's, Yorkster, Lanes, and Tops and Bottoms.

In 1987, in one of Berkshire's rare sales of a business, Associated Retail Stores was sold to Joseph Norban, Inc. of New York.

Buffett's retailing efforts never have really paid off. In the 1970s he owned Munsingwear and the stock never did much.

In the proposed merger of Berkshire and Diversified, Buffett and his wife agreed to vote for the merger only if a majority of the shareholders did. With the combination, Buffett was attempting to bring the far-flung elements of his financial empire under one house, Berkshire.

In the negotiations, Berkshire was represented by Malcolm G. Chace, Jr., the former chairman of Berkshire. Diversified was represented by David S. (Sandy) Gottesman, a director of Diversified who would become one of Buffett's closest friends and a wealthy Berkshire shareholder.

Gottesman, because of his large ownership in Diversified, came out of the Berkshire-Diversified merger with 17,977 shares of Berkshire.

A number of the members of the investment firm he heads, First Manhattan in New York City, also had been Diversified investors and they came away owning another 13,158 Berkshire shares.

Because Buffett owned substantial positions in both Berkshire and Diversified, the negotiations took place without him and were conducted by independent directors of each corporation.

The proxy statement relating to the merger explained: "Berkshire and its subsidiaries are engaged in the underwriting of property and casualty insurance throughout the United States, in the manufacture and sale of woven textiles in the United States and Canada, and, through a subsidiary which Berkshire is required to divest by 1981, in the commercial banking business in Rockford, Illinois. Berkshire and its subsidiaries additionally maintain long-term investments in a number of other businesses . . . Berkshire owns approximately 18.8 percent of the outstanding common stock of Blue Chip, whose shares are traded in the over-the-counter market; and Berkshire's insurance subsidiaries hold in their investment portfolios approximately 22.6 percent of Blue Chip's outstanding common stock."

Blue Chip in turn owned a number of businesses such as See's Candy and the Buffalo *Evening News*, Wesco (which owned 22 percent of Detroit International Bridge Co., operator of an international toll bridge between Detroit, Michigan, and Windsor, Ontario; Berkshire insurance companies owned an additional three percent of Detroit Bridge).

Are you still there?

Then, this is what the proxy statement had to say about Diversified: "Diversified is a holding company which renders financial and operating advice to Associated Retail Stores, Inc., a wholly-owned subsidiary engaged in retailing of popular-price women's and children's apparel, to Associated's wholly-owned subsidiary, Columbia Insurance Company, which is engaged in the fire and casualty insurance business primarily through accepting portions of reinsurance contracts from Berkshire's insurance subsidiaries, and to Southern Casualty Insurance Company, a wholly-owned subsidiary of Columbia engaged in Louisiana in providing workers compensation insurance, almost exclusively to the forest products industry. In the opinion of Diversified's management, Diversified's most significant asset, other than its Berkshire stock, is its beneficial ownership of approximately 16.3 percent of the outstanding common stock of Blue Chip . . ."

The merger planned little in the way of management change other than that Charles Munger, who had become chairman of Blue Chip in 1976 and was a director of Diversified, would serve as a director of Berkshire.

Buffett is well-known for his "hands-off" attitude toward managers: "If they need my help to manage the enterprise, we're probably both in trouble." *(Outstanding Investor Digest,* May 24, 1991)

For years, Buffett, principal stockholder of both Berkshire and Diversified, had wanted to combine the two companies. He wanted particularly to bring together the two corporations' holdings of Blue Chip, to simplify the corporate structure under Berkshire.

The following chart shows the pre-merger and post-merger ownerships:

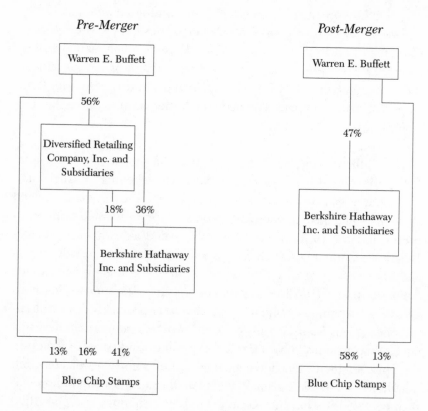

When the merger was over, Berkshire owned 58 percent of Blue Chip and Buffett and his family owned another 13 percent of the stock. It would only be until 1983 before Blue Chip was fully merged into Berkshire.

A little stream had merged with other little streams and was becoming a mighty river.

13 BLUE CHIP STAMPS

"We're actually prohibited from buying other savings and loans. But that's not a prohibition that keeps us up at night."

Over the years, through the Berkshire subsidiary, Blue Chip Stamps, Buffett has acquired such businesses as See's Candy Shops, and the Buffalo *Evening News*, which are to this day Berkshire cash machines.

In the late 1960s Berkshire began accumulating stock in Blue Chip, a Los Angeles, California, trading stamp business with a float of about $60 million in outstanding, unredeemed stamps. In 1972 Buffett took $25 million of the money and bought See's. The candy company's annual sales at the time were $35 million. In 1977 he also bought the Buffalo *Evening News* for about $33 million from the estate of Mrs. Edward H. Butler, Jr.

Wesco was acquired by Blue Chip in 1973.

When Buffett was forty-six years old, he owned about $35 million worth of Berkshire stock and about $10 million worth of Blue Chip Stamps stock. (Fortune, May, 1977) By 1983 Berkshire owned about 60 percent of Blue Chip. And it was through Blue Chip that Buffett for Berkshire bought 80.1 percent of Wesco Financial Corp., which in turn bought Precision Steel, and Mutual Savings and Loan Association.

The relatively small S&L still exists at the building on valuable downtown land, a building owned by Wesco but largely leased out.

The principal Blue Chip businesses are the Buffalo *Evening News*, the promotional services business conducted by Blue Chip itself, a steel service center, and branded metal specialty products businesses carried out by Precision Steel Warehouse, Inc., a wholly-owned subsidiary bought by Wesco in 1979 for about $15 million.

The nine-story Mutual Savings and Loan Association building in Pasadena, built in 1964, has about 124,000 square feet of rentable space (Wesco uses about 22,000 square feet). The block also contains four commercial store buildings and a multi-story garage.

Wesco's Precision Steel has plants and offices in Franklin Park and Downers Grove, Illinois, and in Charlotte, North Carolina.

Blue Chip offers two main kinds of promotional services: those used by business organizations to attract or retain customers and those used by businesses for internal motivational programs.

Blue Chip had started its trading stamp business in 1956. There was a time when a lady's quartz watch, for example, could be purchased for seventeen books of the stamps.

Blue Chip stamp revenues hit a historical peak of more than $124 million in 1970, then dropped to a little more than $9 million in 1982, according to Berkshire-Blue Chip merger documents.

Most of the decline occurred in the early 1970s, when many supermarkets converted to discount merchandising, and service stations, faced with their first major gasoline shortage, decided they didn't need trading stamps for promotion.

Blue Chip's stamp business was dealt an all but fatal blow when a supermarket chain that accounted for 51 percent of trading stamp revenues discontinued the stamps in 1982.

The only benefit the stamp business offered was some continuing float, the cash received in advance of need, which was invested.

Blue Chip Motivation, operated as a separate division, struggled in a competitive environment offering motivation programs for organizations, using awards of merchandise and travel in order to stimulate sales or productivity, promote attendance or safety, or otherwise motivate their employees.

Today the stamp operations of Blue Chip are tiny and are conducted from a modest building in Los Angeles that also houses the small K&W Products business, which makes products for the automotive aftermarket business. Although K&W is small, it has been expanding through acquisitions of late.

In December 1980, Wesco's Mutual Savings, which had operated seventeen locations in Southern California and had ranked about thirty-ninth among California savings and loan associations in assets, sold all its offices, except for its Pasadena headquarters office and a single branch across the street.

It is in the basement of this building, down in the snack room, that Charles Munger holds the annual meeting of Wesco for a small band of shareholders.

In 1966, Mutual Savings foreclosed on a property near Santa Barbara, California, and has since been trying to develop the twenty-two acres of vacant oceanfront property.

Munger often tells stories about how slowly things have gone with regulators over the years, but he says one of these years the property will be developed.

In the 1983 Blue Chip annual report Munger wrote: "We began the 1980s with five constituent businesses instead of one. In order of acquisition they are: (1) trading stamps and other promotional services, (2) See's Candy Shops, Incorporated, (3) Mutual Savings, (4) Buffalo *Evening News*, and (5) Precision Steel."

Munger says in this annual report that the businesses have in common good management and some resistance to inflation. "The second of these two common characteristics gets more important every year as inflation continues. Many businesses, once good investments when inflation was low, are now, under inflationary conditions, unable to produce much, if any, cash even when physical volume is constant . . . Inflation is a very effective form of indirect taxation on capital represented by holdings of common stock. We know of no countermeasure . . . But, even so, we think a habit of always thinking about and trying to serve shareholders' interests in real terms, instead of rationalizing growth of managed assets regardless of real effects on shareholders, is quite useful and may fairly be expected of corporate managements."

Shortly after that report, Blue Chip merged with Berkshire Hathaway, Inc., long a 59.6 percent-owner of Blue Chip Stamps.

At the time of the merger, Buffett personally owned 10.6 percent of the outstanding shares. He was the company's second largest shareholder after Berkshire itself.

At the time of the merger, Berkshire had 986,509 shares outstanding, held by about 1,900 shareholders, and Blue Chip had 5,178,770 shares outstanding, held by about 1,500 shareholders.

As for the prospect of acquiring another S&L like Mutual Savings, Buffett assured the 1988 Berkshire annual meeting that "We're actually prohibited from buying other savings and loans. But that's not a prohibition that keeps us up at night."

14 THE COCA-COLA COMPANY

"I like products I can understand."

A short time before Warren Buffett would make stock market history by buying a billion dollars of Coca-Cola stock, he took a call from Coca-Cola president Don Keough.

Recalled Keough, "I said, Warren, are you buying a share or two of Coca-Cola stock? He said yes and he said it enthusiastically."

"We knew he had an interest in The Coca-Cola Company," Keough continued, admitting that one of the tips occurred when "Warren became America's number one fan of Cherry Coke, which we introduced in 1985."

In fact, Buffett wrote in Berkshire's 1985 annual report that "after forty-eight years of allegiance to another soft drink" (Pepsi) he was switching to Cherry Coke. He even declared Cherry Coke "the official drink" of Berkshire's annual meetings.

Soon, on the afternoon of March 15, 1989, a brief announcement came over the Dow Jones news wire that Berkshire had acquired 6.3 percent of the stock of The Coca-Cola Company!

Buffett, making his largest investment ever, struck during an unusually long period when Berkshire is not required to report—from the end of the September 30 quarter until Berkshire's annual report appears in late March.

He had spent months secretly putting in buy orders and had just finished guzzling down a $1 billion-plus ocean-size helping of Coca-Cola.

"I wish we had bought more," he would say later.

Buffett told Forbes magazine a key reason for his purchase of Coke was that its stock price did not reflect the all-but-guaranteed growth in international sales in a world that is increasingly uniform in its tastes.

Coca-Cola dominates most of the markets it serves, selling more than two billion gallons a year of soft drink syrup and concentrate to bottlers.

The most widely recognized and esteemed brand names on earth, by far, are Coca-Cola and Coke.

Self-described "Buffett wannabe" George Morgan, an Omaha stockbroker, relates the story of Buffett running into a youngster at a mall wearing a Coca-Cola outfit. Buffett asked him how much he paid for it. The youngster replied seventy-five dollars. "That's a lot of pay to advertise someone else's product," said Buffett, even more convinced of Coke's valuable franchise.

About 668 million times a day, from Australia to Zimbabwe, from Omaha to Osaka, from the Great Wall of China to the Great Barrier Reef, someone drinks a Coke.

The company sells almost half of the soda pop consumed on earth, about twice as much as its nearest rival, PepsiCo.

In the United States, the Coke and Pepsi empires claim about three-fourths of the roughly $46 billion-a-year soda business. Coke has 41 percent of that market and Pepsi about 32 percent.

Coca-Cola USA accounts for 10 percent of all America's liquid consumption.

Coke supplies syrups and concentrates to about 1,000 bottling partners in 185 countries.

The sun never sets on the world of Coca-Cola, now Berkshire's shining centerpiece investment. Buffett's stake in Coca-Cola stock is his biggest investment ever.

Coca-Cola sold about 180 billion servings of Coke in 1989. Cuban-born, Yale-educated Roberto Goizueta, Coke's chairman and a big booster of Atlanta, Coke's home town, hopes to double that amount by the year 2000. (Fortune, August 7, 1990)

Goizueta, owner of a large chunk of Coca-Cola stock, knows something about growth. In the decade since he became chairman on March 1, 1981, he has guided the growth of Coca-Cola from a market worth of $4 billion to one worth more than $53 billion.

Buffett's investment, stunning in its size and the stealth of acquisition, came to $1,023,920,000. For that money, he bought 23,350,000 shares of Coca-Cola stock, which subsequently split 2-for-1 in 1990 and again in 1992. Berkshire now has an incredible 93,400,000 shares.

The day after Berkshire's announcement of its Coca-Cola holdings, Buffett told *Wall Street Journal* reporter Michael J. McCarthy that the purchase of Coke was "the ultimate case of putting your money where your mouth is."

"Coke is exactly the kind of company I like," Buffett told him. "I like products I can understand. I don't know what a transistor is, for example." Further, he said, "More and more in recent years, their superb decision-making and the focus of their strategy have emerged more clearly to me."

The *Journal* story suggested that analysts saw Buffett's move as protection against recession. "There could be ten recessions between now and the time we sell our Coke stock. Our favorite holding period is forever," Buffett rejoined.

Shortly after the Coca-Cola purchase was revealed, trading in Coca-Cola stock was halted because of a large influx of buy orders. The stock closed at $51.50, up $1.25. Just a year and a half later Buffett's $1 billion stake in Coca-Cola was worth $2 billion.

Another large Coca-Cola shareholder, SunTrust Banks, Inc., holds slightly more than 10 percent of the stock, but that is split between stock it owns—about two percent—and the some eight percent the bank holds in fiduciary accounts.

The bank itself owns Coke shares worth about a billion dollars. So what if it's taken a lifetime to rise from $110,000, the price the old Trust Company of Georgia paid for the stock in 1919 when it helped underwrite Coca-Cola's first stock offering? The Coca-Cola stock is a nice fat percentage of the worth of SunTrust, which, by the way, has in its vault the only written copy of the Coke formula.

Buffett's cost basis for his Coca-Cola stock was about $21 a share before two subsequent 2-for-1 stock splits.

Berkshire's 93,340,000 shares of Coca-Cola today are worth about $4 billion! That's hefty pocket change, "The Real Thing," one might say.

Buffett has said "his eyeballs connected with his brain" in the summer of 1988 and he began buying Coke all the way through March 1989. Coca-Cola was buying back its own shares, so there were two huge purchasers of Coca-Cola stock in the marketplace during that time.

What Buffett saw, what made him thirst for Coca-Cola, was the world's greatest brand name. The Coca-Cola and Coke names were being carried for zero on the balance sheet of a company with stunning international possibilities for profit growth and efficient global advertising.

Buffett discovered—and it was right there in front of everybody's eyes—a worldwide bulletproof franchise.

You can talk about Coca-Cola's splendid balance sheet with lots of cash and little debt and you can even talk about its world empire and how many servings of Coke there are around the world on any given day.

But here may be the most stunning of all the remarkable statistics about Coca-Cola, again noted in its 1989 annual report: "The Coca-Cola Company began to transform itself into a global enterprise in the early 1920s. For more than sixty years, we have been developing business relationships and investing in a system that today carries an estimated replacement cost of more than $100 billion."

Let's say you wanted to enter the soft drink business and match Coca-Cola. You can't raise $100 billion. *Warren Buffett* can't raise $100 billion. So Coca-Cola can fairly well count on no real competitors because it is so far out in front.

In Berkshire's 1990 annual report, it is little wonder Buffett says he regards Coca-Cola as "the most valuable franchise in the world."

One Berkshire shareholder remarked, "He really doesn't ever have to make another investment."

Buffett assigned a number of reasons for buying Coca-Cola, and others supplied other reasons for him, but in the end, Buffett has said, it may be more than just a list of reasons.

"It's like when you marry a girl. Is it her eyes? Her personality? It's a whole bunch of things you can't separate," he told *Wall Street Journal* reporter Michael J. McCarthy.

When Buffett courted Coke, he did so in a quiet and a huge way. For months he had three brokers at the other end of his phones picking off whatever large blocks of Coca-Cola stock they could find.

About a week after the announcement, Atlanta *Constitution* business writer Melissa Turner interviewed Buffett at his office in Omaha. She asked him why he hadn't bought sooner and he replied, "You wonder what pushes the needle, don't you? Must have just dawned on me." He also told her, "Let's say you were going away for ten years and you wanted to make one investment and you know everything you know now, and you couldn't change it while you're gone. What would you think about? If I came up with anything in terms of certainty, where I knew the market was going to continue to grow, where I knew the leader was going to continue to be the leader—I mean worldwide—and where I knew there would be big unit growth, I just don't know anything like Coke."

Pausing for a sip of Cherry Coke, he continued, "I'd be relatively sure that when I came back they'd be doing a hell of a lot more business than they are doing now."

Coca-Cola has been part of people's lives for 100 years. The world's best known trademark originated on May 8, 1886, when, legend has it, pharmacist Dr. John Styth Pemberton first made the syrup for Coca-Cola in a three-legged brass pot in his Atlanta backyard.

In 1887 a patent was filed for a product listed as "Coca-Cola Syrup and Extract."

Thinking that two C's, derived from two of the drink's ingredients —flavoring extracts from the coca leaf and the cola nut—would look well together in advertising, Pemberton's bookkeeper, Frank M. Robinson, with an ear for alliteration, suggested the name and penned "Coca-Cola" in the flowing Spencerian script now world famous.

In 1886 sales of Coca-Cola averaged nine drinks a day—an inauspicious beginning for an enterprise whose sales of soft drink syrup now well exceed two billion gallons a year.

Pemberton also started Coca-Cola's push into advertising, making it one of the first American companies to make substantial use of advertising.

By 1891, Atlanta businessman Asa G. Candler had acquired complete ownership of Coca-Cola for $2,300. Within four years, his merchandising skill helped expand consumption of Coca-Cola to every state.

A strong believer in advertising, he promoted Coke incessantly, distributing souvenir fans, calendars, clocks and other novelties, all carrying a Coke trademark.

In 1919, the company was sold for $25 million to a group of investors headed by Ernest Woodruff. His son, Robert W. Woodruff, became president of the company in 1923. For more than six decades his leadership took the business to new heights.

Among his contributions were the six-pack and the open-top cooler, vending and dispensing equipment, displays and promotions.

Under him commercially successful Coca-Cola eventually became an institution the world over.

In 1941, as the United States entered World War II, Woodruff decreed "that every man in uniform gets a bottle of Coca-Cola for five cents, wherever he is and whatever it costs the company."

The presence of Coca-Cola not only lifted troop morale, it also gave local people their first taste of Coke and paved the way for future bottling operations overseas. Even after the troops left, Coke stayed, establishing its own beachhead as one of the first American products widely available overseas.

Although Coca-Cola has expanded over the years into other businesses, more and more it is shedding those extra businesses to concentrate on being a worldwide soft drink company. After years of diversification, it is evolving more into a one-product company, un-like Pepsi, more of a snackfood and restaurant business company.

Gone are Coca-Cola's coffee, tea, wine and bottled water busi-nesses and the units that made steam boilers and pasta.

In late 1989, it sold its minority interest in Columbia Pictures, the movie and television studio it bought in 1982, to Sony Corp. for $5 billion, investing much of the money in new bottling systems as well as buying back its own stock, almost always a hallmark of Buffett's investees.

"He really understands the company," says Don Keough. "He's a terrific board member. He knows the company. He knows the num-bers. He's an informed and stimulating director. He has a clear understanding of the inherent value of global trademarks."

And what did Mr. Keough do after Mr. Buffett bought Coca-Cola stock? "I became a modest Berkshire shareholder after his purchase of Coca-Cola stock," said Keough, who had an opportunity more than thirty years ago to invest in the Buffett Partnership but passed on the offer from Buffett.

"I wish I had invested back then," Keough said. Had Keough done so, Buffett would have turned the $5,000 he asked of him into something on the order of $15 million. Oh, well.

Keough once lived directly across from Buffett on Farnam Street. The future Mr. Coca-Cola, who drinks his Coke in diet form, was one of many Buffett solicited to join the Buffett Partnership. "He was exactly the same then as he is now," Keough recalled. "What you see is what you get. He had the same values. His story really is not money. It's values. People should know about his values . . . What he said at the [Berkshire] annual meeting [in 1991] in his response to a question about choosing careers says it all. He said enjoy your work and work for whom you admire."

15 BERKSHIRE'S "SAINTED SEVEN"

"Last year we dubbed these operations the Sainted Seven: Buffalo News, Fechheimer, Kirby, Nebraska Furniture Mart, Scott Fetzer Manufacturing Group, See's and World Book. In 1988 the Saints came marching in."

SEE'S CANDIES

Candy companies are fun and, in the case of See's Candies, both fun and profitable.

See's Candies, wholly owned by Berkshire, has been making candy for sweet-toothed customers for more than seventy years. Berkshire bought See's on January 3, 1972, for $25 million, acquiring it through Berkshire's Blue Chip Stamps affiliate.

Buffett has said that, while Blue Chips sales dropped from $102.5 million in 1972 to $1.2 million in 1991, See's revenues more than made up for things as sales rose from $29 million to $196 million in that time period. In 1991 See's handed Berkshire more than $25 million in profits.

Buffett has said that after he bought See's, it took him five minutes to put Charles Huggins in charge and that, with the record Huggins has notched, he wonders what took him so long.

In the 1991 Berkshire annual report, Buffett said that the compensation agreement for Huggins was "conceived in about five minutes and never reduced to written contract—that remains unchanged to this day."

Over the years Huggins and Buffett have talked every ten days or so, although Huggins said during the Salomon crisis it was more on the order of once a month. (Wall Street Journal, November 8, 1991)

See's was founded in 1921 by a seventy-one-year-old grand-mother, Mary See, who went into the business with little more than an apron and a few pans.

See's makes boxed chocolates and confections with names like Walnut Cluster, Peanut Cluster, Almond Square, Milk Patties, Molasses Chip and Milk Cherry, produced in two large kitchens, one in Los Angeles and one in San Francisco, and distributes candies through its distinctive white retail stores—about 225 of them—in twelve western and midwestern states and Hawaii.

The great majority of the stores, more than 165 of them, are located in California, where the company gets about 80 percent of its profits.

A large volume of candy sales is also carried out through direct shipments nationwide from a seasonally-varying number of order distribution centers. Significant seasonality exists in the business, with heavy sales in cold months and light sales in hot months. About 50 percent of sales come in the last two months of the year when quantity discounts add to extremely high Christmas and New Year's sales.

See's does a splendid job of gift wrapping—the perfect Christmas present. For years, boxes of See's candies have been the gift of choice for a number of congressmen.

In March 1982, Berkshire received a bid for See's Candy from a British firm for $120 million in cash. Buffett didn't bite.

See's has nearly tripled its net income from about $6 million in 1981 to well over $25 million in 1991. But it has difficulty expanding. "We've looked at dozens of ideas of how to expand," Buffett said at the Berkshire annual meeting in 1988. "And in the end we haven't found how to do it . . . It's a tough business."

Buffett himself is a big See's eater—probably just taste-testing all the time, of course. But even when it comes to delicious chocolates,

Buffett strives for discipline, limiting himself to one box a month. That two-pound box arrives regularly at Berkshire headquarters and everyone at the office shares it.

In every box of See's Candy you'll find the See's Philosophy:

"For over sixty-five years we have worked hard to maintain the tradition of quality which literally millions of faithful See's candy eaters have come to expect, year after year.

"Our philosophy is quite simple: Be absolutely persistent in all attitudes regarding quality—buy only the best ingredients obtainable—offer the most delicious and interesting assortments of candies available in the United States—own and operate all See's sparkling white shops, while providing the highest level of customer service.

"This may seem old-fashioned, if not unusual, in this day and age —but it works. At the same time we fully believe that we can always do a better job at what we try to do—ultimately making people happy!"

Buffett says that in 1991 Americans ate 26 million pounds of See's products. Presumably, Buffett's still-top-secret plan for synergy at Berkshire calls for all that candy to be washed through everyone's digestive tract with Cokes.

And that includes the Tim Moylan family of Omaha. Moylan keeps a supply of See's Candy at his office for visitors and one day the candy caught the fancy of Moylan's four-year-old son, Dan.

"Remember our friend, Howard Buffett?" asked Moylan. "Well, Howard's father owns the factory that makes the candy." (Omaha *World-Herald,* April 8, 1992)

Replied Dan, "You mean Howard's dad is Willy Wonka?"

The writer of the story, Robert McNorris, promptly got a note from Buffett saying he planned to pass out samples of See's candy at the Berkshire annual meeting.

"When business sags," Buffett wrote, "we spread the rumor that our candy acts as an aphrodisiac. Very effective. The rumor, that is; not the candy."

oung Warren Buffett and sisters Bertie and Doris (in plain skirt) in front of the family home
Washington, D.C., about 1948, when their father was serving in Congress.
Courtesy of Doris Buffett)

Buffett bought his Omaha home in 1958 for $32,500. The lawn is well taken care of, but not by Buffett who is described as hopeless at household chores. *(Photo by LaVerne Ramsey)*

Warren Buffett with a glass of Coke. When he acquired a stake in Coca-Cola, Buffett said he was "putting my money where my mouth is." *(Photo by LaVerne Ramsey)*

Berkshire Vice Chairman Charles
Munger at Borsheim's traditional party
for shareholders held the day before
the Berkshire annual meeting.
(Photo by LaVerne Ramsey)

Rose Blumkin, "Mrs. B," started the
Nebraska Furniture Mart with five hun-
dred dollars and later sold out to
Berkshire. Although she's established a
competitor, Mrs. B's, across the street,
Buffett still likes to cite her as an exam-
ple of what hard work can achieve.
(Photo by LaVerne Ramsey)

Susan Buffett Greenberg says that when
she told school friends her father Warren
was in the securities business, "they
thought he checked alarm systems."
(Photo by LaVerne Ramsey)

Coca-Cola President Donald Keough (in apron) talks with Bill Ruane, head of the Sequoia Fund, at the Berkshire annual meeting in 1991. Both longtime Buffett friends, they also serve on the board of the Washington Post Co. (*Photo by LaVerne Ramsey*)

Warren Buffett and Fortune magazine's Carol Loomis, who shows off the bracelet Buffett gave her. The charms are replicas of annual reports she edited for him.

Warren Buffett autographing reports
before the Berkshire annual meeting.
Buffett often stands in a Coca-Cola
apron or a See's Candies cap to greet
arriving shareholders.
(Photo by LaVerne Ramsey)

Ed Colodny, chairman of USAir, and his
wife Nancy at a Borsheim's party. "I like
Ed," Buffett says, but considers the
USAir investment "an unforced error."
(Photo by LaVerne Ramsey)

Former Time Inc. Chairman J. Richard Munro says Buffett's offer to acquire a substantial interest in Time, Inc. was rebuffed by the board. "If he had become a major shareholder, we probably would not have gone through what we did," Munro said, referring to Time's subsequent merger with Warner Communications. *(Photo by Steve Fenn)*

Former Salomon Inc. Chairman John Gutfreund was forced to resign after his firm came under fire for rigging Treasury auctions. *(AP/Wide World Photos)*

Deryck C. Maughan learned he was the new chairman and chief executive of Salomon Inc. when Buffett turned to him and said, "Deryck, you're the one." *(AP/Wide World Photos)*

Robert E. Denham, who had counseled Buffett about Berkshire acquisitions for years, was picked as the new general counsel for, and Buffett's personal choice for, chairman of Salomon Inc., the parent company of Salomon Brothers. (*AP/Wide World Photos*)

Four generations: Warren Buffett and his mother, Leila Stahl Buffett; his son, Howard Graham Buffett; and his grandson, Howard Warren Buffett. (*Courtesy of Howard Graham Buffett*)

The Buffalo *News*

Buffett bought the Buffalo *News* in 1977 for about $33 million, sight unseen.

Because of his knowledge of newspapers, he could tell how the paper was doing by looking at its financial statements. It was not necessary, in his view, to go to look at the plant. He already knew what a printing press looked like.

He purchased the newspaper, not through Berkshire, but through the other company he controlled, Blue Chip Stamps. The Washington *Post* and the Chicago *Tribune* had turned down purchase of the *News*, apparently because it was an evening paper.

But Buffett saw it might be a good business if it could launch a Sunday edition.

Its special introductory offers to subscribers and advertisers brought a lawsuit from its competitor, the morning Buffalo *Courier-Express*, which published seven days a week.

The *News* eventually beat back the lawsuit, but both papers continued to lose money for years. From the time of Buffett's purchase, the *News* lost about $12 million.

Then in 1982 the *Courier-Express* folded and what Buffett had was a flourishing monopoly, his favorite kind of business.

The *News* began putting out an earlier edition and today employs 1,000 people and publishes Sunday and seven editions each weekday.

Charles Munger has told one Berkshire shareholder, "Warren was just plain lucky on that one."

The *News* has turned into a quintessential Buffett business. It has a return on assets of "an astonishing 91.2 percent," according to a January 1991 story in NewsInc magazine. "The Buffalo *News* may well be the most profitable newspaper company in the country," it said.

It has a circulation of 308,714 daily and 378,574 on Sunday. Penetration of its area is more than 75 percent.

Buffett's name on the masthead, listed as chairman, is followed by Stanford Lipsey, publisher and president, and Murray Light, editor and senior vice president, who has been with the *News* since 1949.

Slight of build, curly-headed Lipsey has been with Buffett since 1969 when Berkshire acquired the now defunct Sun Newspapers, which Lipsey was managing. Lipsey is a close friend of Buffett's and the two talk on the phone several times a week.

Tim Medley, president of the Medley & Company investment counsel/financial planning company in Jackson, Mississippi, met the modest Lipsey at a Berkshire shareholder party at Borsheim's in 1990. Medley joined a group of fellow shareholders and teased them, "While you all were over talking to those big wigs, I was talking to some regular fellow named Stan who said he was with the Buffalo *News.*" Informed that it must be Stan Lipsey, publisher of the paper and Pulitzer Prize winner, Medley demurred, saying he doubted the fellow was really the publisher, since he said he'd be glad to drop off a couple of copies of the newspaper at Medley's hotel room the following morning.

Medley had the impression "Stan" might be with the newspaper's circulation department. The end of the story is that Lipsey left two copies of the Buffalo *News* at Medley's hotel doorway the following morning.

Generally, a newspaper has a hard time having better economics than the economics of the area it serves. But Lipsey has succeeded in outperforming the economics of his area.

"We don't budget at the *News*," he told *NewsInc.* "We maintain a living, everyday awareness of expenses, and thereby we save an enormous amount of time and aggravation that goes into budgeting."

Buffalo has spent the past decade coming back from its financial collapse of the 1970s, making an enormous effort to shift to a service-jobs metropolis. Education and government now are among its largest employers.

Buffalo lost 23 percent of its manufacturing jobs in the early 1980s as its industrial base declined with such closings as Bethlehem Steel's in 1983. But things began to get better in a hurry for the smokestack, heavily blue collar city after the United States-Canada free trade agreement of late 1988.

The free trade agreement began to change the face of the Buffalo landscape of rusty steel mills, unused auto plants and empty grain elevators, so long a symbol of decay. In its place dozens of Canadian businesses set up offices and branches.

Canadian manufacturers began fleeing their high labor costs and taxes at home. Dozens of Canadian firms crossed the border to set up shop. New businesses came in as Canadians sought services on the cheap, south side of the border.

The unemployment rate in Buffalo dropped from a high of 13 percent to a respectable five percent by the early 1990s.

Buffalo, located on the Niagara River separating the United States and Canada, is just a ninety-minute drive along Queen Elizabeth Way to Toronto, the business hub of Canada.

Real estate prices have been improving as many Canadian businesses looking for growth south of the border open offices in Buffalo.

It also hasn't hurt that the Buffalo Bills have become Super Bowl contenders.

Businesses still are not enthralled with Buffalo's bitterly cold winters. What they do like is that Buffalo industrial land costs are far below those of Toronto, as are taxes and electricity.

All this has not been lost on the Buffalo *News*, which has been enjoying steadily increasing profits even in a sluggish advertising environment.

It is the only metropolitan newspaper published daily within a ten-county upstate New York distribution area that comprises one of the fifty largest primary market areas in the United States.

Among newspapers published in those primary markets, the Buffalo *News* claims the highest percentage of household coverage, 76 percent on weekdays and 84 percent on Sundays.

Berkshire has said it believes the "newshole" percentage (percentage of the paper devoted to news as opposed to advertising) of the Buffalo *News* to be greater than any other paper of its size.

During 1989 the newshole percentage was 50.1 percent and in

1991 was 53.6 percent, one of the highest newshole rates in the country. Buffett is certainly giving his readers their money's worth.

NEBRASKA FURNITURE MART

"He [Buffett] walked into the store and said, 'Today is my birthday and I want to buy your store. How much do you want for it?' I tell him '$60 million.' He goes, gets a check and comes back right away." That's how Rose Blumkin, known as Mrs. B, says Buffett negotiated the purchase of her business.

Actually, Buffett's final purchase price in 1983 was $55 million for 80 percent of the store and it's not as though he hadn't thought about it for a long time.

More than ten years before the purchase, he was telling journalist Adam Smith it was a good business. Smith, in *Supermoney*, recounts the story this way: "We're driving down a street in Omaha; and we pass a large furniture store. I have to use letters in the story because I can't remember the numbers. 'See that store?' Warren says. 'That's really a good business. It has a square feet of floor space, does an annual volume of b, has an inventory of only c, and it turns over its capital at d. 'Why don't you buy it?' I said. 'It's privately held,' Warren said. 'Oh,' I said. 'I might buy it anyway,' Warren said. 'Someday.' "

The Nebraska Furniture Mart, founded in 1935, is a whopper of a store—the largest under one roof in the United States. It operates a home furnishings retail business from a large—more than 240,000 square feet—outlet and sizable warehouse facilities of more than 400,000 square feet.

The store serves a trade area with a radius around Omaha of about 300 miles and sells everything from rugs, sofas, lamps and electronics to cellular telephones. When Buffett was buying the store, he did not even order an inventory until the deal was completed.

When Mrs. B asked where were his accountants, lawyers and investment bankers, Buffett replied, "I trust you more." The contract was two pages long.

As a girl, Rose Blumkin, who was born December 2, 1893, talked her way past a border guard in her native Russia, assuring him she would be back after buying leather for the army and a bottle of liquor for him. She made her way to America and forever after did only two things: run her business and raise her family.

Mrs. B started her business in 1937 with only $500. "Just imagine what she could have done with more," Buffett has said. And following her own advice to "Sell cheap and tell the truth," she eventually made the Nebraska Furniture Mart the success that drew Buffett's attention.

By controlling costs and offering value to the customer, the business flourished. It's now the dominant furniture store in the region. In fact, when Mrs. Blumkin was sued by a competitor for selling too cheap, the judge not only ruled in her favor, but he later bought carpeting from her.

For years Buffett brought friends by to see her, and he bragged at annual meetings and in the annual reports about how she was picking up speed as she got older. His portrait of Mrs. B was of a business heroine.

But in May 1989, at the age of ninety-six, following a dispute with her family about the running of the Nebraska Furniture Mart's carpet department to which she was so devoted, she quit.

Further, she demanded and got $96,000 for unused vacation time, then stormed out and set up shop across the street. She calls her new store Mrs. B's Warehouse, where she still sells carpet and furniture, and still moves around her store on her famous motorized cart. "Their price $104; our price $80," reads one sign in her new store.

Buffett has always favored older managers like Mrs. B. "We find it's hard to teach a new dog old tricks," he said at the 1987 Berkshire annual meeting. "But we haven't had lots of problems with people who hit the ball out of the park year after year. Even though they're rich, they love what they do. And nothing ever happens to our managers. We offer them immortality."

The Nebraska Furniture Mart is always a must-visit for Berkshire shareholders. Once, I wandered in the furniture mart a day prior to the annual meeting, and when I turned into the carpet section, I saw a scene that would have warmed the heart of any Berkshire share-holder. There in the middle of the carpet section was Buffett with a man I would learn was his longtime friend Sandy Gottesman, chair-man of the First Manhattan investment firm in New York and a large Berkshire shareholder. The two were talking to Mrs. B as she sat in her motorized cart. I wish I had been a photographer. You just had the feeling that if Buffett and Mrs. B were actually on the carpet section floor talking business, you were a shareholder in the right company.

Normally shy, I walked right up to Buffett and introduced myself as a Berkshire shareholder. He said, "Good, come to the annual meeting. Ask questions." We had a very brief chat in which, instead of asking about business, I asked him about his tennis and he said he wasn't playing much any more because he had hurt his back.

He and Gottesman wandered around the carpet section inspecting the operations and I wandered around inspecting them.

Yet another year I found Charles Munger, wearing a well-worn travel jacket, blue shirt and dark slacks, wandering around in the lower level of the store, appropriately checking things.

That same year, standing again in the carpet section, I saw an energetic young man in casual clothes come up to Mrs. B's grand-son, Robert Batt, and ask to use the telephone. The man was Buf-fett's son, Howard Buffett, then county commissioner of Omaha's Douglas County.

He talked politics for a time and then I said hello and asked him a question he has probably heard a time or two in his life. "What's your father like?" The younger Buffett replied, "He's great. I've been working on him a long time and he's improving a lot."

Both Washington *Post*'s Katharine Graham and Buffalo *News*' Stanford Lipsey have visited the store.

Of late Berkshire-style synergy has come to the Nebraska Furni-ture Mart. There is now a See's Candy shop at the store. As Buffett wrote in the 1990 Berkshire annual report, "While there, stop at See's Candy cart and see for yourself the dawn of synergism at Berkshire." Installed on October 21, 1990, the See's Candy cart—the first See's outlet east of Colorado—sold 1,000 pounds of candy in its first week. It didn't hurt subsequent sales when Buffett went on an ABC affiliate in Omaha notifying chocoholics of the See's Candy cart's existence.

In October 1991, the Nebraska Furniture Mart opened a new store called Trends just behind the Nebraska Furniture Mart. The store sells mainly ready-to-assemble contemporary furniture such as leather sofas, day beds, children's furniture and cribs. Buffett was on hand for the ribbon cutting and predicted Trends would become the second largest furniture store in sales in the Midwest, second only to the Nebraska Furniture Mart itself.

With synergy apparently still on his mind, Buffett went over to the store's soda fountain and asked Judy Troutman for a Cherry Coke.

Footnote. On December 1, 1991, the day before Mrs. B's ninety-eighth birthday, Buffett paid a call at Mrs. B's Warehouse and presented her with two dozen pink roses and a five-pound box of See's Candy. (Omaha *World-Herald,* February 2, 1992) Mrs. B was quoted as saying, "He's quite a gentleman."

Rapprochement? Could be. The story said Louie Blumkin had recently asked his mother whether she might be willing to sell her business to Berkshire. Would she ever sell? "Who knows?" said Mrs. B. "Time will tell . . . I would sell only one way, if they let me work."

The rapprochement seemed well on its way when Rose Blumkin told the *World-Herald,* July 14, 1992, that she planned to sell her furniture business to her son, Louie.

"I do a very good business there, but it's hard to manage it," she said. "My son offered to buy me out, and I'm going to sell."

She said her son is buying the business for the Nebraska Furniture Mart owned by Berkshire.

Under the agreement, expected to close in the fall of 1992, will Mrs. B. contemplate early retirement?

No way. She plans to keep selling carpet.

THE SCOTT & FETZER COMPANY

Berkshire purchased The Scott & Fetzer Company of Cleveland, Ohio, in early 1986 for $410 million, comprised of $320 million for the company's assets and $90 million assumption of Scott Fetzer debt.

Scott Fetzer, as everyone calls it, doubled Berkshire's revenues to about $2 billion.

It had been on the auction block since 1984, but nothing had clicked until Buffett phoned CEO Ralph Schey and asked for a meeting. Buffett and Munger dined with Schey in Chicago on October 22, 1985. The following week, a contract was signed.

Word of Berkshire's purchase of Scott Fetzer was carried by the Dow Jones news service, which startled Berkshire shareholders by erroneously reporting "Scott Fetzer to acquire Berkshire Hathaway." The report was quickly corrected to read that in reality Berkshire was buying Scott Fetzer.

At Berkshire's annual meeting in 1987, Munger and Buffett were presented with an inch-thick notebook prepared by Scott Fetzer's investment bankers before the purchase. But they handed it back saying they didn't want to get confused. As usual, they just wanted to keep things simple.

With Scott Fetzer, Berkshire acquired three main businesses— World Book encyclopedias, Kirby vacuum cleaners of Cleveland, Ohio, and Scott Fetzer Manufacturing Group, which includes more than a dozen diverse and obscure enterprises.

The largest manufacturing revenue producer of the Scott Fetzer Manufacturing Group is Campbell Hausfield/Scott Fetzer Company, which makes and markets a variety of products related to transmission of air and fluids, such as air compressors, spray painting units, air receivers and high pressure sprayers and washers. Another segment, Wayne Home Equipment, sells furnace burners and sump, utility and sewage pumps. Other businesses sell conduit fittings, roll-up awnings, appliance timing controls, ignition transformers, boat winches, cutlery, maintenance chemicals, and custom steel bodies for truck chassis.

In addition, there's Scott Fetzer Financial Group of Westlake and Columbus, Ohio, which helps customers finance Kirby and World Book products.

There's nothing particularly sexy about any of these businesses, but together they're another little stream winding its way into Old Man River.

The main business, and clearly Buffett's favorite of the businesses acquired in the Scott Fetzer acquisition, is World Book.

But he likes Kirby, too.

KIRBY

With the acquisition of Scott Fetzer, Berkshire became the owner of the Kirby vacuum cleaners business.

"See, it actually picks up the carpet . . . it collects sand," said Hank Smith, vice president of Kirby South in Birmingham, demonstrating the vacuum cleaner's prowess. "If we get in the home, we usually make the sale," Smith explains. In one consumer survey after another, Kirby ranks at the top. "It leaves the others in the dust," Buffett is fond of saying.

Of course, Kirby tends to cost more, $1,289 for its latest Generation 3 model with a power-assisted drive. But users say the strong engine, the space age materials, the strength and durability are all worth it.

Kirbys are sold all over the world, indeed about a third of its sales are overseas. Kirby sells to about 700 factory distributors. They in turn sell the Kirbys to a network of area distributors and dealers. Some of these independent dealers sell the vacuum cleaners door-to-door using in-the-home demonstrations.

Although Berkshire's home cleaning segment is led by Kirby, it also includes Douglas Products, Cleveland Wood, and a host of other profit centers. Douglas makes specialty hand-held electric and cordless vacuums and distributes through department and hardware stores and catalog showrooms. Cleveland Wood manufactures vacuum cleaner brushes. They distribute through discount, hardware and department stores and catalog showrooms.

WORLD BOOK, INC.

Senator Bob Kerrey of Nebraska once happened to tell Buffett he had bought the *World Book* for his two children. "I bought *World Book*, too," replied Buffett, meaning, of course, he had bought the company. Kerrey has said, if ever elected president, he'd turn to Buffett for advice about the economy.

The *World Book Encyclopedia*, as well as Childcraft, a children's resource, and Early World of Learning, a preschool educational program, are among World Book's products. Revised editions of the encyclopedia are published annually.

Almost twenty million pounds of paper are used to print the 1990 *World Book Encyclopedia*, according to the company so fond of compiling facts. The paper would stretch 194 million feet—nearly 37,000 miles—or across the continental United States more than twelve times.

The paper would fill ninety-four railway cars, which means every day during the printing of the 1990 *World Book*, a carload of paper moves from Luke, Maryland, where it's loaded, to the Crawfordsville, Indiana, printing plant.

There are about 100 million characters of type in the 1990 *World Book* and it took three and a half months on the presses to complete the first printing of that edition. Seventeen thousand gallons of ink were used.

In a $500 million encyclopedia industry, *World Book* is found in four of every ten homes in the United States and Canada that own an encyclopedia. And it is estimated that $1 of every $10 spent for books is spent on encyclopedias.

About 270,000 sets of *World Books* were sold in 1990.

In the first quarter of each year an updating yearbook is published and marketed by mail to owners of earlier editions. Otherwise, products are marketed primarily through demonstrations made in homes, schools and libraries by a commissioned sales force of about 42,000 people located throughout the United States, Canada, Australia and the British Isles.

The company itself has about 500 employees and a 40,000-member salesforce. It had 1990 profits of more than $20 million. *World Book* is sold in more than seventy countries and its products have been translated into many languages including Arabic, Chinese, Finnish, Indonesian, Japanese, Korean, Malay, Portuguese, Spanish, Swedish, Thai and Turkish.

Education is always a World Book selling point. About half of World Book's sales force consists of current or former teachers.

World Book also publishes *The Childcraft Dictionary; The World Book Dictionary; World Book of America's Presidents; The World Book Encyclopedia of Science; The World Book Medical Encyclopedia; The World Book Atlas; World Book Reading Development Program; The World Book Year Book; Science Year; The World Book Annual Science Supplement; The World Book Health and Medical Annual; Childcraft Annual;* and *Play It Safe!* with the Alphabet Pals℠ safety program.

The encyclopedia industry has four major players—the others being Encyclopedia Britannica, Grolier and Collier's. World Book is the market leader, selling more than twice as many sets as any competitor and selling more sets in the United States than its top three competitors combined.

A large portion of encyclopedia sales are made on an installment basis. Buyers can finance their purchases through World Book Finance, Inc., a subsidiary of Scott & Fetzer.

In 1988 World Book made a major revision of its format. The seventieth anniversary edition was three years and $7 million in the making, featuring its most extensive revision in twenty-six years. For the revised edition, World Book mobilized more than 1,000 editors, artists, researchers, cartographers, contributors, production specialists and illustrators, checked about 13,000 information sources and reviewed 160,000 photographs.

The publication is known for extensive fact checking. For example, to actually determine that Quebec, Canada, had what was reputedly North America's narrowest street, World Book employees measured the width of the Sous-le-Cap Street and found it to be 8 feet by 10 inches.

The twenty-two-volume set includes 14,000 pages and 18,000 articles by some 2,000 of the world's leading experts in their fields, such as Dr. Michael DeBakey, "heart" contributor; former Dallas Cowboys coach Tom Landry, "football" contributor; and the recently deceased author Isaac Asimov, "science fiction" contributor.

The encyclopedia also includes 29,000 photographs and illustrations and 2,300 maps. Three new features include:

- 24,000 color illustrations, of which 10,000 are new
- 7,000 revised articles
- new typeface and binding

It is estimated that more than 111 million people have grown up with *World Book* from 1917 to 1988 and that there are 12 million *World Book* sets in use worldwide. Buffett has to be proud of these numbers.

The *World Book* was introduced by J.H. Hanson of the Hanson-Bellows Co. in Chicago in 1917 as *The World Book—Organized Knowledge in Story and Pictures.* He created *World Book* by spending $150,000 to revise his then-popular encyclopedia, *The New Practical Reference Library.*

In 1918, Hanson's money ran out and he sold World Book to one of his former accountants, W.F. Quarrie, also of Chicago, and the company flourished.

Celebrities such as the late FBI director J. Edgar Hoover, etiquette expert Emily Post, and Bishop Fulton J. Sheen became *World Book* contributors.

In 1945, Marshall Field II bought World Book to be the flagship of a new company that ultimately became Field Enterprises Educational Corp. Field believed that "education is the keystone of the democratic form of government" and that *World Book* was a key tool for education.

In 1978, World Book was bought by Scott Fetzer.

There are many stories about the gentle persistence of dedicated World Book sales agents, not the least of which is the story of Joyce Fishman, of Marshfield, Massachusetts, a top World Book saleswoman who was once bitten by a dog and still managed to make the sale.

World Book's part-time and full-time sales people make anywhere from $6,000 to more than $20,000 a year and generally have the luxury of flexible hours. They get about $100 commission for a set of *World Books,* which in 1990 ranged in cost from $599 to $899 a set, depending on binding quality. Managers, who get a cut of all the sales force under them, make substantially more. A top branch manager can make as much as $250,000 a year.

Ever the advocate of eating one's own cooking, Buffett has gently pushed sets at his children and grandchildren.

He keeps a *World Book* set at both his home and office.

Fechheimer

Berkshire acquired its 84 percent ownership in Fechheimer Brothers Co. of Cincinnati, Ohio, in June 1986, after Bob Heldman, a longtime Berkshire shareholder, wrote Buffett he had a business he believed met Buffett's famous acquisition tests.

Buffett has frequently referred to his *Wall Street Journal* "ad" for what he is looking for in businesses: large size; demonstrated, consistent earning power; good returns on equity while employing little or no debt; management in place, ("we can't supply it"); simplicity ("if there's lots of technology, we won't understand it"); and an offering price ("we don't want to waste our time . . . by talking, even preliminarily . . . when price is unknown").

Heldman wrote Buffett about Fechheimer, a uniform manufacturing and distribution business owned and operated by the Heldman family—Bob and his brother George, now retired, and a subsequent generation of Heldmans. "We wrote several times and I think convinced him the business fit the tests he lists in his ad. I had a meeting with him in Omaha," recalled Bob Heldman. "We had the parameters of a deal set and met just one last time. It turned out it was in Middle Fork, Idaho, on the Snake River. There are no roads. You have to fly in. We had planned a board meeting at a lodge there and decided that was a good time to settle it. He [Buffett] flew into Boise and I met him and then we got on a little plane and went to Middle Fork. Munger flew in from California and we all met most of the afternoon with our lawyers and we were going to meet the next day but a storm warning came up and we left," said Heldman.

Heldman remembers that Munger asked him, "What are you least proud of?"

"I really couldn't think of anything. We have made a few bad deliveries," Heldman said.

Buffett never went to Cincinnati, either before or after Berkshire's purchase of the Cincinnati concern.

The deal for Berkshire to acquire Fechheimer was closed shortly afterward with Buffett paying about $46 million for the stake in Fechheimer based on a $55 million valuation for the whole company.

Buffett has said the only problem with Fechheimer is its small size, but it remains a steady contributor to Berkshire's earnings stream and has been expanding. Fechheimer now has forty-three stores in twenty-two states.

Around the country, the Fechheimer stores go by different names. For example, the stores in Birmingham and Mobile, Alabama, are called McCain Uniform Co.; in Arizona they are Pima Uniforms; in Tennessee they are Kay Uniforms; and in Texas they are Uniforms of Texas stores.

The Heldmans are hands-on managers known for starting their day sitting around a table and personally opening the company's mail whether it be bills, a complaint, a compliment or a new business idea. They believe it keeps them in close touch with every aspect of the company. One investment-type person showed up to make a business pitch and was told to go ahead and make his case while the Heldmans went right on reading the mail. The inscrutable Heldmans, hardly looking up, finally nodded approval and went right on poring over the mail.

Not much gets by the Heldmans.

During the cocktail party at Borsheim's the day before the Berkshire annual meeting in 1990, Buffett and the Heldmans slipped off to a back office of Borsheim's for a game of bridge. Buffett teamed up with his friend, lawyer George Gillespie, and they squared off against the Heldman brothers.

Afterward, one shareholder had the audacity to ask Buffett if he had won. Grimacing a bit, he replied he had not. "Hard to believe, isn't it?" Buffett quipped.

The slightly built Heldmans had outslicked their boss at the bridge table, but later would not confirm it even in response to a casual inquiry made during a ride back to a hotel after the Borsheim's party. They just grinned ever so slightly and looked out the window to check out the Omaha scenery. Two years later, Bob Heldman said with quiet pride, "Well, we don't like to talk about it, but we did win."

You will not get a lot of fast and loose talk when the Heldmans are around. And you simply cannot tell what their bridge or business hand holds.

You do get attention to business and the right uniform size.

The acquisition of Fechheimer now meant that Berkshire had seven operating businesses—Buffalo *News*, Fechheimer, Kirby, Nebraska Furniture Mart, Scott Fetzer Manufacturing Group, See's Candies and World Book.

"Last year we dubbed these operations the Sainted Seven," Buffett declared in the 1988 Annual Report. "In 1988 the Saints came marching in."

Later acquisitions, such as H.H. Brown Shoe Co., would mess up Buffett's alliteration, but he settled for the rising profits instead.

16 THE STOCK PRICE

"Our goal is to attract long-term owners."

One of the most unusual things about getting to know Berkshire is its stock price.

"I never bought Berkshire because I always thought it was too high," says Ed Conine, head of J Braggs Department store in Omaha, who has been familiar with Buffett's record for years.

Echoes a man who sports a Harvard MBA and one of the top jobs at one of the largest securities firms on Wall Street and who is well aware of Berkshire: "I just couldn't buy the stock because of the price . . . I realize it's what's behind the price but I just can't think in terms other than round lots." The man said he looked at the stock once and it was more than $1,000 a share.

You can go down the list on the New York Stock Exchange past many stocks selling for $30 or $40 a share. Then you work through the B's and find Berkshire trading in the high four figures.

The price itself has left many an investor and stockbroker aghast. "What the hell is that?" is a refrain from any number of brokers to the inquiry of "How's Berkshire?"

For fun sometime, call your broker and ask for a quote on Berkshire.

"What's that? There's something wrong with my machine," will probably be the reply.

Many brokers just don't know the stock. Those who do, don't recommend it. Commissions on it are unusually low.

Because of its high price, only a few shares make a big trade. A quirk in brokerage commission schedules involving the combination of the price and number of shares makes for a comparatively small commission on trades of Berkshire stock.

At some discount brokerages you can buy 100 shares of Berkshire for a $38.50 commission. Trades of that dollar volume for lower priced shares of another stock would be in the hundreds of dollars, thousands at a full-service brokerage.

Once investors are in Berkshire stock, most don't sell. Therefore, a broker is less likely to get a round trip on commissions. Berkshire stock just does not fit into the scheme of things for brokers.

"I began buying Berkshire in the early 1980s. I bought from 1981 until 1987," said Chad Brenner, a lawyer in Cleveland, Ohio, who said Buffett's insistence on quality management and long term outlook appealed to him. "I'm not a smart seller. I've never sold any shares . . . My kids will inherit my stock and I'm thirty-seven."

That is probably good news for Brenner and his children, but it is not good news for any broker casting about for commissions.

"I began buying it at under $1,000 a share . . . and I'd have no problem with buying it here [about $8,800]," Brenner said.

But Brenner indicated whether he buys more shares or not, he will live out his life only on the buy side of Berkshire stock.

Buffett said in 1984 that more than 90 percent of Berkshire's shareholders were the same people who were shareholders five years before that and that 95 percent of the shares were held by investors for whom the next largest investment was less than half the size of their Berkshire holdings. Thus, Berkshire has a loyal group of shareholders and ones with a big percentage of their net worth riding on Berkshire's fortunes.

The float is so thin and shares so infrequently sold that days can pass between Berkshire trades on the New York Stock Exchange. Buffett likes that. "Our goal is to attract long-term owners who, at the time of purchase, have no timetable or price target for sale but plan instead to stay with us indefinitely," Buffett wrote in the 1988 Berkshire annual report.

Brokers and journalists are often embarrassed by their lack of knowledge about Berkshire's high stock price.

On a day in September 1989, when Berkshire was up $100 to $8,550, an office worker at one brokerage firm said, "Something's wrong here. I need to get you a broker . . . Boy, I was about to blow my mind!"

Frequently, the first digit gets left off and any number related to the stock price can be suspect. For example, the Associated Press on November 18, 1989, listed the price-earnings ratio at 11,100. Ouch! On September 2, 1990, the P/E, actually about 17, was still higher at 11,636. But that was nothing compared to the listing March 22, 1991, which carried the P/E at 112,857, hardly in the range for value investors.

The high P/E business never seems to get fixed. On July 1, 1991, the P/E was listed as 248,525 and on July 14, 1991, Barron's carried the P/E as 258,625!

The price of Berkshire shares is so high, many newspapers have trouble squeezing the full price into their listings. In December 1989, at the Associated Press, a computer program that processes stock prices had to be modified when it was discovered the share price exceeded the program's previous per-share ceiling of $8,192.

For a string of days late in 1989 the Stock Phone stock quote service in Atlanta carried Berkshire at $–83. So you always have to be a little suspect of any Berkshire quote as well as other information related to the quote.

In September 1990, when the early trading volume was ten shares, Berkshire was listed as trading 6,000 shares. It would be a rare day indeed if Berkshire were to trade 6,000 shares because the stock has a very low turnover rate of about four percent a year. It trades an average of about 200 shares a day.

At the same time that a brokerage firm's quote machine indicated 6,000 shares were trading, it correctly listed the high for the year in 1990 at $8,725, but listed the low at $175. Although 1990 was a bad year, it was not that bad.

Still, on October 2, 1990, a time of worries about Iraq's August 2 invasion of Kuwait and doubts about whether Congress would ever reach a budget agreement, Berkshire fell $100 to close at $6,000. But the tape read a garbled "BRKBRO 5 1/4."

Back on September 11, 1989, Berkshire's share price shot up $175 to a new all-time high of $8,300. The next day the *Wall Street Journal* tables reported the previous day's high was $158, the low $8, and the closing price $108, down $801 for the day. Say what?

In January 1990, during a nasty spill in the market, Berkshire shareholder George Eyraud of Birmingham called a broker from an airport for a quote and was told that Berkshire was down $700, trading at $200 a share. His bankruptcy was just around the corner. "I went and got a bowl of soup and tried to pull myself together, but I couldn't eat anything," he said, hoping that still once again the quotes were awry, which they were.

Another time he called a discount brokerage in Birmingham and asked to transfer $3,000 to his bank account. "Sir, you only have $2,400 and you owe us $45,000. You'll be getting a big bill from us," the voice at the other end of the line said. "How can that be when I have thirty-two shares of Berkshire in the account?" he asked. "Well, your Berkshire stock is selling at $77.50," the broker replied. "Ma'am, that stock is selling for $7,750—," Eyraud said. "Well, we'll check into it," the skeptical broker responded.

Eyraud once suggested to a woman stockbroker she buy a share of Berkshire. Her reply was "$8,000! I could get a full-length mink coat for that. You've got to get your priorities straight."

Once, a young stockbroker, seeing Berkshire's high stock price for the first time said, "Boy, am I going to short that thing!"

On August 13, 1990, I got a margin maintenance call from my broker saying I must put $919,938 into my account within two days! That is not funny when you've been a low paid reporter all your life. It became somewhat more amusing, however, when my broker said it all happened because the computer had the wrong price for Berkshire.

But the margin maintenance calls kept coming. In January 1991, one arrived for $1,064,341. Okay, I had grown accustomed to the drill, but there was an added problem with the next one that came in March 1991, for $1,107,912. It arrived in my mother's mail and she inadvertently opened it. Mother takes $1 million margin maintenance calls to her son very seriously.

"I knew you had some debts . . . ," she started.

Investors entering the land of Berkshire simply cannot get over the stock price. Joanne Englebert of Birmingham, a Berkshire shareholder, once suggested to a friend, Dr. Martha Wingfield, of Chapel Hill, North Carolina, that she buy a share of Berkshire, then trading at about $7,000. That way, Mrs. Englebert reasoned, she too could go to the Berkshire annual meeting in Omaha. "I think $7,000 is a little much for a weekend in Omaha, don't you?" Wingfield replied.

Berkshire shareholder Michael Assael, an attorney in New York, tells of a time he called a stockbroker who punched up a Berkshire quote. The broker took a hard look at the four digit figure, then suddenly began apologizing, saying he couldn't read his screen. "I recently had an eye operation," he explained.

The price has thrown off investors, even experienced ones. One lawyer/investor who took a look at a Berkshire report and kept hearing about the stock price stated in 1988, "All the gravy's been taken out of that thing." The price then: $4,200.

Of course, Berkshire has its slow periods. Sometimes long-time shareholders who know better wind up selling. Such was the case with Henry Brandt, Harvard's number one student in 1949 and long a senior vice president with Shearson Lehman Hutton. In 1982, he sold more than 1,500 of the family's Berkshire shares for more than $15 million less than they are worth today. "I'm very embarrassed about that," he told Fortune magazine. His embarrassment was complete only when he later learned that the buyer of his shares was a Berkshire subsidiary.

An investor first taking a look at Berkshire is usually floored by the price and then put off again because it pays no dividend.

Of course, the price is high because the underlying value is high and because Buffett has never split the stock, reasoning that such actions are cosmetics, involve paperwork and attract the wrong kind of investor. Buffett wants investors, not speculators.

Although it's fun when dividends arrive, dividends are paid out in after-tax money that is taxed again at the shareholder level. Dividends may look good and they may feel good, but Buffett's not about falsely looking or feeling good. It makes more sense—and that is what Buffett is about—not to have dividends, particularly if Buffett is your money manager.

With Berkshire, the investor is leaving his share of the retained earnings within the company for Buffett to reinvest and keep growing, which he has generally done on the order of 25 percent a year. That is just one of many reasons Berkshire stock trades at more than $9,000, a figure many people look at, laugh at and then ignore.

Of course, most people ignored it at $13 a share in 1965 when a young man with a bizarrely offbeat manner was already planning bigger things.

17 BORSHEIM'S

"Are there any more at home like you?"

Borsheim's, the Omaha jewelry store that Buffett bought 80 percent of in February 1989, is now the site for a shareholder shopping spree and cocktail party the day before each Berkshire annual meeting.

Buffett himself shows up and so do the likes of Katharine Graham and other luminaries.

A string quartet plays, champagne and salmon are served, and shareholders swap Buffett stories. My own story is that I walked up to him, as scores of shareholders do, to shake hands. Thinking he could not possibly know me or where I was from, I told him my name. His instant reply was, "Up from Birmingham, are you?"

The party is great fun. Everyone peers at the Borsheim's merchandise, which ranges from inexpensive coffee cups to jewelry priced at hundreds of thousands of dollars. A thirty-five-karat diamond ring has sold at Borsheim's for $450,000. Some of the sapphires are the size of golf balls.

For Berkshire shareholders, Borsheim's planned something a little special for April 25, 1992—an exhibition of a $6 million Patek Philippe watch. Made of gold and 126 jewels, it's the most expensive watch ever made. The collection also included pocket watches owned by Queen Victoria, Albert Einstein and Rudyard Kipling.

If you are interested in—you know, something a little special, for your "significant other"—a Fabergé egg, some Lalique crystal, a Cartier necklace—Borsheim's will be glad to accommodate you. Maybe you want a Waterman pen, made by Gillette. Please notice. Synergy at Berkshire is coming along. Perhaps a set of china or flatware. Borsheim's carries more than 400 china patterns and 375 flatware patterns.

Even a vendor can enter Borsheim's with goods and leave with cash.

At the 1991 annual meeting some of the jewelry was priced in Berkshire stock. Cute little signs announcing two shares of Berkshire for this diamond, three shares for that necklace. One diamond ensemble went for fifteen shares—$120,000 at the time.

Borsheim's was founded in 1870 by Louis Borsheim, and in 1948 it was purchased by Louis Friedman and his wife, Rebecca, the younger sister of Rose Blumkin of Nebraska Furniture Mart fame. Their son, Ike Friedman, and Ike's son Alan and sons-in-law Donald Yale and Marvin Cohn, owned and managed Borsheim's when Berkshire bought it.

Donald Yale, who came to Borsheim's management team after a successful accounting practice, played a role in the business going to Buffett. One day when Buffett was looking at a ring while Christmas shopping in 1988, Yale yelled out, "Don't sell Warren the ring, sell him the store!"

After the first of the year, Buffett called and asked if a sale were possible. A short time later Buffett bought the store. Buffett and Ike Friedman have agreed not to disclose the price, but it's believed to have been more than $60 million. (Lear's magazine, October 1991, article by James Traub) Ike Friedman told Traub, "We buy it right, we sell it right. That's the difference between us and the other stores. I would say that seventy to eighty percent of our jewelry is cheaper than what a jeweler would pay to buy it. We make money on volume. And compared to other jewelers' expenses, ours are nil."

Of his purchase of Borsheim's, Buffett has said, "I neglected to ask Mrs. B a question that any schoolboy would have asked. That is, 'Are there any more at home like you?'"

Ike Friedman said the entire negotiations between him and Buffett took less than thirty minutes. During the first ten-minute meeting with Friedman, Buffett asked him five questions: What are sales? What's the annual net increase in sales? What's in inventory? What's the debt? Are you willing to stay on?

Without referring to books, Friedman answered the questions. Although we now have the questions, we do not have the answers except for the ones about how much debt—answer zero—and whether Friedman would stay—yes.

Friedman then discussed the sale with the rest of the family and he and Buffett met briefly again. At the second meeting Buffett asked Friedman how much he wanted for 80 percent of the business. Within ten minutes, the price was set and the papers drawn. One page, that is, and a handshake between Buffett and Friedman sealed it. The final touches on the agreement were made at a restaurant, not at a corporate office. As usual, Buffett paid cash. Friedman was suddenly a rich man and a happy, fruitful business partnership with Berkshire was born.

Buffett said at the time: "Ike, there are only a handful of people I do business with this way. And none of them is a Fortune 500 company." Friedman told Buffett, "I'd never have guessed when I was selling newspapers downtown that I would one day sell a business for this kind of money! I'm a lucky man."

Once the agreement was reached, Yale has recalled: "Buffett said, 'Now, forget that it happened, and just keep doing what you were doing.' There was no discussion of future growth and absolutely no discussion of changing our way of making decisions, planning expansion or bringing in additional profits. He made it very clear that he was not in this as a quick-return deal."

In delineating the fundamentals of Borsheim's business, Buffett has listed these attributes:

1. Huge inventories and enormous selection across all price ranges.
2. Daily attention to detail by top management.
3. Rapid turnover.

4. Shrewd buying.
5. Incredibly low expenses.

"The combination of the last three factors," he says, "lets the store offer everyday prices that no one in the country comes close to matching." (*The Goldsmith,* November 1989.)

"Ike has a big smile on his face today," Buffett announced at the annual meeting in 1990. He should. Borsheim's previous days' sales had reached $1.5 million.

Later, Berkshire redeemed Alan Friedman's (Ike Friedman's son) share of the business so that Berkshire now owns 85.72 percent of Borsheim's. (Omaha *World-Herald,* February 23, 1992)

Today the Yale and Cohn families each own half of the remaining 14.28 percent of the business, which Buffett has said he believes sells more jewelry than any other single store except Tiffany's store in New York.

Between Thanksgiving and Christmas in 1991, 58,500 customers —an average of 2,250 a day—bought 38,500 items. (Omaha *World-Herald,* February 23, 1992)

In 1986, Borsheim's moved from its 6,800-square-foot location in downtown Omaha to what is now a 37,000-square-foot site in the Regency Fashion Court Mall. The new store claims more than half the jewelry market share in Omaha. About 40 percent of its sales come from outside its market, largely from business done over the telephone.

Borsheim's customarily sends trusted customers a smorgasbord of the store's collection. They can look it over, buy what they want and send back the rest. Buffett says there's never been a single case of dishonesty in connection with the honor system.

Borsheim's is one of the largest independent jewelry stores in the country, employing 200 people full time and adding fifty to seventy-five people during peak seasons. Employees do not work for commissions since management feels that would force employees to worry more about making the sale than serving the customer.

The store traditionally has advertised little, but does more and even offers a special bridal package and uniform packaging plan.

Borsheim's first catalog was sent to 23,000 people around the United States, including 11,000 preferred customers and 6,000 Berkshire shareholders. Shareholders get a discount.

The store buys in great volume, often directly from the source, and sometimes even cuts its own stones.

Also, the store is a part owner of an amethyst mine in Brazil, which accounts for the large piles of geodes on the floor by the outside entrance to Borsheim's.

Berkshire's 10-K form—a detailed financial report filed with the SEC—explains: "The size of this operation, like several of the Scott Fetzer operations, currently precludes its classification as a 'reportable business segment' of Berkshire. However, it contributes meaningful added diversity to Berkshire's activities."

That it has. Many a Berkshire shareholder has tugged at her man saying, "Honey, please take me to Borsheim's."

The day before the 1991 Berkshire annual meeting, Buffalo *News* publisher Stan Lipsey and his girlfriend, Judi Hojnacki, spent hours checking out practically everything in Borsheim's. The moment Buffett passed by the couple, giving Judi a quick kiss on the cheek, they finally settled on an emerald ring. That was a happy note.

But on a terribly sad note, Ike Friedman, long a heavy smoker and seriously ill with lung cancer, died September 12, 1991.

Yale was named president and chief executive officer and Marvin Cohn, also a son-in-law of Friedman's, was named executive vice president. Buffett was named chairman of the board of Borsheim's at a time he was already chairman of Berkshire and interim chairman of Salomon.

18 BONDS

"Junk bonds will one day live up to their name."

During 1983 and 1984, Buffett quietly bought up $139 million worth of the bonds issued to finance Projects 1, 2 and 3 of the Washington Public Power Supply System (WPPSS), a nuclear power plant utility in the state of Washington so notoriously troubled it was dubbed "Whoops."

In the Berkshire 1984 annual report revealing this unusual purchase, Buffett explained how on July 1, 1983, WPPSS had defaulted on $2.2 billion worth of bonds issued to help finance Projects 4 and 5. For Buffett, that calamity created a buying opportunity. The stigma of the Projects 4 and 5 default spilled over to the other projects and, as is his fashion, Buffett was able to buy the bonds at a steep discount.

The bonds Buffett bought had a special appeal, offering a fixed 16.3 percent, tax-free current yield, a $22.7 million annual return on the investment.

As usual, the investment worked out very well for Buffett. The projects went well and the bonds rose to the occasion. The 16.3 percent after-tax payoff arrived like clockwork at the Berkshire account. Buffett explained he bought the bonds because he probably would have had to pay almost twice his WPPSS purchase price for a business bringing in that much after-tax money.

At year-end 1991, Berkshire still held about $200 million worth of Whoops bonds.

Although Buffett is not a great fan of bonds, he will buy them under special circumstances and he has a history of buying the bonds of troubled companies. In the 1970s he bought the depressed bonds of Chrysler when the firm was close to collapsing. He also purchased Penn Central bonds at about fifty cents on the dollar after the railroad went bust. Both companies rallied back.

In 1986 he bought an additional $700 million of medium-term tax-exempt bonds, which he considered the least objectionable alternative to stocks.

Berkshire's bond portfolio is run by William J. Scott, a long-time Berkshire hand who once was manager of the Buffett Partnership.

Deep in the annual report for 1990, Buffett mentioned that Berkshire had acquired $440 million worth of RJR Nabisco's junk bonds. By the time he was writing the letter, March 1, 1991, he said the market value had increased by $150 million.

That's the kind of time Buffett sits down at the table and says, "Please pass the junk bonds and I'll have Oreos for dessert."

RJR NABISCO BONDS

The first hint that Buffett might be entering the junk bond market came at the Berkshire Hathaway annual meeting in 1990 when a shareholder asked if the junk bond market could ever become a place for a professional investor. "I'll let you know in a year or two," Buffett said, a man known for saying, "Junk bonds will one day live up to their name."

In late 1989 Buffett started accumulating the RJR bonds issued to help finance the takeover and in 1990 he added heavily to the holding. Of course, no one knew this until the Berkshire annual report came out in late March 1991.

Even then, you could have missed the news because it was not until page seventeen of the report that Buffett wrote, "Our other major portfolio change last year was large additions to our RJR

Nabisco bonds, securities that we first bought in late 1989. At year-end 1990 we had $440 million invested in these securities, an amount that approximated market value. (As I write this, their market value has risen by more than $150 million.)"

Had almost any other company made a quick $150 million, it would have, in newspaper parlance, been in the "lead" paragraph of the chairman's letter.

Fortune reported the Nabisco purchase and asked if he wished he had bought more. "There are lots of things I wish I'd done in hindsight. But I don't think much of hindsight generally in terms of investment decisions. You only get paid for what you do," he replied.

Many of the RJR Nabisco bonds were paying about 15 percent so Buffett was hauling in a splendid return while he waited for management to sell some assets and keep their Oreo cookies stocked at the stores.

As junk bonds were tanking, Buffett had spotted a gem. But he didn't just wing it and buy large well-known company bonds at random. Only after intensive study of the massacred junk bond market in which he has said he found more carnage than he expected, did he pick RJR as offering the best hope of a good return.

After the investment there began to be talk of RJR buying back some old bonds and issuing new ones at lower rates.

Junk bonds, called high yield bonds for their double digit interest rates, were popularized in the 1980s by firms trying to raise money to finance takeovers. The bonds are extra risky because the issuers are saddled with extra debt. But again Buffett's reading of the overall financial landscape and his precise timing produced another bonanza for Berkshire. Just about the time his RJR investment was made public, financial writers began offering stories about a comeback in the junk bond market.

Not only that, RJR was beginning to get more notice for paring down its debt. Its losses were dropping dramatically. Its creditworthiness was upgraded. And RJR was making moves to refinance at lower rates.

RJR seemed on its way back to life under Louis Gerstner, who left a top job at American Express to run things at RJR.

On May 3, 1991, RJR announced it was retiring most of its junk bonds used to finance the buyout, using money it had raised in a stock offering. The company said it planned to redeem the bonds at face value, bonds which Buffett had purchased at a steep discount.

Buffett and Berkshire had made a large and quick profit and now, apparently, Buffett would end up with a lot of cash, which he knows how to deploy better than anyone. Once again, Buffett was creating permanent value for Berkshire shareholders.

The repetitiveness, the steadiness of the success of his remarkable investments is Buffett's hallmark.

At year-end 1991 Berkshire held more than $1 billion of bonds in such entities as Washington Public Power System, RJR Nabisco and ACF Industries.

THE ZERO-COUPON BOND

Berkshire raised $400 million in cash on September 21, 1989, by offering zero-coupon convertible subordinated notes to the public. The bond-like investment offered investors a kicker—a chance to buy Berkshire stock at $9,815 at a future date. The notes were priced at a 15 percent premium to the value of the underlying stock with a closing price of Berkshire at $8,535 a share on September 9, 1989.

Apparently, with Berkshire already trading above $8,000, Buffett was playing on the popularity of the stock to raise some always welcome fresh cash.

The underwriter was Berkshire's old friend, Salomon.

Syndicate officials said the size of the issue was increased from an originally planned $585 million face amount to $902.6 million because of the strong demand.

Institutional investors were eager to buy the notes because the purchase would enable them indirectly to acquire Berkshire Hathaway common stock.

The note offering marked the first time that Berkshire has sold stock, albeit indirectly, since Buffett gained control of Berkshire in

1965, and one of the few periods Berkshire investors would have been about as well off in a money market fund.

The fifteen-year zero-coupon bonds due September 28, 2004 were rated double A-2 by Moody's Investors Service and offered at a price of 44.314 to yield 5.5 percent. Each $10,000 face amount note can be converted at any time into Berkshire common at a price of $9,815, a 15 percent premium over the stock's closing price of $8,535 the day before the offering. Since the notes were sold at such a deep discount (at a price of about $4,400 each) and the stock price is high, it would take more than two $10,000 face amount notes to acquire one share of Berkshire common.

The issue is non-callable for three years and notes can be put back to the company in the fifth and the tenth year.

Stock whiz Mario Gabelli recommended the security in a Barron's article January 18, 1991, saying: "You have a triple-A-equivalent security, with a put on September 24, 1994, selling at 42.75, which is an imputed compound return to the put date—which is a cash put—of close to nine percent. In other words, in buying this LYON (Liquid Yield Option Note), you get a three year bond with a nine percent compound return vs. about eight percent now on a 'govie.' Plus, you get an upside kiss—if, in fact, they come up with a cure for cancer—not that Warren Buffett is working on that—but if he comes up with some magic and the stock goes up substantially, you have full upside. I like that!"

With Berkshire then trading at about $6,800, Gabelli admitted the conversion premium of the zero-coupon bonds was pretty rich, about 40 percent of the conversion price of $9,815.

Berkshire can deduct the 5.5 percent interest accrual each year, even though it is not actually making any payments to bondholders. Thus, the net effect to Berkshire is positive cash flow.

The bond offering trades under the symbol BRK RA.

"I've always said that I don't like issuing new stock," Buffett has said, but in this case, "we feel we are getting value received. The combination of paying no interest on the [bonds] while selling the stock at a premium" made the prospect more palatable.

Although Berkshire stock almost never gets a writeup by brokerage firms, there was a writeup from Prudential Securities recommending the bonds. The last paragraph of the research review said, "From a practical point of view, Berkshire Hathaway is a 'prestige investment.' Very few investors own BRK shares, and those that do consider it a 'core' holding. The stock trades maybe 100 shares a day, and is not related to computer program trading or fundamental research recommendations. Berkshire Hathaway transcends Wall Street. It represents an investment in one of America's foremost capitalistic institutions, and shareholders perceive themselves as a very special class of sophisticated (and deep-pocketed) investors. The bonds are an extraordinary opportunity to join that group with the added advantage of having a locked-in positive rate of return. I rate these bonds a strong buy only for our firm's top one percent clients: those who can appreciate an extraordinary opportunity."

Well, most Berkshire shareholders would blush about how special or rich they are.

There are a number of shareholders who are struggling to hold just one share. And one share certainly is a core holding for them.

Another nit: If Berkshire is so great for one percent of humanity, why isn't it good for everyone?

19 WESCO

". . . all of a sudden you meet someone . . ."

Wesco was written up in a *Wall Street Journal* piece on April 17, 1990, as a "tourist-class ticket" to investing Berkshire-style because Wesco, which has many of the same investments as Berkshire, trades in two digits rather than in four digits.

Wesco Financial Corp., of Pasadena, California, is 80.1 percent owned by Berkshire through Blue Chip Stamps, the trading stamp company in Los Angeles. Wesco has three main businesses.

It owns a thrift, Mutual Savings and Loan Association of Pasadena, California; Precision Steel Warehouse, Inc., of Chicago, Illinois, a steel business which has steel service centers in Franklin Park, Illinois, and Charlotte, North Carolina, and operations in Downers Grove, Illinois; and Wesco-Financial Insurance Co. ("Wes-FIC"), of Omaha, a member of the Berkshire Hathaway Insurance Group.

Wesco also wholly owns a small insurance agency, WSC Insurance Agency in Pasadena, and owns 80 percent of the stock of New American Electrical Corp., of Anaheim, California, which it bought in late 1988 for $8.2 million. The other 20 percent of the electrical products company is owned by New America Electrical's chief executive officer, Glen Mitchel, a friend of Wesco chairman, Charles Munger.

164

Wesco's Mutual Savings and Loan Association is located across the street from a See's Candy shop in the Plaza Pasadena shopping center.

Wesco's headquarters is not far from Cypress Insurance Corp. of Pasadena, one of Berkshire's insurance businesses, which does a good amount of business with Wes-FIC. Wes-FIC reinsures about half of the book of workers' compensation insurance business of Cypress.

Cypress gets some of its insurance business from See's. More synergy at Berkshire? After all, there are Coke machines at many of Berkshire's operating units as well as the See's Candy cart at the Berkshire-owned Nebraska Furniture Mart.

Wesco's building sports an American flag by the door and a prominent sign saying "Warning. This facility permits smoking and tobacco smoke is known to the State of California to cause cancer."

Of the 7.1 million Wesco shares outstanding, Berkshire owns about 5.7 million. The stock is thinly traded, with about 1,300 hundred shares a day changing hands. Some days no shares are traded.

Many of the other shares are held by the Caspers and Peters families, who have family members on Wesco's board.

In many ways Wesco, which has about 1,000 shareholders, is indeed something of a baby Berkshire, holding some of the same stocks and bonds as Berkshire. It owns small preferred stock positions in Salomon, Champion, and USAir and small positions in Coca-Cola, Gillette and Wells Fargo stock.

One of its main holdings is about 7.2 million shares of Federal Home Mortgage, better known as Freddie Mac. Wesco's cost for the stock purchased in late 1988 was $71.7 million. Now it's worth more than $300 million, and in 1991 Berkshire boosted its overall Freddie Mac holding to about 7.5 million shares.

Wesco's Mutual Savings and Loan Association is a strong thrift, ranking about fiftieth in size among California savings and loan associations. It had assets of $367 million at year-end 1991.

As a result of a foreclosure in 1966, Mutual owns about twenty-two acres of oceanfront property near Santa Barbara, California, carried on the books at $15 million. The land is worth much more and is being slowly developed for about thirty-two houses and recreation facilities.

Other properties include several buildings in a small shopping center in Upland, California, leased to small businesses.

Wesco's chief financial officer, Jeffrey Jacobson, portrays Wesco as a company where nothing fancy happens, where management just tries to keep things in the middle of the road. In short, things are on track.

"We still have the Freddie Mac stock," he said.

As for the long trial of trying to make something of the Santa Barbara property, Jacobson said, "We're starting to sell some of the units. A number of the houses have been built."

Apparently, Munger and his wife have taken a fancy to the land, paying Mutual Savings $2.1 million in cash for two lots on the Santa Barbara real estate development, according to Wesco's 1992 proxy statement.

"He keeps a low profile," Jacobson said of Munger, adding that Munger has lots of irons in the fire. He serves on the board of Good Samaritan Hospital in Los Angeles and he's chairman of The Daily Journal Corp., an over-the-counter company that publishes the Los Angeles *Daily Journal,* a sort of *Wall Street Journal* to the legal profession.

Each year Munger writes to Wesco's small band of shareholders in much the same vein that Buffett does. In the 1990 report he wrote, "It is quite conceivable that Mutual Savings will decline in size because it should decline in size. Even so, we expect that Mutual Savings will muddle through in a manner satisfactory to Wesco shareholders with moderate expectations. Our optimism comes mainly (1) from an expected minor profit boost from our foreclosed seaside property, and (2) from an expected major profit boost caused by ownership of our large holding of Freddie Mac stock."

There is no pulling of punches and usually some heavy criticism and sarcasm over the S&L crisis or leveraged buyout operators.

But the industry's mismanagement has not spilled over to Mutual. In the Wesco Form 10-K there appears the following shocking statement: "No loan losses have been recorded or required to be reserved for during the past five years . . . Mutual Savings has no 'troubled assets.' "

Still, Wesco overall has not had particularly fast growth, nor has it found enough of the right acquisitions.

At the 1986 Berkshire annual meeting Buffett compared the acquisition search to selecting a wife: "You can thoughtfully establish certain qualities you'd like her to have, and then all of a sudden, you meet someone and you do it."

In 1989 Wesco, in a stinging letter from Charles Munger, resigned from the United States League of Savings in protest over its lack of calling for proper reforms in light of the national S&L crisis. Wrote Munger, "It is not unfair to liken the situation now facing Congress to cancer and to liken the League to a significant carcinogenic agent. And, like cancer, our present troubles will recur if Congress lacks the wisdom and courage to excise elements which caused the troubles."

Wesco is a steady, if unglamorous, part of Berkshire, and perhaps can be thought of as having the safety and about the same steady and sure return of a money market account.

In fact, once a Berkshire shareholder suggested to Munger he might want to turn Wesco into a money market account one day. Munger did not totally dismiss the idea.

That should not suggest he is about to liquidate things, but then Munger has no problems with cash in the bank earning sure money either.

Munger has always thought that quality businesses and stocks will carry the day.

Buffett has said that Munger has influenced him greatly by emphasizing concern about the quality of a business rather than just buying for a cheap price.

The *Journal* story about Wesco also noted that Wesco's businesses were not considered as good as Berkshire's. A day after it ran, Munger was talking at the Nebraska Furniture Mart to Berkshire shareholder/First Manhattan Corp. chairman Sandy Gottesman about the story. "Well, I hate to see it says our businesses are less good than Berkshire's," Munger lamented, although Munger has said much the same thing himself. He wound up saying, "We'd be fine if we had bought quality stocks in 1968."

Berkshire acquired Wesco in 1973 at about $6 a share by present day prices. At year-end 1991, it traded at about $70 a share and it pays a modest dividend.

That's on the order of 15 percent on his money annually, a "money fund" even Buffett could be proud of.

20 SALOMON REDUX

"I like to put meaningful amounts of money in a few things."

Buffett made his $700 million preferred stock investment in Salomon Inc., on September 28, 1987, after a lifetime of denouncing Wall Street's ways.

"It's a huge commitment," he announced at the next stockholders meeting. "We'll know in ten years whether it was a great idea." He was wise to allow himself such a long time-frame.

"Without borrowing, it pretty much empties the piggy bank for now," he told the *Wall Street Journal*, September 30, 1987. But as usual with his investments, Buffett was totally committed. "I like the fact it's a big transaction," he added. "I can't be involved in fifty or seventy-five things. That's a Noah's Ark way of investing—you end up with a zoo that way. I like to put meaningful amounts of money in a few things."

One of his most constant themes over the years has been to criticize Wall Street's short-term trading mentality. In the 1991 Berkshire annual report he opined that, "We believe that according the name 'investor' to institutions that trade actively is like calling someone who repeatedly engages in one-night stands a romantic."

So why Salomon? Why did Buffett invest in the heart of Wall

Street? And why particularly in a firm widely known for aggressiveness and shrewd, hair-trigger trading?

"Why are we vocal critics of the investment banking business when we have a $700 million investment in Salomon? I guess atonement is probably the answer," he said at the Berkshire annual meeting in 1991.

The real answer may be is that he got a sweet deal on a worldwide business franchise. Salomon, founded in 1910, is one of the largest and most profitable brokerage firms in the United States.

Before looking at the deal, let's examine the matter of Buffett's timing, which, in hindsight, simply could not have been worse.

The stock market crash of 1987 was only three weeks away—the day the market would drop 508 points, or almost 23 percent, its worst single day loss ever.

The crash sent almost all stocks nosediving. Brokerage stocks were particularly hard hit because of their cyclical nature and partly because overexpansion in the securities industry had knocked down margins. The crash triggered a longlasting tailspin for brokerage stocks, suctioning Salomon's stock price right along with it.

Salomon's common stock was trading at about $32 a share when Buffett bought the preferred issue. After the crash the common stock eventually sank to a low of $16 a share.

Some studies, in fact, suggest Salomon's own huge selling that day was one ingredient in the mounting panic.

Instead of buying Salomon common stock in the first place, what Buffett and former Salomon chairman John Gutfreund (pronounced Good Friend) agreed to was that Berkshire would buy a newly issued preferred stock—a Salomon financial instrument paying a nine percent dividend.

If Buffett's timing was off, the deal—the first in a string of preferred stock investments for Berkshire—decidedly was not.

Preferred stock is hybrid investment containing some characteristics of both stocks and bonds.

Common stock is a security representing ownership in a company, and although common stockholders can benefit most if business is good, they assume the primary risk if the business goes sour.

Preferred stockholders, on the other hand, get dividends paid before they are paid to common stockholders. If the company goes under, a preferred stockholder has a claim to the assets before the common stockholder.

As long as Salomon continues to pay dividends, Berkshire is not affected by a drop in Salomon stock. Essentially, Berkshire is insulated, short of bankruptcy, through its preferred investment.

Salomon's nine percent dividend, $63 million a year paid to Berkshire, is largely exempt from corporate taxes because corporations do not have to pay taxes on 70 percent of their dividend income on preferred stocks.

Moreover, Berkshire can convert its preferred stock investment into Salomon common stock at any time before October 31, 1995, should the common stock reach $38 a share.

Perhaps it was the attractiveness of the deal that triggered Buffett into making a move that could well be a miscalculation of upside potential. Certainly Berkshire shareholders were surprised by the deal. After all, they had listened to him deride Wall Street for years.

In any event, Buffett got into bed with Salomon, and although it may work eventually, it literally caused Buffett some sleepless nights.

Gutfreund had to do some hard selling to the Salomon board to get it to bite on the deal clearly so favorable to Berkshire.

Salomon was under great pressure from a takeover threat from Revlon chairman Ronald Perelman in 1987. Backed with financing by junk bond king Michael Milken, Perelman was trying to buy a 14 percent stake in Salomon stock held by Minerals Resources Corp., a Bermuda-based company controlled by the Oppenheimer family of South Africa.

In the end Buffett got his investment and Perelman backed off.

For this and his subsequent preferred stakes in The Gillette Company, USAir Group, Inc., and Champion International Corp., where often there was a real or a perceived takeover threat, Buffett became known as a "White Knight," stepping in to save the takeover targets.

In *Liar's Poker*, Michael Lewis's account of his bond trading days at Salomon, Gutfreund is quoted as saying that if the Buffett plan were rejected in favor of Perelman, he, Gutfreund, would resign. "I never stated it as a threat. I was stating a fact," Lewis quoted Gutfreund.

Lewis's portrayal of hardball bond trading tactics at Salomon would hardly give potential customers confidence, and his account paints a picture of a fast and loose corporate culture at Salomon.

Whatever the financial astuteness of most Salomon employees, its reputation at times has been less than impeccable.

The company has broken the law and has a checkered history of oil trading infractions. It has been fined as a result of charges it cheated customers on both securities and commodities trades.

The high living of Gutfreund and his socialite wife, Susan, was publicized in articles describing an estimated $20 million fixup of their $6 million duplex on New York's Fifth Avenue. And they spent millions more on a home in Paris.

Buffett must have had second thoughts about Gutfreund along the way. A Los Angeles *Times Magazine* piece on February 16, 1992, said Buffett "hit the roof" in October, 1990 when Gutfreund came to a Salomon board of director's compensation committee with a plan to boost bonuses by $120 million at a time when Salomon was struggling.

Buffett asked Gutfreund to revise the figure downward, but Gutfreund soon returned with a request for another $7 million. Buffett voted against the plan, but it passed.

Even operationally, Salomon had a record of overexpansion, exorbitant bonuses, and an overly ambitious plan to invest and occupy a dramatic new office tower at New York City's Columbus Circle. Salomon decided to scrap its plans for the Columbus Circle location, causing it to forfeit about $100 million.

In February, 1991, Salomon moved from One New York Plaza, known for the football-sized trading rooms that Gutfreund roamed, to nineteen floors at 7 World Trade Center.

A number of Salomon's investments have done poorly.

Its forays into merchant banking using its own money for investments in leveraged buyouts of Revco and Southland (which would end up in bankruptcy proceedings) have been lackluster.

Finally, for all Salomon's remarkable worldwide business expertise and range and the gilt-edged resumés of its employees, it has done little for shareholders. Its stock price is about where it was a decade ago although its book value has tripled in that time, up from about $11 a share to about $30 a share.

Salomon's stock has been in the doldrums since the crash of 1987 despite a hefty stock buyback program. Of course, Salomon also had done a lot of things right—Berkshire and many others will attest to superb underwritings performed by Salomon.

Still, it had been operating in recent years in a virtual industry depression.

Salomon has three main divisions: Salomon Brothers, Inc., for securities; Philbro Energy, for energy; and Philipp Brothers, Inc., which became the commodity trading division of Salomon in 1983.

Few trading companies could equal Philipp Brothers international network. But after a string of losses it has been largely disbanded. Profitable units have been merged into the company's main operating groups and others have been let go.

Although the Salomon Brothers securities businesses were faltering since even before the crash, the money has been rolling in at Salomon's Philbro Energy group, where its trading and refining businesses have been basically strong.

Ever since Buffett and Munger came on the Salomon board in 1987, there had been real cost cutting and streamlining of operations. And with a better securities environment in the early 1990s, the firm was making a quick leap forward.

Buffett himself had thrown a lot of business Salomon's way.

For example, Berkshire's zero-coupon note offering was underwritten by Salomon, and Salomon and Berkshire have traded huge amounts of securities back and forth. Salomon's 1990 proxy statement provides some details: "Among the company's transactions, in the ordinary course of its business in 1989, Salomon Brothers Inc. purchased from Berkshire entities in which it is informed Berkshire has a material interest, marketable securities having a value of approximately $884,663,000. Additionally, Berkshire paid commissions and fees of $3,086,000 to Salomon Brothers Inc. in connection with securities transactions. The company believes that its transactions with Berkshire and such entities are upon terms which are no less favorable to the company than those obtainable from other sources."

In 1990 there were again large transactions between Berkshire and Salomon. The Salomon 1991 proxy statement put it this way: "Salomon Brothers Inc. purchased from Berkshire and entities in which it is informed Berkshire has a material interest, marketable securities having a value of approximately $135,359,769, and sold to Berkshire and such entities marketable securities having a value of approximately $800,337,873. Additionally, Berkshire paid commissions, fees, service charges and interest of $3,981,309 to Salomon Brothers in connection with securities transactions."

The pattern continued in 1991, when Berkshire bought about $920 million worth of marketable securities from Salomon and in turn Salomon bought from Berkshire about $392 million worth. Berkshire paid about $5.3 million in commissions and fees to Salomon.

When Buffett needs a stockbroker, he calls Salomon.

Not until early 1991 did Salomon publish a handsome earnings report as the overall markets began to recover with the Persian Gulf War. Earnings then continued to move up and the stock price rose.

Salomon, whose underwriting business was picking up markedly, was named lead underwriter for the huge Time Warner financing in the summer of 1991.

But just as things finally began to look up after four long years, all hell broke loose.

On August 9, 1991, Salomon, which had become a Wall Street powerhouse largely by trading government bonds, disclosed it had uncovered "irregularities and rule violations" in connection with its bids at Treasury securities auctions, the most important of all financial markets. Salomon said that the 35 percent threshold—intended to keep one buyer from dominating the market—had been breached by it in some instances. In addition, the firm said bids were submitted in the names of firms that had not authorized Salomon to make them.

Although Salomon itself revealed the infractions and suspended four employees, it was hardly out front with the disclosures, making them known only after the government was six weeks into an investigation of a "squeeze" in the May auction of two-year Treasury notes. A squeeze occurs when one buyer controls a disproportionately large amount of securities and forces other buyers to pay more for securities later, thus undermining fairness in the market. In short, Salomon had "cornered" and "monopolized" the market.

The government probe occurred after other firms complained that Salomon, which has dominated Treasury auctions in recent years, had corralled too big a piece of the $12.26 billion notes sold in May and then squeezed competitors by driving up prices. (*Wall Street Journal*, August 12, 1991)

But even though Salomon had plenty of time to think things over, the Gutfreund management team released information about only part of its maneuvers.

On August 14, the firm said that although top Salomon officials, including Gutfreund, president Thomas Strauss and Salomon Brothers unit's vice chairman John Meriwether, knew in April of an earlier illegal bid, Salomon had disclosed nothing until faced with a federal investigation.

It also said it bought $1.1 billion in government securities from customers under questionable arrangements and, further, that a bogus bid for $1 billion of bonds was carried out inadvertently as a result of a botched practical joke!

Reaction to the scandal was incredulity, summarized best by William Simon, a former Treasury secretary and a former Salomon partner: "Good God. I'll be damned. Good God. That can be my only reaction." (*Wall Street Journal*, August 15, 1991)

Within a few days Salomon's stock fell from about $36 to $25 a share, eventually plummeting to a low of $16 a share. Its bonds plunged as credit agencies threatened lower ratings and some big investors ceased to do business with Salomon.

A crisis swept the firm, with investigations underway into every facet of its activities while lawsuits hurriedly were stamped in at the courthouse.

During tense meetings on August 16, Gutfreund said he would

resign and a frantic call was placed to Buffett, "Mr. Clean," who offered to take the job. He immediately flew to New York.

During the afternoon, financial wires—which had already reported that trading in Salomon stock had not opened pending a news announcement—were hopping:

"S&P puts Salomon ratings on creditwatch: Negative."

"Salomon stock, bonds plunge on spreading scandal news."

"Salomon says Gutfreund, Strauss prepared to resign."

Then at 2:27 P.M. the Dow Jones news wire flashed:

"Salomon says Buffett to become interim chairman."

From that moment of management overhaul forward, Buffett would never again be unknown. But that was hardly the point. Buffett faced a dangerous situation in trying to fix the mess at Salomon.

By 6:45 A.M. that morning, Gutfreund—who told a colleague that reading the *Wall Street Journal* story about top Salomon officials knowing about illegal bidding was like reading his obituary—called Buffett and said that he and Strauss were going to resign. Later that morning, Buffett called Gutfreund back and volunteered to head the firm on an interim basis. "You won't believe this—because I don't look that dumb—but I volunteered for the job of interim chairman. It's not what I want to be doing, but it will be what I will be doing until it gets done properly." (Institutional Investor, September 1991).

Buffett immediately faced enormous issues: appeasing investors and clients, dealing with criminal and civil investigators and worrying about some new bomb exploding on his watch. But Buffett was the logical person, magician or not, to turn to, and he got things off on the right foot when he quickly met with Salomon's managing directors at the World Trade Center, telling them the firm's reputation for staying just within the bounds of the rules would NOT be acceptable. (New York *Times*, August 17, 1991)

Of course, the story was covered by everyone including *Barron's* (August 16, 1991) Alan Abelson, who took his usual satirical approach, saying, "The caretaker appointed to look after Salomon in the absence of Gutfreund and Strauss is an out-of-towner, from Omaha, Nebraska, to be exact, and he runs a textile company. But he's supposed to be a fast learner, so we've no doubt he'll pick up enough about the securities business while on the job to keep the traders from sneaking off to play paddle ball or catch the 3 P.M. showing of *Terminator 2.*"

So here's what Buffett did on the Sunday afternoon of August 18, 1991: accepted the resignations of Gutfreund, Strauss and Meriwether; fired government-bond trading chief Paul Mozer as well as Thomas Murphy; named Deryck C. Maughan, the Tokyo-based chairman of Salomon Brothers Asia Ltd., chief operating officer, telling Maughan ten minutes before the press conference, "Deryck, you're the one"; and successfully appealed to Treasury secretary Nicholas Brady to partially lift an hours-old government suspension of Salomon trading in Treasury securities auctions.

Then Buffett met with the press for about three hours, saying the illegal trading first came to the attention of Salomon in April, when Mozer received a carbon copy of a letter indicating the Treasury was aware of a problem in one of its auctions. The letter from a federal regulator was sent to a customer whose name Salomon had used without authorization to make a bid. Mozer approached Meriwether and "showed him a letter which was clearly going to lead to Mr. Mozer being in trouble," Buffett said. Top management discussed the matter with its lawyers and determined that the government should be told, Buffett said, but it was not done.

"I cannot explain the subsequent failure to report," Buffett said, adding that he had long been an admirer of Gutfreund but that he was distressed by management's actions. "The failure to report is, in my view, inexplicable and inexcusable." Buffett and Gutfreund, on September 3, 1991, agreed not to talk to one another during the investigation.

Buffett pledged to root out the scandal and try to improve the firm's reputation for honest dealings. The next few days were enormously hectic.

Coincidentally, an abortive coup in the former Soviet Union led to the photo mix-up at New Jersey's Asbury Park *Press*, which misidentified a photo of Buffett as being Gorbachev's momentary successor, Gennady Yanayev.

And, clearly, Salomon itself was acting under a lot of pressure during the crisis. Once a reporter called asking to speak to Salomon's spokesman, Robert Baker, and was told, "I'll have Mr. Buffett call you." The reporter replied, "Gosh, that'd be great." When Baker called back, he soon said he'd have to hang up and call back. "Warren's on the line," he announced.

Later, Baker said Buffett had set the company on a new path, even while working both from New York and Omaha. Baker continued: "Warren has given the company its strategic direction . . . He has kept his focus on the regulators and the capital structure. It's our belief that those who misbehaved are gone. New management dealt with that very swiftly. Warren has cleaned house. I see no reason for the government to shut us down . . . We are cooperating with the government in an unprecedented way. We are cooperating to a greater degree than in any case in the history of Wall Street."

Salomon's business, he said, began rebounding with the return of such clients as the World Bank and the state of Massachusetts. "Our bond underwriting is returning fast. We still have some trouble on some of the equity underwritings because of the two, three, four month lead time. Some clients don't want to deal with the uncertainty for that long. This has to hurt us in getting some new business," Baker added.

As for a report in the *Wall Street Journal* that said Buffett stays at the Plaza Hotel and wears expensive suits, Baker said Buffett doesn't stay at the Plaza, that he stays at either Katharine Graham's apartment or at the Marriott near the World Trade Center. "He stays at the Marriott for $192 a night so he can walk to work," Baker said. Okay, said Baker, he has a few expensive suits. "They're not even tailored and he jokes that when he wears an expensive suit, he makes it look like a $300 suit."

As for staying at the Plaza, Buffett has stayed there in years past, largely because Mrs. Buffett liked it, says Buffett's daughter, Mrs. Susan Greenberg. She said he did not stay at the Plaza during the Salomon crisis. "He'd just as soon stay at Motel 6 . . . He's been staying at either the Vista or the Marriott for about $125 a night."

In the subsequent days of the Salomon scandal, Buffett fired Salomon's top lawyer, Donald Feuerstein, and replaced him with Robert Denham, a managing partner of Munger, Tolles & Olson, the Los Angeles based law firm founded by Charles Munger. Buffett described Denham, who was the top student in his first year at Harvard Law School, as his first and only choice. For seventeen years Denham had worked with Buffett on such Berkshire investments as American Express, Champion and even Salomon itself. (Business Week, September 9, 1991)

Soon Buffett told the Salomon sales force, "It's my job to deal with the past. It's your job to maximize the future, and it can be a huge future. Everyone must be his own compliance officer. That means that everything you do can be put on the front page of the newspaper, and there will be nothing that cannot stand up to scrutiny."

Buffett even accepted the resignation of Salomon's outside counsel—the Wachtell, Lipton, Rosen & Katz law firm—a highly regarded firm that had represented Salomon for years and that had helped Gutfreund bring in Buffett as an investor in 1987. (Wall Street Journal, September 3, 1991)

As for the amount of litigation the firm faced, Buffett later said, "I may be the American Bar Association's Man of the Year before the year is over."

Buffett set about slashing bonuses and making them payable in stock rather than cash, reducing debt and demanding new procedures whereby every bid was cross-checked at least twice. He told Salomon's Philbro Energy unit to cut all ties with Marc Rich & Co., a major client of Philbro's, saying Salomon wasn't going to do business with Rich, a U.S. fugitive.

Amidst the crisis, what about Berkshire?

"Berkshire works pretty well, some say, without me," Buffett said. "It really is a lot less complicated operation than Salomon. I've always said I could run [Berkshire] working five hours a week. Maybe we'll test that. But I hope not for too long." Added Buffett, "I was practically looking for a job. The only thing I am is an addressee on the envelope when they send me the check . . . I can spend whatever time is needed . . . If I quit thinking about this, I'd probably just have a big hole up there."

Maughan began picking up Buffett's lead on humor, pointing out he was not from Salomon's trading culture and there was no way he could be. "You cannot graft the head of an investment banker onto the body of a trader and not get tissue rejection," Maughan said.

And here's how the Buffett-Maughan combination reacted to a question about whether Buffett would take a salary.

Buffett: I was thinking of making it one dollar a year, but I could be negotiated downward.

Maughan: The new corporate culture.

But that's not the end of the Salomon story. If Buffett can work his magic here so that Salomon's stock can stage a comeback and surpass the $38 a share mark by October 31, 1995, Berkshire will be able to make a handsome profit on its $700 million investment by exercising its conversion rights, when Salomon starts redeeming the shares.

In any event, a new era of high visibility for Buffett and Berkshire has dawned.

Soon Buffett was testifying before Congressional committees. On September 4, he testified before the House Energy and Commerce finance subcommittee, and at the end of the session subcommittee chairman Edward Markey asked him to sum up his recommendations in one minute. "I'm not sure I can drag it out for one minute," Buffett replied. "Integrity is paramount."

Here's what he told Congress on September 11, 1991:

"A week ago when I testified before the House subcommittee, I began by apologizing for the misdeeds of Salomon employees that have brought us here. Normally I would not wish to be repetitious. But in my opinion this particular message bears repetition many times over. The nation has a right to expect its rules and laws to be obeyed, and Salomon did not live up to this obligation.

"Our customers have a right also to expect that their names will not be drawn into some underhanded scheme. So to you and them and the American people I apologize on behalf of more than 8,000 honest and decent Salomon employees as well as myself.

"Mr. Chairman, I also want to thank you for holding these hearings in such a timely manner. You and the American people have a right to know exactly what went on at Salomon Brothers and I am here to tell you the full truth as I know it to date. When and if I learn more, it will immediately be disclosed to the proper authorities.

"Many decades ago J.P. Morgan stated the objective of his firm: 'First class business run in a first class way.' I have yet to hear of a better goal. It will guide me at Salomon Brothers and I invite you to measure our future conduct by that yardstick."

When the dreaded results for the third quarter were in, they were better than expected. Even with a $200 million charge set aside to cover expected costs and fines, the firm actually registered a profit of $85 million for the quarter. A revamping of Salomon's compensation system lowered Salomon's payroll by about $110 million.

Salomon took out an unusual two-page newspaper ad on October 29, 1991, in the *Wall Street Journal,* the New York *Times* and the Washington *Post,* at a cost of about $600,000. The ad set forth Buffett's letter to shareholders as well as the firm's newly shrunken balance sheet.

"I believe that we had an extremely serious problem, but not a pervasive one," Buffett said.

It was a piece of solidly good news for Salomon and its stock price rose eight percent that day, and shortly thereafter the World Bank, after a three month suspension, resumed business ties with Salomon, a major plus for the firm.

But even under Buffett, Salomon still occasionally has its snakebit days. On March 25, 1992, a clerk mistook a customer's order to sell $11 million of stock as an order to unload 11 million shares, some $500 million. The huge sale in the closing minutes of the trading day wiped out a twelve-point rally on the Dow, which closed instead with a one point loss. Buffett said it was an honest mistake and did not fire him. In fact, he asked that he not be told the clerk's name.

"I believe Salomon would have gone under without Warren Buffett," said Malcolm S. Forbes, Jr. "There is no question he saved it."

Now the world knew just who Warren Buffett was.

In the end he saved Salomon.

He ousted the old management and overhauled the firm with a new management, emphasizing ethics, openness and compliance rather than risk-taking and bravado.

He cooperated in an unprecedented way with the government, even handing over records from Salomon's own lawyers, waiving attorney-client privilege.

Overseeing Robert Denham's legal team in its strenuous and skillful negotiations with the government, Buffett managed to guide Salomon, against heavy odds, in avoiding criminal penalties that could have brought the firm to its knees.

Indeed, Salomon—while settling civil matters for $290 million—was able to avoid criminal charges, in part because of its full cooperation with government investigators.

"If he had not repositioned the firm, he would not have been able to get anything in the negotiations with the government," said Omaha stockbroker George Morgan.

Buffett's impeccable reputation helped smooth the intense talks with the Treasury Department, the Securities and Exchange Commission and the Justice Department.

Taking a more conservative fiscal stance, Buffett reduced Salomon's balance sheet by selling about $50 billion in assets, thereby lowering the firm's exposure to high leverage and huge borrowings. His message here was that ultra-easy access to funding often leads to undisciplined decision making.

He slashed bonuses, setting up new, fairer standards for both bonuses and compensation. He restructured Salomon's stock and bond trading departments, cutting back on its stock trading and moving the firm back to its bond-trading roots, through which it had grown to prominence.

He assuaged clients, employees, shareholders and the government itself, asking all to look for a new first-class Salomon that would set the highest standards in its business dealings. Here he teaches us that good profits and good behavior go hand in hand.

Buffett said Salomon had learned an expensive lesson but was ready to move forward as both an ethical and profitable company, indeed that those elements should complement and reinforce one another.

He kept his pledge about staying on with the firm until the investigations were completed. Better, he kept his pledge about turning the firm around and rebuilding its reputation.

"We have managed to preserve a firm with a proud history and promising future," he wrote Salomon shareholders. "You have our pledge that we will conduct our business in the future so as to merit your continued trust."

Along the way, Buffett had some setbacks. There were a large number of defections from the firm and there was some grousing about Buffett's not wanting to play near the edge of the court. There was kidding about his "Jimmy Stewart" ways, his supposed naiveté about Wall Street's quick-buck operations.

But in the end the mild-mannered, straight-arrow, determined Midwesterner had come to town and put a stop to Salomon's brash, fast-buck mentality.

The emphasis would be on solid business relationships and understandings—not on rigging Treasury market bids or hiding wrongdoing. The new style would be on less leverage, not more. It was on honesty, not fast talk or running over the customer.

In short, Buffett was able to bring about a corporate culture change at Salomon based on his own history and personality of honesty, openness, caution and fair-mindedness. As a result, Salomon righted itself and its stock steadily rebounded.

You shouldn't cut corners. You should do things simply, ethically, and without a lot of loud talk. You should do things in an honorable, open manner—indeed, in a way that would not be embarrassing should it appear on page one of a newspaper. If at all possible, you try to have fun.

You should try to be a good guy.

"He demonstrated that an honest person could come in and clean up Wall Street's ways," notes George Morgan of Omaha. "He showed that honesty, hard work, good relationships, openness are good—that honesty works.

"That *Liar's Poker* stuff scares me and that's what the world perceived those guys as being . . . He put in a compensation plan that rewards honest money-making for the firm—not money just because you are there or generating a lot of activity." Morgan adds that bonuses are now based on meaningful, honest moneymaking activity for the firm.

When Buffett stepped down, he named Deryck Maughan to head Salomon Brothers, and Andrew Hall continued to run the Philbro Energy oil trading and refining unit.

Then there was much speculation about who Buffett would name as chairman of the parent firm, Salomon Inc.

The guessing ranged from Paul Volcker, former chairman of the Federal Reserve, to John Byrne, head of Fund American Companies, to John Whitehead, former co-chairman of Goldman Sachs & Co., to Thomas Murphy, chairman of Capital Cities/ABC, Inc.

But Buffett said his "sole recommendation" for the job was Robert Denham, the lawyer who had served Buffett so well during the Salomon crisis.

Buffett remains chairman of Salomon's executive committee.

As always, it was all so simple. Keep control of the firm by putting in charge a brilliant lawyer and trusted friend who advised you through the crisis, someone who would ensure Buffett's reforms remain.

Denham was certainly the person to oversee the remaining lawsuits against the firm, and Buffett said Denham's job—exactly in line with Buffett's philosophy of running things—would include evaluating the performance of the Salomon units, setting compensation for top executives, ensuring legal compliance, allocating capital and avoiding undo risk.

Having imposed those duties on a wayward firm he successfully reined in, Buffett returned to Omaha full-time to continue to carry out those duties for his beloved Berkshire Hathaway.

Buffett, who has hunkered down in his modest home and office in Omaha most of his life, and also has seen the bright lights of the world, has chalked up extraordinarily vast achievements and riches, all of which he is handing back to society.

A great student and teacher, Buffett has taught us that honest and traditional values can work and can prevail.

Buffett has made us think and made us laugh out loud. He has amply enriched the world.

21 THE GILLETTE CO.

"We thought we made a good investment or we wouldn't be in it."

"He's glad there are more people growing hair on their face," says one Berkshire employee. After all, it has to be shaved off.

From a Berkshire point of view, shaving should be done with a Gillette razor. Twice a day!

As with the investment in Coca-Cola, Buffett again chose a U.S. domiciled company overseeing a huge overseas business. Gillette, with nearly 70 percent of its sales and profits coming from overseas, is an international firm engaged in the manufacture and sale of personal care products.

As a major force in providing grooming aids, it's looking sharp. Lines include blades and razors, men's and women's, along with toiletries, cosmetics such as Jafra skin care products, stationery products, including writing instruments and correction fluids (Liquid Paper), Braun electric shavers, and Oral-B oral care products.

The company was founded in 1901 by King C. Gillette, who was working for Crown Cork & Seal Company as a salesman when his boss, William Painter, advised him: "Why don't you invent something that is thrown away, once used, and customers will have to come for more?"

Gillette later described how the whole idea for a disposable razor came to him while he was shaving one morning in 1895: "The way the blade could be held in a holder; the idea of sharpening the two opposite edges of the thin piece of steel; the clamping plates for the blade, with a handle halfway between the two edges of the blade. All this came more in pictures than conscious thought, as though the razor were already a finished thing, and held before my eyes. I stood there before that mirror in a trance of joy. My wife was visiting Ohio, and I hurriedly wrote to her. 'I've got it! Our fortune is made!' Fool that I was, I knew little about razors and nothing about steel, and I could not foresee the trials and tribulations I was to pass through before the razor was a success. But I believed in it with all my heart." (Peter Hay, *The Book of Business Anecdotes*)

In 1903 Gillette's firm began selling the Gillette safety razor and twenty blades for five dollars.

Unfortunately, for all his success, Gillette died virtually broke in 1932 as a result of poor investments and debts in the 1920s.

By 1960, the company developed a technique for applying a silicone coating to the blade edge, vastly improving shaving quality. The Trac II shaving system introduced in 1971 ushered in the era of twin blade shaving, a concept refined with the Atra pivoting head twin blade system in 1977 and the Atra Plus system in 1985, featuring a lubricating strip for extra smoothness.

The company is currently riding high on its new Sensor—the first razor that continuously senses and automatically adjusts to the contours of the face, offering a close, safe and smooth shave. Gillette launched the Sensor in January 1990 and sold 20 million Sensors in the first eight months. By October 1991, Gillette had produced one billion Sensor replacement cartridges and captured fifteen percent of the U.S. razor and blade market. As the world's economies become more united, Gillette's value as the leading brand name in razors can only increase.

Gillette broke into the writing instruments business with its purchase of Papermate pens in 1955. In 1987 Gillette chairman Colman C. Mockler bought Waterman Pen Co. of France and expanded it internationally. Waterman is a top-of-the-line pen known for its superior craftsmanship. Today Gillette is the world's largest writing instruments business, but margins in the business are thin, not nearly those of razor blades.

Its toiletries and cosmetics lines, not as successful as Gillette would like, include deodorants, antiperspirants, shave creams, hair sprays, shampoos, conditioners, home permanents, styling aids, ethnic hair care products, and bath and skin care products.

Gillette claims about 17 percent of the $1.6 billion U.S. deodorant market, with its Right Guard, Dry Idea and Soft & Dry brands, second behind a 31.5 percent market share held by giant Procter & Gamble Co.

Its Braun electric shaver and small household products lines are among international leaders. Braun is the number one marketer of electric shavers in Germany and is among the leaders in Europe, North America and Japan. Gillette's Flex Control electric razor, made by Braun, the first swivel-headed electric razor, is available only in Europe, where demand is outpacing supply. The Braun unit, bought by Gillette in 1967 for just $64 million, now has sales of about $1 billion a year.

Gillette's Oral-B division is the leading seller of toothbrushes in the United States and several international markets. The Oral-B toothbrush is regarded as a topnotch toothbrush, often recommended by dentists.

Gillette is the leading seller of blades and razors in North America and most other areas of the world. Now it's making an all-out effort to sell razors and blades in the former Soviet Union, and is solidly along in plans for a joint venture to operate a razor blade plant there with a capacity for making 750 million blades a year.

Gillette chairman Mockler, a Harvard Business School graduate who took over management of the company in 1975, stabilized Gillette, guided it through a brief period of negative net worth in the late 1980s, and oversaw the development and launch of the extraordinarily successful Sensor razor.

After fighting off two major takeover attempts in three years—one by Revlon's chieftain Ron Perelman in 1986 and one by the now-defunct Coniston Partners in 1988—Mockler restructured the company. The work force was reduced by eight percent and under-performing operations were sold. To escape the takeovers, Gillette bought back almost 30 percent of its common stock, ballooning its debt from $436 million to nearly $2 billion, but it has been paying that down quickly.

Although Gillette's balance sheet looks like that of an LBO, Gillette can pay down debt because of its superior cash flow and Berkshire's $600 million investment in July 1989. Buffett pulled off the investment by calling up his friend Joseph J. Sisco, a Gillette board member, and proposing "an equity issue that might make sense." (Business Week, August 7, 1989.)

In a privately arranged transaction, Buffett purchased $600 million worth of Gillette's 8.75 percent convertible preferred stock. With the common stock trading at about $41 a share at the time, the preferred stock was convertible after two years into 12 million shares at $50 a share. If not converted, the preferred stock would have had to be redeemed by Gillette within ten years.

At the time of the preferred stock purchase, Buffett issued a short, simple statement: "Gillette is synonymous with highly successful, international consumer marketing and is exactly the sort of business in which we like to invest for the long term."

Newsday columnist Allan Sloan, who has followed Buffett's career off and on for twenty years, argues that Buffett's stake in Gillette was immediately worth about $40 million more than Buffett paid for it:

"The stock bought by Buffett's Berkshire Hathaway, Inc., carries a dividend of 8.75 percent a year, and he can trade $50 worth of it for one share of Gillette common stock. In other words, he agreed to pay 'a conversion premium' of $8.375 a share over the $41.625 that regular investors were paying for Gillette at the time the deal was negotiated.

"But look. Buffett is getting $4.375 a year in dividend income [the 8.75 percent dividend times $50] for each Gillette share he controls. The holder of a share of Gillette common stock gets a dividend of only $.96 a year. So, while Buffett has agreed to pay a premium of $8.375 a share for Gillette, he gets an extra $3.415 a year in dividend income [$4.375 minus $.96] while he's waiting. Work it out, and in less than two and a half years, the extra dividends that Buffett will receive make up for the premium he has agreed to pay.

"You still with me? Now watch. In the arcane world of convertible securities, three and a half years is the norm for breaking even in a security such as this Gillette convertible. Run the numbers through Gillette's black box, which the company graciously did for me, and you'll find that to reach the break-even point in three and a half years, Buffett would have had to pay $53.50 a share, rather than $50. That's a seven percent difference. Now, multiply that by $600 million, and Buffett is $42 million ahead . . ."

Sloan reported that Buffett and Gillette agreed with his math, but not his interpretation.

"Gillette claims that certain aspects of the stock—the fact that Gillette can call it in for early redemption, that Gillette has the right of first refusal to buy the stock should Buffett decide to sell, and other arcana—offset the relatively high dividend and relatively low conversion price."

He reports that Buffett told him, "We thought we made a good investment or we wouldn't be in it," and noted that Gillette was getting his services. "Charlie and I agree to work on the company for ten years. We don't charge a fee, we don't even bill for transportation services to come to board meetings."

Buffett's preferred stock was not normally convertible until 1991. *Forbes* magazine in its November 12, 1990, issue pointed out a loophole. "If the common stock price exceeds $62.50 for at least twenty consecutive trading days, Gillette is likely to offer to redeem the preferred at par. In that event, Buffett would score a quick $150 million pre-tax profit on his $600 million investment [excluding the 8.75 percent dividend on the preferred], assuming that he converted and then sold. This summer [1990] it looked as if Buffett would indeed score. Driven by the stunning success of its new Sensor razor, Gillette's common stock rose from about $45 a share early in the year to close above $62.50 for sixteen consecutive trading days, from July 11 through August 1, when it ended the day at $63.50. If the common stock had stayed above $62.50 for four more working days through August 7, Buffett could have converted his $600 million worth of preferred into $750 million worth of common."

Saddam Hussein spoiled Buffett's fun by invading Kuwait August 2, 1990, and sending the stock market reeling.

It was a close shave. But before too long Buffett would get a second chance.

With the rally that began with the first bombs of the Persian Gulf War, Gillette's stock price began moving up. Then, on February 21, 1991, all sorts of good news tumbled out. Sales, profits and per share income were solidly higher for the year and fourth quarter of 1990. Also, the company announced a 2-for-1 stock split and a hike in the dividend rate. Further, Gillette said it had planned to redeem Berkshire's preferred stock investment of $600 million on April 3, 1991, but that Berkshire planned to convert its stake of Gillette common stock into about 11 percent of the common stock.

With the split of May 1991, Berkshire had 24 million shares of common stock in a company enjoying increased cash flow because it no longer had to pay dividends on that Berkshire preferred stock that had been converted to common stock.

All along Berkshire had been making 8.75 percent on its $600 million investment, which in two years and a half more than doubled in value.

It was at Gillette's Boston headquarters that chairman Mockler died of a heart attack on January 15, 1991. At about the same time, the February 4, 1991 edition of Forbes magazine featured a cover picture of Mockler reaching the top of the mountain against competitors and inside a story highlighting Gillette's many achievements.

Buffett had referred to Mockler as one of those people he could "like, admire and trust." Mockler planned to retire at the end of 1991 and Alfred Zeien, an amateur architect who designed and built his own home on Cape Cod, had been named president. Zeien succeeded Mockler.

Gillette had turned out to be a brilliant investment and Buffett was left with a major stake in a fully-turned-around global franchise, an irreplaceable consumer products company with a wonderfully reinvigorated international brand name.

22 USAIR GROUP, INC.

"I like Ed."

Berkshire made its preferred stock investment in USAir Group, Inc. on August 7, 1989, to the tune of $358 million, or about a 12 percent stake.

Buffett said at the time, "It is unusual for Berkshire Hathaway to invest in a capital intensive, labor intensive industry, such as the airline industry. Our enthusiasm for the investment in USAir Group preferred stock is dramatic evidence of our high regard for Ed Colodny's management."

"I like Ed."

Buffett's strategy here must have been spotting an industry that had only a few large players, was in a state of consolidation, and had the possibility of some synergy for Berkshire, perhaps with PS Group's travel, leasing, and fuel operations. PS Group's Rick Guerin has said Buffett is a believer in the future of the travel industry.

But in this case, Buffett's strategy, in the early flying at least, backfired, as any number of factors came to bear to cause USAir's stunning decline amidst heavy airline industry turbulence.

When Buffett made the investment, USAir common stock was trading at about $50 a share. Each $1,000 face value preferred share is convertible two years from the purchase date into 16 2/3 common shares. The investment pays Berkshire a 9.25 percent dividend a year.

Because of corporate tax benefits, that 9.25 percent return is as good as a fully taxable investment that yields about 12 percent.

USAir could buy back or call the preferred stock after August 7, 1991, for $100 a share higher than the $1,000 purchase price. Until then Berkshire is free to convert its stock, selling any remaining shares of the preferred stock to USAir at the original $1,000 a share price.

What Buffett apparently saw through his preferred stake was this: a way to gamble safely. If he lost, he would earn 9.25 percent. If he won, he would control an airline in a consolidating industry capable of healthy returns.

USAir had started out in the East, as Allegheny Airlines. It acquired Mohawk Airlines in 1972, and established a hub in Pittsburgh in 1978. With a bunch of monopoly routes, USAir had it made in the early 1980s.

It didn't do much marketing. It didn't buy jumbo jets. It didn't offer first class service. It wouldn't even give customers an extra bag of peanuts.

With confidence, it undertook one of the biggest airline combinations in history in 1987, acquiring both Pacific Southwest Airlines and Piedmont Aviation, Inc.

Although the mergers made USAir into the nation's fourth largest airline, size isn't everything. Some of its planes were old and the airline missed out, for the most part, on international growth.

And because USAir's flights are shorter, it's a relatively high-cost producer.

USAir president Ed Colodny himself said in the annual report that 1989 was a difficult year because of deteriorating industry fundamentals and merger-related problems. Planes were late. Bags were lost. Useless Air became one moniker.

On the West Coast USAir got clobbered in a five-way battle with American Airlines, United Airlines, Delta Airlines and low-cost Southwest Airlines, making many of its Western routes unprofitable.

Justice Department trust-busters began looking into whether USAir's Pittsburgh hub was monopolistic.

Moreover, in absorbing two successful carriers into its system, USAir adopted what it called a "Mirror Image" strategy of making them do everything exactly its way.

For years, Piedmont had promoted the fact it served a whole can of Coke rather than handing out a plastic capful at a time. When USAir cut out the tradition, Piedmont frequent flyers put their foot down.

Cost-cutting was one thing, but this was downright stingy. Cost-cutting and large layoffs were the order of the day in 1990.

At the same time, competition became more fierce, and when Iraq invaded Kuwait August 2, 1990, jet fuel prices soared and USAir came in with a loss of $454 million. In a January 26, 1991, press release Colodny said, "During 1990, and more particularly in the fourth quarter, the airline industry was faced with soft domestic traffic caused by a weak national economy, huge increases in the price of jet fuel and widespread, unrealistic fare discounting." He added, "Most of these factors continue to be present. It is unrealistic to think the airline industry economic environment, which is adversely impacted by the Gulf war, will change significantly in 1991."

Eventually 7,000 furloughs were announced, or 14 percent of the work force. Orders for planes were deferred and the number of flights reduced as the airline struggled in an economic no-man's-land: too big to be a regional airline and still too small to compete with the major national carriers.

The airline industry has been described as an industry where perhaps only four or five carriers will survive. All airlines have faced such severe pressures that one could only recall a cartoon which ran in Barron's. It's caption read: "Arrivals, Departures, Bankruptcies."

Indeed, in the year prior to mid-1991 six of the top dozen airlines in the nation filed for bankruptcy protection. A competitor's bankruptcy is no break for USAir, as Buffett pointed out at the 1991 Berkshire annual meeting: "Once an airline goes into bankruptcy, they're in effect debt-free. Eastern picked up hundreds of millions of dollars essentially by selling off gates and other assets to subsidize operating losses at a time when they were effectively debt-free—because they weren't paying anything on their debt. And USAir can't compete with that. To compete with someone who's bleeding copiously, you need a blood bank."

But Buffett hung in there, telling Martha H. Hamilton of the Washington *Post* early on, "There are no plans—just to be an investor for ten years or longer. We think when you've got an able management, they should have time to play out their hand."

Colodny retired in June 1991, after thirty-four years with the company, but remains chairman of the board. Seth E. Schofield succeeded Colodny as president of USAir Group.

In 1991 Buffett was calling the USAir investment "an unforced error."

"Buffett still walks on water. He just splashes a little bit," said Marshall Lewis, senior vice president of the Blunt, Ellis & Lowei investment firm. (Omaha *World-Herald*, October 20, 1991)

During May 1991, USAir began service to Omaha's Eppley Airfield, perhaps beginning a happier chapter in its existence but hardly signaling the major turnaround needed. The overall outlook at USAir remains cloudy, even though in July 1991 it could run ads boasting that in the previous twelve months it had the best on-time record of any of the seven largest U.S. airlines.

At year-end 1991 Buffett slashed his estimate of the value of the $358 million investment to $232,700,000. Meanwhile USAir employees, officers and board members took pay cuts.

At the Berkshire annual meeting in 1991, Buffett described the airline industry as a "terrible business," adding, "My mistake was I didn't think price competition would get that bad. The cost side, of course, has been abysmal as well as the result of events in the Middle East."

23

NHP, INC., FREDDIE MAC, AND LOW INCOME HOUSING

*"I look on it as an investment with pro-social aspects . . .
I don't view it in a philanthropic context."*

NHP, INC.

Berkshire bought a 50 percent stake in national Housing Partnership, Inc., better known as NHP, Inc., in 1986 for $23.7 million. NHP of Washington, D.C., mainly owns and operates multi-family rental apartments and is the nation's largest apartment landlord.

Buffett came up with the idea to invest in the housing partnership, but Munger has always seemed a bit skeptical about the investment.

On October 31, 1990, NHP, headed by J. Roderick Heller, III, announced that Berkshire had sold its stake, most of it to Harvard University.

Institutional investors agreed to buy 62 percent of the privately held company's shares.

Harvard University, through its $5 billion investment management company, bought 50 percent of NHP shares from Berkshire and Weyerhaeuser. Before the transaction, Berkshire owned 50 percent and Weyerhaeuser owned 25 percent, and afterward Harvard owned 50 percent and Weyerhaeuser and other institutional purchasers owned 12.5 percent each. Management, and certain shareholders, who invested at the time NHP subsidiaries were organized in 1970, owned the remaining shares.

Said Heller in a press release at the time, "We are very pleased that Harvard, with which we have had business relationships for over three years, has become our major shareholder, and we are looking forward to a long and fruitful association. At the same time, we regret that Berkshire Hathaway will no longer be an owner of NHP. Warren Buffett has been an outstanding shareholder, and his advice has been invaluable during our successful turnaround of recent years."

Terms of the sale were not released, but NHP, whose portfolio of apartments includes about 81,000 units, did say the sale price was more than half the $72 million book value of the company, which would have given Berkshire a 50 percent profit on its investment.

This particular investment appeared to be small and mediocre by Berkshire standards, and the final sale price was most certainly affected by the fact that in 1990 the words "real estate" were two of the worst words around. A five-year period for a lot of Buffett's and Munger's time and energy and some money, in the end, brought only fairly small potatoes. For Berkshire the investment would have to be classified as so-so—one that went from $24 million to about $35 million in value in five years. It received no mention in the 1990 annual report.

Then maybe it shouldn't have. Buffett could have done better in government bonds.

Buffett has said that, given Berkshire's size, small ideas will not help much—only big, successful ones will make Berkshire grow.

FREDDIE MAC

In late 1988 Berkshire's Wesco unit beefed up its theretofore minor stake in the stock of Federal Home Loan Mortgage Corp., more affectionately known as Freddie Mac, to 7.2 million shares.

It was the maximum amount, at that time, that any single shareholder could own under government rules. The cost of the purchase was $71.7 million, and had some investors asking themselves, "Who is Freddie Mac?"

Explaining the investment to Fortune magazine in its December 19, 1988, issue, Buffett said, "Freddie Mac is a triple dip. You've got a low price/earnings ratio on a company with a terrific record. You've got growing earnings. And you have a stock that is bound to become much better known to equity investors."

Freddie Mac helps make the American dream of owning a home come true. Over the years, Freddie Mac has helped finance one in eight American homes, including more than 700,000 apartment units.

About 97 percent of Freddie Mac's business is with single family home mortgages.

Chartered by Congress in 1970, the stockholder-owned company buys home mortgages from lenders, guarantees the mortgages against default, packages them as securities and sells them to investors, such as S&Ls. It creates a continuous flow of money to mortgage lenders in support of home ownership and rental housing.

In 1984, it issued about 15 million shares of participating preferred stock to Federal Home Loan Board-member S&Ls, with trading generally restricted to board members.

In 1988 the company began offering the stock on the New York Stock Exchange on a when-issued basis.

The company had been owned by thrifts that owned the stock through the country's Federal Home Loan Bank System and were allowed to resell the stock starting in January 1989.

The lifting of trading restrictions on Freddie Mac preferred stock allowed public investors to come in.

So what is Freddie Mac and how does it work to link the nation's mortgage markets with its financial markets?

Freddie Mac provides stability in the secondary market for home mortgages.

The moment you drop your monthly mortgage payment in the mail is merely the start of a long odyssey for your money.

If your lender has kept the loan in its portfolio—in other words, kept it on its books—your payment will be processed, your check deposited, and the money used to pay interest on deposits and make more loans to new buyers in your area.

Let's say you take out a 10 percent fixed-rate home loan of $150,000 from a bank. The bank may not want to carry it on its books for the next thirty years. One reason is because the bank will wind up losing money if rates skyrocket in the future. To eliminate the risk, the bank sells your loan to someone like Freddie Mac.

If your lender has sold your loan to another institution, there is a good chance that part of your monthly check may go to a farmer in Nebraska, an elderly widow in Florida, a big pension fund in New York or even to an investor in London or Tokyo. Mortgages are bought and sold in the "secondary market"—by a vast network of lenders, like the federal government, quasi-government agencies and private investment Wall Street companies.

Among such agencies are Freddie Mac, the Federal National Mortgage Association, better known as Fannie Mae, and the Government National Mortgage Association, or Ginnie Mae.

Freddie Mac's only real competition is Fannie Mae, making them duopoly businesses which benefited with the decline of the S&L industry nationwide. If Buffett can't locate a true monopoly business, he is usually glad to settle for a duopoly.

The secondary market accomplishes several things. Lending institutions can make long-term mortgage loans knowing they can sell them to someone like Freddie Mac, and at the same time mortgage-backed securities make it easier and safer for more investors to participate in the mortgage market.

After Buffett made the investment in the stock at a cost per share of about $30, it rose in 1990 but then began to plummet, along with anything that had to do with the suddenly suspect world of real estate.

At its low in 1990, the stock had lost two-thirds of its value from its 1989 peak and was trading at a price/earnings ratio of about five.

The Freddie Mac plummet rocked the stock of Wesco, which owns the Freddie Mac stock directly, and didn't help Berkshire in the rocky stock market of 1990.

In late 1990 Freddie Mac was reporting problems in its apartment-backed mortgage business, particularly in New York and Atlanta, but, even so, profits from the company's single-family home mortgage business remained strong and the stock began to rebound.

In its 1990 year-end report, Freddie Mac chairman Leland Brendsel said, "We estimate that property values underlying our single-family mortgage portfolio stood at approximately $600 billion at year-end, reflecting a decade of home price appreciation. This means, on average, there is almost two dollars of property value underlying every mortgage dollar represented in our single-family portfolio."

In 1991 Freddie Mac stock rebounded strongly as fears about real estate eased and interest rates dipped dramatically.

Despite the 1990 scare, Steady Freddie has been profitable in every quarter since 1971.

Again Buffett's strategy of patience paid off.

On May 15, 1991, it was disclosed that Berkshire in a first quarter filing with the Securities and Exchange Commission didn't include the 2.4 million shares in Freddie Mac it had held at the end of 1990.

But the *Wall Street Journal* reported that Freddie Mac said that Berkshire's Wesco unit reported it still owned the stake.

The story quoted an analyst saying that Buffett may have wanted the filing status kept confidential because he plans to increase or decrease his stake. At year-end 1991, Berkshire had upped its Freddie Mac stake to 2.5 million shares.

Freddie Mac turned in a strong performance in 1991.

"Despite a very difficult year for the economy, Freddie Mac kept money flowing to the housing market throughout 1991 by purchasing $100 billion in mortgages," said Leland Brendsel in a company report. "It was an outstanding year for us with record earnings and record revenues."

In March 1992, the company proposed a 3-for-1 stock split and a 14 percent dividend increase. With the split, Berkshire has about 7.5 million shares of Freddie Mac.

LOW INCOME HOUSING

In 1990 Berkshire invested $25 million in the non-profit National Equity Fund to help finance low-income housing. And in 1991 it invested $20 million in low income housing, split evenly between the National Equity Fund and the Enterprise Fund. The money was to go for creating low income housing in several cities, including Houston, Los Angeles, Detroit, Chicago and, possibly, Buffett's home town of Omaha.

"I look at it as an investment with pro-social aspects," he said at a press conference. "I don't view it in a philanthropic context."

The investment, which Buffett termed "financially and socially responsible," should earn 15 to 20 percent a year for over a decade in the form of tax credits created through the federal Low Income Housing Tax Credit program, part of the 1986 tax law revision.

In its first three years the National Equity Fund collected $141 million to build more than 5,200 housing units in twenty-six cities. Buffett's investment is the largest ever made in the fund.

Buffett made the investment in part to encourage other corporations to follow suit. Salomon pledged $10 million in the program and American Express has made a small $2 million investment.

Because the only profits investors receive are derived through tax benefits, their equity investments reduce the financing costs of the housing developments, thus reducing the cost of rent to the tenants.

Of the law providing for the investment credit, Buffett said, "It seems to me to be a fine marriage between the corporate community and the local community development organizations. The marriage should provide affordable housing for low-income groups."

The tax credit was assured when President Bush signed the new housing bill into law at the White House on November 28, 1990.

Sitting at Bush's side at the ceremony was a man whose initials are WEB. Before the signing Bush and Buffett had a private chat. What they said to each other was not disclosed.

We may never get the details, but here's basically what happened:

The discussion was about business, not politics. The President of the United States, George Herbert Walker Bush, peppered Buffett with questions about the economy.

Let's hope the President's secretary didn't erase the White House tapes.

24 CHAMPION INTERNATIONAL CORP.

"It has been helpful to me to have tens of thousands turned out of business school taught that it didn't do any good to think."

One hugely accepted notion that Buffett has shot holes through is the so-called "efficient-market" theory, which holds that every stock price is a fair price because it incorporates all known information about a company. The theory argues there is nothing to be gained by analyzing a company and ferreting out new information.

In other words, the theory postulates that market prices at any given moment reflect all knowable public information; the prices you read in the stock tables of your newspaper every day are, therefore, fair prices. There are no bargains. The efficient-market theory holds that it's useless to try to outperform the market. Furthermore, all future prices are subject to new, random information. Future stock prices, the theory holds, are independent of what has come before.

Many times Buffett has said, "It has been helpful to me to have tens of thousands turned out of business schools taught that it didn't do any good to think."

Buffett has often joked that he wished more people would subscribe to the efficient-market theory so there would be fewer investors trying to figure out where the market has gone astray, where it does not accurately reflect intrinsic value.

He would just as soon people go on believing in an efficient market while he picks over the inefficiencies, the discrepancies in the marketplace, finding value the market has not yet recognized. It is how Buffett has made his living.

One typical such move came with the announcement of Berkshire's eight percent preferred stock stake in Champion, the giant forest products company based in Stamford, Connecticut, on December 5, 1989, at the time of a hostile bid for Great Northern Nekoosa by competitor Georgia-Pacific Corp.

Andrew C. Sigler, Champion's chief executive officer since 1974, has long been a vocal critic of takeovers in general and a takeover of his company in particular. With Berkshire's large stake in Champion, the company had reduced its chances of being swallowed.

A Champion spokesman has said the company approached Buffett who agreed for ten years he would not boost his stake to more than 18 percent of the company.

Champion had acquired St. Regis Corp. in 1984 as a so-called "white knight" after raiders threatened a takeover of St. Regis.

Sigler has said of Berkshire's $300 million investment: "We wanted to raise capital to help support our cost-cutting, quality improvement, and capacity enhancement programs. Berkshire's CEO Warren Buffett is a remarkably astute investor, and his commitment to the long-term performance of the companies in which he invests is well matched to Champion's needs and goals. This infusion of capital from such a stable source is particularly valuable for a capital-intensive company such as ours during this period of economic uncertainty. It improves our balance sheet and strengthens our capability to complete our announced capital improvement program."

Champion, with operations in the United States, Canada and Brazil, makes printing and writing papers, publication papers, newsprint, kraft, pulp and forest products. The company's many facilities nationwide and internationally make bleached paperboard, newsprint, packaging and pulp and forest products, including plywood, newsprint, lumber and studs.

Champion has long been a laggard in the forest products industry. Its stock price, well under book value, is trading about where it was a decade ago. Buffett bought the preferred when the stock was at about $30 a share.

The company cited a litany of reasons for its sluggish earnings showing: severely depressed conditions in the wood products industry, weakening world pulp markets, lower prices for some of the company's paper grades, startup difficulties in connection with several major rebuilds, and higher tax rate, largely attributable to the company's Brazilian operations as a result of economic reforms in that country.

In 1989 the company produced about 1.4 million tons of coated and uncoated paper at four mills: Canton, North Carolina; Courtland, Alabama; Hamilton, Ohio; and Pensacola, Florida.

One of every three paperboard milk containers in the United States is made from Champion paperboard. Champion has a large building-product business that has been hurt by the housing slump.

Laurence Tisch's Loew's Corp. now owns about 16 percent of Champion's 93 million shares.

In addition to stakes by Buffett and Tisch, the Templeton funds and Primark have taken stakes, apparently all believing the company, which has about $5 billion in sales annually, is undervalued.

The company has been unable to get good profits from its investments and is trading at a P/E of about 7.

Over the years the company has earned a reputation for making large capital investments that have not paid off particularly well.

But what apparently intrigues investors is the vast amount of timberlands the company controls—6.4 million acres in the United States and 2.5 million in Canada, where Champion owns about 85 percent of Weldwood, a pulp and paper products company.

That nine million acres of land is a lot of land. It's a lot of trees.

In recent years the 30,000-employee company has spent more than $2 billion on capital projects, according to the company's 1990 annual report, completing major portions of its large modernization program.

In January 1991, Champion dropped the poison-pill defense it has had in place since 1986 to ward off potential takeover bids. With little money around available for takeover attempts, the threat seemed largely past.

Or did it? In its February 19, 1991, issue, *Financial World* magazine carried a small story about Champion, noting that among its big investors were Buffett, Tisch, and John Templeton, as well as the Manning & Napier and Dean LeBaron's Batterymarch financial firms.

And it listed another interesting investor, Sandy Gottesman, chairman of First Manhattan, noting he happened to be Tisch's neighbor. Of course, Gottesman is a very close friend of Buffett's. Let's just leave it that a lot of heavyweights are circling around Champion.

Value Line, in its April 26, 1991, issue, said flatly, "Champion's three-to-five years prospects are poor." It went on to note that value investors had been buying the stock but added, "Perhaps they see something Wall Street's missing." Of course, Buffett thinks in longer than three-to-five year time frames. That's what makes him Buffett.

Value Line, in its July 26, 1991, issue, kept to the same theme: "Champion shares are untimely . . . The stock is no more compelling as a long-term investment."

Is this a case of Wall Street not seeing the forest for the trees? While Wall Street looks at the short term, Buffett's strategy apparently is to wait for a payoff further out when a consolidation in the industry brings higher margins.

In the meantime he's getting nine percent and the trees are at least growing, if not to the sky.

25 AMERICAN EXPRESS CO.

"He has not offered to let me pay for this transaction on my credit card."

American Express announced on August 1, 1991, that it would accept a cash infusion of $300 million from Berkshire.

Buffett immediately gave his best punchline to the Omaha *World-Herald:* "He [American Express chairman Jim Robinson] has not offered to let me pay for this transaction on my credit card."

Buffett had now returned to the scene of one of his early investment victories. With his newly acquired stake, Buffett became a major shareholder in the giant company known for its credit cards, travelers checks and struggling Shearson Lehman Brothers brokerage firm, which American Express pumped more than $1 billion into in 1990 to restructure. The hard-hit subsidiary had lost $900 million that year.

American Express, founded in 1850 by Mr. Wells and Mr. Fargo, who also founded Wells Fargo, another current Buffett favorite, also owns the Atlanta-based Robinson-Humphrey, Inc. brokerage business.

American Express credit cards are accepted as far away as the Mongolian People's Republic. The card is accepted in 180 countries.

The company is also a leader in financial planning, securities brokerage, asset management, international banking, investment banking and information services.

This time around, Buffett has a much larger amount invested and may have a much surer investment, since American Express is pledged to pay him an 8.85 percent dividend on it, a return made even better because of the 70 percent corporate-tax exemption on the dividend income, so that Berkshire is actually earning more than 11 percent on a taxable equivalent basis.

But this investment, what Buffett calls a "perc," was somewhat different from the earlier convertible preferred stakes and in the end offered Buffett less of a topnotch prospect and gave American Express more control over its outcome.

"There's not much upside potential with this one. I'm not sure why he did it," says *Newsday* columnist Allan Sloan.

The preferred shares are exchangeable into common shares at the option of American Express, not Buffett, making them different from convertible shares.

"Convertible preferred shares have unlimited upside," Buffett told the *Wall Street Journal* (August 2, 1991). "With this, we get less of an investment opportunity."

"When I heard they needed some equity funds, I told Jim [Robinson, chairman of American Express] that Berkshire would be interested in investing $500 million. I was willing to buy more, but Jim didn't want to sell more than $300 million," Buffett told the *Journal*.

In this case, Buffett did not join the board. Robinson told *USA Today* (August 2, 1991), "I don't think he needs to be on the board to provide that [counsel]. We would have welcomed him on our board, but he's on a number of boards. He has a pretty full plate. Also, he's on the Salomon board and we own [rival] Shearson."

As for Buffett, he told the Associated Press he won't play a role in running American Express, but that he would "speak when spoken to." (He'll be spoken to.) It's not as though the men can't talk. There's always the phone, and Buffett and Robinson, whose roots are from a prominent family in Georgia, both serve on the board of Coca-Cola.

Presumably the two could slip off after a Coca-Cola board meeting, have a chat over a Cherry Coke, and put the charges on an American Express card.

Taking on a lot of interviews in connection with the announcement, Buffett told the Omaha *World-Herald* (August 2, 1991) that recent losses at Shearson were temporary.

"It really doesn't take any of the luster off the really great franchises—the cards, the travelers and the information systems," Buffett said, shortly before the company experienced more setbacks in its Optima card operations.

American Express owns Omaha-based American Express Information Services Corp., the parent firm of First Data Resources, Cable Services Group, Integrated Payment and Integrated Marketing Services, all Omaha companies.

The Berkshire-American Express agreement calls for Buffett's non-transferable preferred shares to be exchanged for common stock within three or four years. The private placement investment would have a maturity of three years, unless extended for an additional year.

American Express would redeem the securities issued to Berkshire no later than maturity by exchanging common shares for the preferred stock. The number of common shares to be issued will be determined by the American Express share price at the time of redemption. If American Express doesn't redeem before maturity (three years with the possibility of a one year extension if American Express stock is below $24.50 at that time), it will exchange about 12 million common shares for the preferred stake. That would be about a 2.5 percent stake in American Express common stock, which was trading at about $25 a share when Buffett bought the preferred issue.

As usual, when Buffett made his investment, things did not look good at American Express.

In addition to its problems at Shearson, the company took a $30 million loss in 1989 when it had to restate earnings for another unit, The Boston Co., which specializes in lending money to wealthy individuals.

American Express loans to Prime Computer and Balcor Co. were described as "worrisome" by some money managers.

Further, a wave of merchants were complaining that American Express cards had been taking too large a commission from sales billed to its cards, and the entire credit card industry was more competitive than ever.

Value Line at the time was saying, "These shares seem unexciting . . . not confident that the stock will show any special strength for the year ahead. And prospects for 1994–96 aren't well defined." Enter Warren Buffett.

26 TORCHMARK CORP.

"I know where you are, I'll just walk over."

In late 1986 I wrote Buffett a letter boldly suggesting he might want to look at the stock of Torchmark, the insurance and financial services company in Birmingham, Alabama, and noting that I liked Berkshire so much I had margined things for more of its shares.

Several days later I received the following note from him dated December 1, 1986: "Thanks for the nice comments—and I'll look at Torchmark. I'm glad you are a shareholder, but you are right—I'm not keen on margin buying. However, we'll try to keep you out of trouble. Sincerely, Warren E. Buffett"

Although he tried to keep me out of trouble, even he could not swim against the tide. During the crash of 1987, Berkshire stock fell from about $4,000 to about $2,900 a share over a several day period, about in line with the rest of the market.

But before that disaster, I was *the* most surprised person in the world when Dan Dorfman reported in August 1987 that Berkshire had amassed a small stake—by Berkshire standards—in Torchmark, a stake never even announced publicly by Berkshire other than through the briefest sort of filings.

Torchmark officials have confirmed such a stake and Berkshire has filed forms with the SEC acknowledging ownership. I have absolutely no proof that my letter had anything to do with Buffett's purchase, but it was a fun day when I learned he was in the stock. Obviously, only Buffett can say how he reached the decision to invest in Torchmark.

One industry report by Bloomberg, L.P., says that Berkshire filed a Form 13F with the SEC acknowledging ownership of 1.6 percent or 863,550 shares of Torchmark.

The SEC releases the form one year after it is filed. Although the form generally is used by institutional investors to give a quarterly report of their holdings, the SEC sometimes allows individual investors to make a confidential filing on the form. Obviously, Buffett likes to keep his investments as quiet as possible for as long as possible so that he doesn't attract copycat investors pushing the price up before he can get his full stake.

The 13F report, made known in November 1990, would therefore have reflected the situation in November 1989, when the investment would have been worth about $26 million. It was worth about $50 million in early 1992, if Berkshire still holds the investment.

In spite of the big numbers, Buffett remains a regular guy.

"He's like talking to a neighbor," says Ronald K. Richey, chairman of Torchmark Corp. "He called up one day and said he'd like to meet with us," Richey recalled for this author. Richey was in Torchmark's New York office at the time, and said he'd be glad to meet with Buffett wherever he liked, including Omaha. Buffett, in New York at the time, said, "Oh, no, I know where you are. I'll just walk over."

Richey said a short time later Buffett walked in, basically told him and Jon Rotenstreich, then Torchmark's president, that he was not a threat to the company, just an investor, and left. "I did not detect his brilliance," said Richey, who acknowledges it's there. "It was just a simple chat."

Torchmark is the parent firm of a battery of insurance companies, the largest of which is Liberty National Life Insurance Co., employing agents who, in some cases, still go home-to-home selling insurance policies, generally seeking a niche market of customers at the modest end of the income scale.

The company also owns Waddell & Reed, a financial services

company that manages a group of mutual funds. Waddell & Reed representatives sell life and health insurance policies from another Torchmark subsidiary, United Investors Life, and oil and natural gas partnerships managed by another subsidiary, Torch Energy.

Torchmark's other main subsidiaries are United American Insurance, which sells Medicare supplement insurance, and Globe Life and Accident Insurance, which sells health insurance.

In a turbulent time for financial services firms, Torchmark has set a record as a model of consistent profitability. For the past forty years it has compiled both per share earnings and dividend increases every year, a record unmatched by any other company listed on the New York Stock Exchange.

The company has a reputation for tight control over expenses and its investments appear solid.

Less than three percent of the company's fixed-maturity investments are in securities of less than investment grade and three-fourths of the investments were in short-term maturities or government securities. Only slightly more than two percent of total invested assets were in mortgages or real estate.

Since 1986 Torchmark has bought back more than a third of its outstanding stock. It is by far Alabama's most profitable company.

Torchmark's bid to buy much larger American General Corp. for $6.3 billion in 1990 did not come off.

Berkshire's stake in Torchmark has made nice, steady progress as Torchmark's businesses have made nice, steady progress.

It's not as inspiring as Whitney Houston singing the National Anthem, but it'll do.

27 WELLS FARGO & CO.

"Most of our shareholders pay their bills in U.S. dollars."

Wells Fargo & Co., the California bank with the stagecoach symbol, announced on October 24, 1990, that Buffett had bought five million shares or almost 10 percent of its common stock, thereby becoming its largest stockholder.

Berkshire also holds 30,600 other shares in defined benefit plans for certain Berkshire employees.

Once again, as almost always, Buffett struck when there was a stigma surrounding the purchase. The very idea of buying a bank stock seemed outrageous at the time he did it. What the word "bank" meant on that day were layoffs, real estate loan writeoffs, slashed dividends, and some smear by association with the S&L crisis. Some pundits were suggesting that real estate exposure could bring down the banking system.

The price-to-earnings ratio of Wells Fargo on the day of the announcement of Berkshire's investment was a minuscule 3.7!

Now, that's an out-of-favor company, even to someone who is not a stock market aficionado. Buffett bought his shares of the San Francisco-based bank holding company at about book value.

So how were Wells Fargo's earnings at that time? Doing quite nicely, thanks. The bank would wind up making $643 million in

1990. Wells Fargo has long enjoyed a good reputation. Its management was so well thought of that other bankers often trained under it.

Henry Wells and William G. Fargo founded the company as an express delivery service and banking operation in 1852, just two years after the men founded American Express.

Dating from the Gold Rush, the company has long provided banking services and operated an express line, transporting passengers, mail, gold, silver and currency throughout the western United States, Canada and Mexico—both by stagecoach and rail.

In those days, a stagecoach traveled only about five miles an hour and holdups were constant. The company earned an important spot in the commercial development of the West.

Wells Fargo separated its banking business from its express business in 1905, and the banking company established a long history of acquiring other banks. The bank acquired Crocker National Corp. in 1986, Barclays Bank of California in 1988, the California branch network of Great American Bank in 1990 and others along the way.

Today Wells Fargo, one of the most profitable banks in the country, is the tenth largest bank in the United States, with assets of about $56 billion.

Wells Fargo stock had traded as high as $86 a share and as low as $41.25 in 1990. Buffett's cost was about $58 a share. The stock began to rise late in the year and Berkshire soon began enjoying Wells Fargo's hefty $4 dividend.

At the time Buffett was buying Wells Fargo stock—he had started with a tiny stake back in 1989—any number of bright investors, including the Feshbach Brothers, well known short sellers, were shorting the stock, that is, betting it would drop. In recent years the stock has been fought over by short sellers and value investors.

"Wells Fargo's a dead duck," Tom Barton, a money manager for the Feshbach Brothers, told the *Wall Street Journal* for the "Heard on the Street" column of November 1, 1990. "I don't think it's right to call them a bankruptcy candidate, but I think it's a teenager," Barton said, meaning the stock price could fall to the teens. "It has one of the highest exposures to real estate of any bank."

George Salem, an analyst with Prudential Securities, Inc., was quoted in the same piece, "He picked the management that underwrites real estate the best. But one thing he didn't realize is that even Mark Spitz [the former Olympic star] can't swim in a hurricane in the middle of an ocean." Wrong. No one could possibly be more profoundly aware of trying to swim against business tides than Warren Buffett. A year after he bought Wells Fargo, it was up about 25 percent.

Buffett's trick is to swim with the tide when it looks to others as though he's swimming against it.

Just what tide did Buffett see? Buffett often kids about how little he thinks about macro-economics, but Berkshire shareholder Yves Mojonnet thinks, in the case of Wells Fargo, Buffett made some macro-economic decisions. "I think he sees California as one of the largest industrial powers in the world and I think he saw bank consolidation," Mojonnet said. And Mojonnet thinks Buffett saw good management, which Buffett has acknowledged. "Wells Fargo was the first to recognize bad loans to the Third World in 1986–87. Management was on top of it then and is on top of it now, cutting the dividend and increasing loan loss reserves."

Buffett is on record as preferring to invest at home. "It's hard enough to understand the peculiarities and complexities of the culture in which you've been raised, much less a variety of others," he told the Berkshire annual meeting in 1985. "Anyway, most of our shareholders have to pay their bills in U.S. dollars."

With Wells Fargo he once again has taken an important stake in a major American enterprise, a strong franchise, with about 20,000 employees, headed by bank chairman Carl Reichardt, a friend of Buffett's.

The stake came just a month after word that Buffett was increasing his stake in PS Group from roughly 10 to 20 percent.

In the worst of times, such as in the midst of the recession in the fall of 1990, Buffett managed to find the cash to become a major shareholder in some of the best businesses in the country. But the Wells Fargo investment did carry with it plenty of risk in the way of exposure to commercial and real estate loans in a rapidly deteriorating real estate market as well as to HLTs, highly leveraged transactions.

On the other hand, Wells Fargo is one of the most profitable and efficient banks in the country. Its return on assets in 1990 was 1.4 percent and its return on equity was 25 percent. It has the lowest exposure to foreign loans of any major bank in the country.

And the Wells Fargo earnings stagecoach drove through plenty of badlands and avoided robberies in 1989.

In Buffett's view, the reward was going to outweigh the risk.

On the day following the announcement, the *Wall Street Journal* said Buffett's filing with the SEC didn't indicate when he accumulated most of his shares but said that, under regulatory rules, he had to file a report within ten days of the time his total stake exceeded five percent.

Wells Fargo stock had traded roughly in the mid-40s range for several weeks, meaning Buffett got about half his stock in that range. But he also got plenty at higher prices.

The *Journal* said Buffett had invested about $225 million. Actually, it turned out the cost was $289 million. Financial reporter Dan Dorfman had reported earlier in the year that there were rumors Buffett was buying Wells Fargo stock. Dorfman, sometimes right, sometimes wrong, was right on the money on this one.

In July 1991, after rumors that Wells Fargo and Security Pacific were talking marriage, Bank of America and Security Pacific said they would merge, creating the second largest bank holding company in the nation after Citicorp.

In 1991 Wells Fargo stock recovered, flying in the face of the shorts. And the shorts had been burned, in part because of Buffett's heavy buying. It was little wonder that, in certain short-seller circles, T-shirts appeared inscribed, "[Expletive deleted] Warren Buffett."

One more time, while almost everyone else was panicking, Buffett appeared to have struck gold, this time out on the West Coast.

Forbes, in its April 15, 1991, issue, quoted Munger about the Wells Fargo purchase: "It's all a bet on management. We think they will fix problems faster and better than other people."

It has been said that when cost-conscious Reichardt found out one of his executives wanted to buy a Christmas tree for the office, Reichardt told him to buy it with his own money, not the bank's. "When we heard that, we bought more stock," Munger said at the Berkshire's 1991 annual meeting.

Buffett's interest in Wells Fargo apparently continued. On May 14, after the market closed, Wells Fargo announced that Buffett was seeking permission from the Federal Reserve Board to more than double his stake to as much as 22 percent. In early August, Buffett got the approval. (Federal change-of-control laws require the Federal Reserve Board to review purchase requests if a buyer intends to acquire more than 10 percent of a bank holding company stock.)

In the meantime Wells Fargo's gravity-defying ability to stay away from bad loan problems ended with a late-in-the-second-quarter announcement that the company would post a large loan loss jump and that earnings would be paltry, far below analysts' expectations. The loan loss figure late in 1991 was a stunning $700 million.

Whether Wells Fargo flops to earth or flies remains an open question.

The stock swan dive drove the price of the stock back into Buffett's original buying range, but the price then slowly recovered as a bank consolidation move swept the country. But whatever the ups and downs, Buffett, no doubt, is in for the long haul.

And it wouldn't be surprising if he had increased his stake during the recent swan dive. After all, that's exactly his style.

28 PS GROUP, INC.

"All our investments usually appear undervalued to me—otherwise we wouldn't own them."

By the end of 1990, Berkshire Hathaway owned about 22 percent of PS Group, Inc., long headed by J.P. "Rick" Guerin, who owns about 700,000 shares of the San Diego-based company heavily involved in aircraft leasing and travel and fuel distribution.

For more than twenty-five years, Guerin has been a disciple and friend of both Buffett and Munger.

According to Portfolio Reports, Berkshire and related companies owned just over 11 percent of PS Group common stock by April 1990, paying an average of $32.40 a share for 373,575 of those shares during a two month period ended April 25, 1990.

On September 17, 1990, the PS Group board approved a Buffett request to own up to 22.5 percent of the company, and later in the year the board granted Buffett permission to buy up to 45 percent of the stock, which he may do, depending on market conditions, price, availability of funds and the attractiveness of other investments.

Over the past two years, Buffett gradually has been increasing his stake in PS Group. During some of the time Buffett was buying PS Group stock, it carried a P/E ratio above 50, so there must be something more to stock selection than just searching for low P/E ratios.

"I think Warren senses the possibility of a baby Berkshire here. Guerin is a top-notch investor, one of America's finest. He and Munger would make a great team should anything happen to Warren," says Berkshire shareholder Michael Assael, adding, "This company sure smells like Berkshire Hathaway to me. But, this time they're in the right business. Travel in the Nineties should do a lot better than textiles in the Seventies."

What is it that Buffett is intrigued by in what appears to be a hard-to-understand firm with a strange mix of businesses?

PS Group traces its roots back to Pacific Southwest Airlines, which was sold to USAir in 1987. After the sale, PS Group was left with an aircraft leasing operation, a fuel distribution unit, and oil and gas operations. Much of the oil and gas operations were sold in 1989. The company's largest investment is in aircraft leasing. It leases about sixteen aircraft to USAir (synergy with a question mark), which accounted for about 60 percent of the company's aircraft leasing revenues in 1990. The company also leases aircraft to troubled Continental Airlines, Inc., and American West Airlines, Inc., all three of which have filed for bankruptcy protection.

In 1987 PS Group, pouring $84 million into the travel agency business (plus another $49 million in 1989), acquired 81 percent of USTravel Systems, Inc., now the third largest travel management system in the country. Founder Peter Sontag and his partner, Ralph Manaker, own the remaining 19 percent of USTravel Systems, Inc.

Through rapid acquisitions by USTravel, the Rockwell, Maryland-based firm now owns and operates 467 locations and has 206 domestic affiliate agencies as well as a small number of locations abroad.

Tall and lean, sixty-two-year-old Guerin said at PS Group's 1990 meeting that Buffett "really believes strongly that the travel business is going to grow." (San Diego *Daily Transcript,* May 29, 1990) But he said there were no advance conversations with Buffett about the company before Buffett invested.

At the 1991 annual meeting chairman Charles Rickershauser, also a friend of Buffett's, and CEO George Shortley (Guerin had stepped down to vice chairman of the firm) said Buffett remains a friend of the company, is available for counsel at any time, but in no way tells them how to run their business.

PS Group now is a combination holding and leasing firm with a powerfully strange business mix. It is also a major investment for Guerin, who holds his 13 percent stake in PS Group through Pacific Partners, a limited partnership investment firm he heads in Los Angeles.

Clearly one thing Buffett sees in PS Group is Guerin's money managing abilities.

PS Group has three main on-going businesses: aircraft leasing, travel distribution through its 81 percent-owned USTravel Systems, Inc. subsidiary, and fuel distribution through PST in Dallas. More than 90 percent of the firm's revenues come from these sources. It also has a small oil and gas business, Statex Petroleum, Inc., and a subsidiary, Airline Training Center, which trains pilots for Lufthansa Airlines, among others.

Also, the firm came into a splendid chunk of 5,750 shares of Berkshire in 1986 as a result of a pension plan reversion. The Berkshire shares were acquired at a cost of $27.6 million, but were sold in 1991 for $47.8 million after PS Group ran into trouble with its banks as a result of the recession. *(Wall Street Journal,* December 20, 1991)

At the time of the PS Group 1991 annual meeting, when PS Group still held Berkshire stock, making for cross ownership of Berkshire and PS Group, Rickershauer, a former head of the Pacific Stock Exchange, said, "I wish we owned 22 percent of Berkshire."

The mystery business at PS Group, the one that has sent PS Group's stock on a roller coaster ride, is a fledging hazardous waste and metals recycling business called Recontek, Inc.

Recontek? Again, it hardly sounds like something of interest to Buffett, who is so insistent on here-and-now earnings, on fresh cash that can be used right now.

But it's also typical of Buffett to defy easy predictions. As far back as 1966, he was telling the Buffett Partnership: "All our investments usually appear undervalued to me—otherwise we wouldn't own them."

Those around Buffett, and Buffett himself, say he has little interest in future projections about business prospects, little interest in startup businesses that may be profitable in the by and by. Recontek may be the exception.

Early in 1989, PS Group agreed to make an equity investment in Recontek, also of San Diego, getting 50 percent control by September 1989, 81 percent by early 1991, and, ultimately, 100 percent. Recontek is PS Group's big bet for the future.

Recontek has developed a proprietary recycling process that takes liquid and solid hazardous waste—generated primarily from the plating, metal finishing, and circuit board industries—and extracts saleable metals such as copper, nickel and zinc from the sludge by mixing chemicals with waste. The metals, chemicals and salts can be resold.

The process provides industry a far cheaper disposal method than hazardous waste landfills, deep wells or incinerators and reduces the liability for potential cleanup costs for underground and soil contamination.

The primary customers of Recontek's proprietary process are expected to come from the electronics industry (which produces metallic hazardous waste during the manufacture of circuit boards), the automotive and aerospace industries (which rely heavily on metal etching and the processes which generate such waste), and the metal plating industry.

Under existing disposal methods, companies that generate hazardous waste remain liable for groundwater contamination and other problems associated with landfill storage. The Recontek process eliminates that contingent liability, a crucial concern for producers of waste.

Recontek, after operating a pilot facility in San Diego, California, built its first recycling plant in Newman, Illinois. The company has reached agreements with seven more communities to build recycling plants.

PS Group executives say they believe they have about a four-year head start on the difficult-to-enter business of recycling metallic hazardous waste in both liquid and sludge forms. And they think margins could run as high as 40 to 50 percent!

"The potential for the Recontek subsidiary is enormous," said the *Wealth Monitors Research* publication of September 16, 1991. "This subsidiary can generate over $37 a share to PS Group by 1996. Given a waste treatment industry multiple of 16 to 20, these earnings reflect a potential share value for Recontek of $592 to $740 a share."

But the business also has many unknowns. Recontek has no patents; securing sites is a difficult proposition; and perhaps someone could come along with a better mousetrap one day. Also, the EPA has expressed concerns, ranging from inadequate piping to problems with storage tanks, and some say it's very difficult to extract high grade metals from metallic sludge because so many metals have similar properties. So Recontek is anything but a sure thing, but Buffett has a nice option on the business should it pan out.

PS Group, which has had a long practice of buying back its own stock, has about 2,100 shareholders and about 2,000 employees.

By the spring of 1991, PS Group stock had soared to about $70 before falling back sharply to less than half that price on the EPA concerns, but the Berkshire annual report at that time made no mention of PS Group. In the spring of 1991, PS Group planned a public stock offering of 1.5 million shares. Three guesses who got that underwriting—Berkshire friend, Salomon Inc. (synergy without a question mark). However, the offering was later canceled as volatility in the stock developed.

Late in 1991 things were going more slowly than expected at the Newman plant and there were some aircraft leasing writedowns. Short selling set in, driving the stock down further. Some sixteen of the company's aircraft leased to USAir were not flying. A weak economy kept pressure on the travel business and Recontek remained unproved.

Some people were starting to yell "bankruptcy" in a crowded theater.

Bankruptcy is a certainty for PS Group by the end of 1992, Gilford Securities president Robert Holmes told *USA Today*'s Dan Dorfman in an April 3, 1992 column. Holmes was shorting the stock.

At the annual meeting in 1992 Buffett was asked about PS Group. He pointed out that the company had denied it would file for bankruptcy and, pressed about its future, he tried to be positive.

"We'll see," he said.

29 THE OMAHA ROYALS

"At a million and a quarter a pop, I can't afford it."

In July 1991, Warren Buffett and Walter Scott, Kiewit's chairman and a Berkshire board member, stepped in to buy a stake in the Omaha Royals minor league baseball team when a deal with the previous owner fell through.

The switch occurred when Philadelphia real estate developer Craig Stein backed out of an ownership plan because he couldn't live with a requirement that Union Pacific have veto over any plan to move the franchise from Omaha.

Union Pacific had announced that it would buy 49 percent of the Omaha Royal AAA franchise with Stein, but when he backed out, Buffett and Scott came to the rescue with $1.25 million each. Union Pacific contributed $2.5 million and the deal was done.

Buffett, a longtime baseball fan, told the Omaha *World-Herald* that he and Scott would sell $100,000 blocks of their ownership to interested investors. For Buffett, this was a quick fix to save the local baseball team, not a long-term investment that would add to his billions.

The franchise, which is the farm team for the Kansas City Royals, might well have been lost had Buffett not stepped in with what was the act of a good citizen rather than the act of a good investor.

The hasty announcement was made in the office of Omaha mayor P.J. Morgan, who said he was surprised to learn that Buffett hadn't visited the mayor's office before then. Replied Buffett, "At a million and a quarter a pop, I can't afford it."

30 THE BERKSHIRE HATHAWAY ANNUAL MEETING

"If any of you would like to withdraw your proxy at this time, just raise your hand. As soon as we can get around to you, you will be ejected from the meeting." Annual meeting in 1988.

Of course, the highlight of the year for a Berkshire shareholder is the annual meeting, now held the last Monday in April in Omaha. It is one of the great shows on earth.

At the annual meeting in 1991 Buffett and Coca-Cola president Don Keough donned bright red Coca-Cola aprons and served shareholders Coke as they arrived for the meeting. In 1992 Buffett and See's Candies manager Chuck Huggins donned caps with a See's logo and passed out small boxes of See's chocolates to shareholders.

From their perch in front of a display of Coke cases, Buffett and Keough provided a small sip of Coke from the Fountain of Wealth in 1991, and Buffett and Huggins cared for everyone's sweet tooth again in 1992.

"The [Berkshire] annual meeting is the best thing I've ever seen in all of commerce," says Keough.

A record 1,700 happy shareholders journeyed to Omaha in 1992 to see Warren Buffett and Charles Munger at the dais sharing Cokes and See's candies and giving them a quick course in the wisdom of the financial ages.

In the early years as few as seven to a dozen people showed up for the annual meetings when they were held in New Bedford, Massachusetts, home of the Berkshire Hathaway textile business. Later they were held in a small cafeteria at Berkshire's National Indemnity office in Omaha.

"He was the same back then as he is now," says James A. Earl, a physics professor at the University of Maryland whose family invested in the Buffett Partnership in the late 1950s.

Still later the meetings were held in the cafeteria of Kiewit Plaza with twenty or thirty shareholders showing up, then later at the Red Lion Inn, where about 250 shareholders showed up in 1985.

There were about 1,000 Berkshire shareholders at the time Diversified was merged into Berkshire at the end of 1979. There were about 1,900 shareholders in 1982 and 2,900 in 1983, many of those coming in with the Blue Chip merger.

Over the years, with Berkshire's mighty growth and the spread of Buffett's reputation for wit and wisdom, more shareholder/fans came, creating the need for ever larger meeting places.

Eventually, the annual meetings were held at the Joslyn Art Museum in Omaha, where there were 580 shareholders present in 1988. The annual meetings are now held at the Orpheum Theatre in downtown Omaha.

In 1990 Buffett welcomed his audience to the new meeting place explaining, "Most of you know we held our annual meetings at the Joslyn Art Museum the past several years until we outgrew it. Since the Orpheum Theatre where we're meeting today is an old vaudeville theatre, I suppose we've slid down the cultural chain. Don't ask me where we'd go next."

When Adam Smith, who did a "Money World" television show about the 1990 Berkshire meeting, asked shareholder Charles Dennison of Princeton, New Jersey, why he was at the meeting, Smith got this reply, "I hear it's a great show."

Robert Baker, a retired lawyer from Chagrin Falls, Ohio, who died in 1992, was among the Berkshire shareholders who regularly made the annual trek to Omaha to hear Buffett. Baker said he had read about Buffett in the early 1980s. "I read enough to know he was terrific and then on April 8, 1983, the 'Heard on the Street' column in the *Wall Street Journal* quoted from his annual report. On April 11 I went and bought five shares. I asked to get them at $920. The broker called me back and said I had bought them for $910."

A year or so later Baker started going to the annual meetings. "They are fully worth it for the wisdom . . . It's worth every penny," Baker said. "He always expresses the great truths so simply. We're always too busy making things so complex. He reminds us not to play games or make things complex . . . I think he looks at the bottom line and looks to see if the managers are having fun, if they love what they do."

There is a great camaraderie among shareholders, whether they own one share or are Berkshire millionaires. It is a communion for kindred spirits who believe they have found investment heaven. "It's the Club Med for investors," says Berkshire shareholder Pat Mojonnet of San Francisco, California. "And when you come home and tell people about it, nobody believes you."

Usually, the only real status check comes from the query, "How long have you been a Berkshire shareholder?" Obviously, the longer, the wiser.

For the uninitiated, a shareholder's first Berkshire annual meeting can be a jolt.

Most chairmen drone on, overstating the progress and rosy outlook. Meanwhile, the public relations department quivers because they dread certain questions from disgruntled shareholders. Worse, there are sometimes no questions at all.

Not so at Berkshire, where you get no excuses on how the sluggish economy hurt company results, or some pie in the sky about how wonderful next year will be.

You get no gadfly—no Evelyn Y. Davis or the Gilbert brothers—questioning the chairman's motives.

Here's what happens: first Buffett and Munger walk on stage. Buffett is often carrying a can of Cherry Coke, sometimes several cans. Berkshire's duo sits at a plain table on which is a box of See's candy.

Buffett normally makes a joke or two, sometimes ostensibly testing the microphone, saying, "Testing . . . Testing . . . One million . . . two million . . . three million."

He distrusts things mechanical and his distrust only increased at the annual meeting in 1990 when Berkshire's chief financial officer Verne McKenzie tried to fix the faulty microphone system. Said Buffett, "Vern McKenzie is our resident technology expert. Can you hear me. Can you hear me? . . . This is why we don't buy technology stocks." In 1992 a screen was set up so people could see Buffett and Munger better, and when, at first, there was noise and flickering, Buffett said, "We're masters of technology here."

Sometimes Buffett, sitting next to Munger, quips, "This is our version of Bartles and Jaymes. We'll let you know after the meeting which is which." At the 1990 meeting, Buffett explained that "Charlie [Munger] is our macro-economics expert. Actually, I handle Omaha and Council Bluffs and Charlie handles the rest of the country."

And in 1992 he assured shareholders that he and Munger "plan to be here until we're both sitting here wondering, 'Who's that guy sitting next to me?' "

Buffett will often warn the audience to be careful not to say anything off-color about him because he has relatives strategically placed throughout the audience.

Then he will make pleasant introductions of the heads of the businesses in the Berkshire portfolio. Sometimes he introduces Munger as his "junior partner in good years and senior partner in bad years," and adds something along the line of, "It's no breach of etiquette to walk out during his answers."

He also likes to rib the shareholders, as he did in 1988: "If any of you would like to withdraw your proxy at this time, just raise your hand. As soon as we can get around to you, you will be ejected from the meeting."

In 1992 Buffett explained that the meeting would go until noon or until Munger said something optimistic. Munger, known for pessimistic and laconic answers, never did say anything cheery and throughout the meeting, after each Munger answer, Buffett kept saying, "We'll be here until noon."

Then Buffett will take up a few housekeeping matters such as electing his wife to the board of directors, noting that attendants "hired from a local modeling agency" are on hand to give you a proxy card should you wish to change your vote.

In 1992 Buffett made his usual introductions of the managers and the board and when he introduced his wife, Susie Buffett, Buffett said, "It's a name we got out of the phone book." He then introduced his niece, Cynthia Zak, and he explained she has a son named Berkshire. "That's a not-too-subtle method of trying to get into my will," Buffett added, laughing.

And he'll make his pitch about how shareholders can visit local businesses. In 1991 it went like this: "At noon we'll break. And there'll be buses to take you to Borsheim's, Nebraska Furniture Mart . . . or anything else that we have an economic interest in."

But it's all just an exercise since Buffett owns about 42 percent of the stock and the holdings of his wife, insiders, and a couple of friends quickly make up well over 50 percent of the stock, making any potential dissenting votes academic.

All shareholders go along with Buffett's litany of business matters and after everyone has said aye to some unarguable point, Buffett will utter, "You're doing fine."

Often he notes that Berkshire meetings are not meant to be democratic and take their "Stalinist manner" from somewhere in the old Soviet Union. He says these things every year and they always elicit chuckles.

The whole routine takes just five or ten minutes and if you have not been to a Berkshire meeting before, you are suddenly surprised to hear Buffett call for a move to adjourn the meeting.

Yes, in less than ten minutes the annual meeting of Berkshire is over.

Well, not really. It's just the beginning as Buffett leans back from the table a bit and says, "Any questions?"

To these Buffett offers responses stunning in speed and originality.

At one meeting, longtime shareholder Irving Fenster started out by saying he was from Oklahoma, Nebraska's big football rival. Buffett yelled, "Who let you in?"

At the same meeting in 1988 Buffett gave the following answer to a question about what makes for a good business: "The best business is where no one else competes, where you buy for one cent and sell for a dollar and it's habit forming and no one else has it. That's the best business."

When he was asked for advice to young investors, he said, "Look at stocks as businesses, look for businesses you understand run by people you trust and are comfortable with and leave them alone for a long time."

The questions roll on for almost three hours, often with shareholders from the Northeast addressing him as "Warren" and shareholders from the South using "Mr. Buffett."

The meeting lasts several hours and then, for the hard core who still can't get enough, Buffett often stays around for even more questions, fielding everything the audience can throw at him and Munger.

It is Munger who usually plays the straight man to Buffett. But sometimes Buffett will go on describing how some business is deteriorating and Munger will interrupt, saying, for example, "He means it went to hell."

Munger sits stone-faced, arms folded, usually offering comments like "Yes" or "No" or "No comment" or "I have nothing to add." After one "That's exactly right," from Munger, Buffett said, "He's learning. Susie take notes," referring to his wife, Susie Buffett, who was elected to Berkshire's board in 1991.

Frequently, Munger will invoke the fate of the whole society as in "Civilization needs program trading like it needs more AIDS."

In the midst of the latest annual meeting Floyd Jones of Seattle stood up and praised Buffett's handling of the Salomon scandal. Jones explained he had worked for the collapsed Drexel firm, adding that he felt Buffett had averted what could have been an international financial crisis had Salomon gone under. "I think you are a hero in world corporate society."

Early in the meeting, for the sake of rotating the questions around the large crowd, Buffett had divided the audience into various zones, and it so happens Jones's question came from zone four. After Jones's eloquent remarks, Buffett said, "Let's stay in zone four for a while."

"It's great to hear Warren and Charlie answer every question openly. And it feels good to know your money is in their hands," says Coca-Cola's Don Keough. "It's the best thing I've ever seen in all of commerce."

There is plenty of free-wheeling give and take.

One Berkshire shareholder, LaVerne Ramsey of Birmingham, asked at the 1991 meeting what would be revealed if Kitty Kelley wrote an unauthorized biography of him and Munger. Buffett slyly shunted the question off to Munger. "I'm afraid not very much," Munger said. "But that wouldn't stop Kitty Kelley." Buffett's answer was, "What you see is what you get with the two of us." Mrs. Ramsey, a Buffett admirer, explained later she really asked the question as a test of Buffett's wit. "He passed," she said.

A small sequel to that story is that, later, Mrs. Ramsey sent a note and some photos to Buffett, explaining the question was just in fun, as Buffett well knew, and he wrote her back, "LaVerne, Thanks for the pictures. I always enjoy them. Charlie should have some 'Kitty Kelley' material for next year; don't let him off the hook. WEB."

Later at the meeting, a shareholder asked him how he spent his day and Buffett started out with, "More of the Kitty Kelley bit, eh?" He went on to say he spends most of the day and night reading and talking on the phone, then turned to Munger. "That's what I do," he said, "Charlie, what do you do?"

Munger replied, "That reminds me very much of a friend of mine in World War II in a group which had nothing to do. A general once went up to my friend's boss, we'll call him Captain Glotz. He said, 'Captain Glotz, what do you do?' His boss said, 'Not a damn thing.' The general got madder and madder and turned to my friend and said, 'What do you do?' And my friend said, 'I help Captain Glotz.' That's the best way to describe what I do at Berkshire." He drew one of the biggest laughs of the day.

One shareholder, in 1992, asked Buffett what books he read, and he said before the Salomon scandal he had read a lot of books. Then he tossed the question to Munger, who said one book he'd enjoyed was *The Third Chimpanzee.* "Are we going to add him up here?" Buffett quipped.

Also, a shareholder asked about the billionaire Ross Perot's entry into the presidential race and whether that gave Buffett any ideas. Buffett said it gave him no ideas whatsoever and added, "We'll see if he's a billionaire when it's over."

There are also sober reminders from Buffett of the dangers of the marketplace. "You shouldn't own common stocks if a 50 percent decrease in their value in a short period of time would cause you acute distress," he told a shareholder at the 1988 meeting.

Among those sure to attend will be Peter Kenner and his young son Nicholas. Kenner, who heads Kenner Printing Co. in New York City, introduced himself to Buffett at the intersection of Madison Avenue and 55th Street in 1986. "Excuse me. Aren't you Warren Buffett?" asked Kenner. "Yes, how did you know?" replied Buffett. When Kenner said his father, Morton Kenner, had been an investor since the days of the Buffett Partnership and he himself was a long-time Berkshire shareholder, Buffett insisted he come out to the annual meeting next time around. Kenner had never been, but started going and hasn't missed one since.

In fact, one time when Buffett was in New York he invited Kenner to fly back with him to Omaha for the meeting. "It was that first plane and it had E.T. on it from the movie," recalls Kenner, who flew out with Warren and Susie Buffett and another shareholder.

By 1990, Kenner's nine-year-old son, Nicholas, a third generation Berkshire shareholder, was begging to go. "He had been asking me about going to the meeting," says Kenner, who thought it a bit odd. But he said his son, who inherited ten shares of Berkshire, explained that, if this was his investment for a college education, he wanted to go.

Kenner told his son he could go, but that it was a grown-up affair and he'd have to be quiet and not ask questions. But young Kenner said he wanted to ask why Berkshire stock price was dropping (from a high of $8,900 to a price at the time of $6,700) and his father finally gave in.

The Kenners ran into Buffett just before the meeting and Buffett encouraged young Nicholas to ask whatever question he wanted. So young Kenner, posing the first question at the Berkshire annual meeting in 1990, asked the ultimate question of Buffett: "Why did Berkshire's stock go down?"

Buffett, feigning anger, joked, "You're underage! Throw him out!"

The greatest financial mind of our time finally replied that he really did not know, that there was no good answer to that question. Young Kenner had stumped the master.

After an explanation about the Berkshire stock price usually trading near intrinsic value of the company, Buffett ended by saying, "Hold it for your old age."

As it happened, after the meeting Buffett and the Kenners again ran into one another, and Buffett asked young Kenner if he could pose for a picture with him, a picture that ran with the Omaha *World-Herald*'s story about the annual meeting. Posing for the picture, Buffett said, "Let's do this right," and handed the youngster his wallet.

"Can I keep it?" said young Kenner.

"I was just making a wisecrack," young Kenner explained later.

A short time later Buffett sent young Kenner a copy of the photo with a letter urging him to come to future annual meetings and ask more questions.

"He's a nice guy. He's very funny," young Kenner said of Buffett. "I just wanted to ask him why the stock price was down. You know, if it's fallen from over $8,000, you want to know why. I definitely want to hold it unless something absolutely amazing happens and it goes down thousands of dollars," he added.

Young Kenner, such a hit at the annual meeting in 1990, was given the first question at the annual meeting in 1991. He came prepared with two. The first was why Buffett picked Coke instead of Pepsi as an investment. The second was why, if Buffett listed Kenner's age as eleven in the Berkshire annual report when he was actually nine, should he trust Berkshire's financial numbers in the back of the annual report. That question sent Berkshire shareholders into convulsions of laughter. Buffett later said he planned "a written response." (Fortune, June 3, 1991)

Kenner had started out his questioning of Buffett by saying he owned ten shares of Berkshire, to which Buffett quipped, "I'd like you to meet my granddaughter."

Buffett, calling on the help of Coca-Cola president Don Keough, took on Kenner's first question by explaining that Coca-Cola is a superb business, serving soft drinks in 170 (now 185) countries where consumption is increasing. Keough said that consumption internationally was fifty-nine servings per capita a year, compared with 300 in the United States, suggesting Coca-Cola's enormous growth potential. Buffett added that he drank five Cokes a day and noted that Munger drinks diet Coke "for obvious reasons."

As for young Kenner's second question about the age discrepancy, Buffett started out with, "Charlie wrote that section" and then ducked it with, "That is a very good question. I look forward to seeing you again next year."

Drawing a big laugh, Kenner said, "I'll be back!"

"I know!" Buffett replied.

The repartee was becoming part of Berkshire lore and Buffett wrote at the end of his letter in the 1991 annual report: "Nicholas will be at this year's meeting—he spurned my offer of a trip to Disney World on that day—so join us to watch a continuation of this lopsided battle of wits."

Walking out of the 1992 meeting, Berkshire shareholder Paul Cassidy said of Buffett, "He's a great education. I bought a couple of shares early on. He gave me the financial security to open my restaurant (The Loft in North Andover, Massachusetts). I try to carry on in my business the ways he talks about. And I tell my children to be long-term investors. They've been buying Coca-Cola stock. I believe that will help send them to college. Our family gets great laughter and enjoyment from Buffett."

After the meeting you may go to Borsheim's or the Nebraska Furniture Mart and stay a bit too long and suddenly need to get back to your hotel and off to the airport. No problem. A car will suddenly appear to take you there. Your driver may well be Louie Blumkin, head of the Nebraska Furniture Mart, and your traveling companion may be one of the Heldman brothers, of Fechheimer.

It's all pretty high cotton at a Berkshire annual meeting.

31 SOME PROMINENT ADMIRERS

"He's one of the more interesting people of our time."
—J. Richard Munro

Few things could give Buffett more pride than knowing the names of the shareholders he has drawn to his unusual enterprise.

They are a wide ranging lot: yuppies, investment bankers and money managers of all stripes; corporate executives; and a number of shareholders who have known Buffett and his family for years.

The Berkshire shareholder list also includes some of the outright rich and famous. To name-drop: U.S. Senator Bob Kerry (D. Neb.) *Washington Post*'s Katharine Graham, Coca-Cola's Don Keough, Capital Cities/ABC's Daniel Burke, GEICO's William Snyder and Lou Simpson, CBS's Laurence Tisch, USAir's Ed Colodny, Sequoia Fund's Bill Ruane, First Manhattan's Sandy Gottesman, PS Group's Rick Guerin, bridge champion Sam Stayman of "Stayman bidding" fame, noted investor Phil Carret, also known for following eclipses, Wall Street's Mario Gabelli and Archie MacAllaster, children's author Martha Tolles, Ann Landers, investment banker John Loomis and his wife, Fortune's Carol Loomis, and Miami Dolphins head coach Don Shula.

"Yes, I'm a shareholder," says Shula. "I had heard about Warren Buffett, and a couple of years ago John Loomis of First Manhattan, who handles my finances, arranged for me to meet him. I was on my way to a league meeting in Dallas and I stopped off in Omaha," recalls Shula. "We were supposed to have dinner, but my plane was late, so we had breakfast the next morning," he said. "It was at the Red Lion." Shula, another friend of Loomis's, and Buffett shared eggs and issues that morning.

Shula recalls that Buffett interspersed much of his conversation with sports references. "I mostly enjoyed his anecdotes. He knows a lot about football. He knew even more about baseball," Shula said. "He was interested in our accomplishments. Of course, he's a big University of Nebraska fan," the coach said.

"After breakfast he took us over and showed us his office [Shula agreed that the description of throw rugs and linoleum is not far off the mark] and to the Nebraska Furniture Mart. I enjoyed it. I came away from meeting him thinking that his message is simplicity. What he says helps you in your own profession, in your own life. You can take what he says and apply it to your own profession," Shula said, agreeing that blocking and tackling—the kind of message Buffett delivers—should always be kept in mind even at the Miami Dolphins level of football.

"I think Berkshire is as solid as ever. It's been down lately but I remain a shareholder . . . I'm pleased with the investment." And Shula, a savvy stock market investor, admits to keeping a pretty close eye on the stock market. "I don't live or die over it," he said with the tone of voice of a man who might say the same thing about the outcome of a Miami Dolphins Super Bowl game.

Ann Landers has a date with Warren Buffett . . .

From her Sioux City, Iowa, home, Ann Landers used to visit her sister, Helen Brodkey, of Omaha, to date the Nebraska boys.

"No. I didn't date Warren Buffett," she laughed, but in the mid-1980s when Ann went to Omaha, she did indeed have a date with him.

Ann was invited to an Omaha Press Club Gridiron function that involved skits. "I was asked to perform and wrote a little skit that had me doing the shimmy in a fringed evening gown. I think Warren was struck by the incongruity of it all—an advice columnist doing the shimmy. He came up afterward and asked if he could take me to lunch the next day. When I told him I already had a luncheon date, he asked, 'Do you think you can get me included?' I told him I was sure that I could, since I was having lunch with people from the Omaha *World-Herald.*" The luncheon host was to be Harold Andersen, the publisher, an old friend of Buffett's. "Of course, they were thrilled to include Warren Buffett.

"We went to the lunch and sat next to each other and behaved shamelessly. We hardly spoke to anyone else. Warren is a fascinating man and has a marvelous sense of humor. He said, 'Let's stay in touch,' and we have. One of the fringe benefits is See's candies, which are not available in Chicago. He owns the company, you know.

"I bought Berkshire Hathaway stock immediately after I met Warren. I'm not a plunger in the market, but I do buy when I know the management. I thought if Warren is running a company, then I want to be in on it. When I saw the price, I almost flipped.

"I've been in his home and met Astrid Menks, who is a very warm and winning person. I also know his delightful daughter Susie and the grandchildren. I attended a formal party in Lincoln given by Kay Orr, who was then the governor, and we all went in our formal attire on a bus. I sat with Warren's wife, who is totally captivating and a real stunner. He wanted me to get to know her. He's very proud of Susie, and well he might be. Not only is she a knockout, she has all the right values. They have a remarkably warm and pleasant relationship for a married couple who live apart.

"I've talked to Warren about his immense wealth and asked the logical question: 'What are you going to do with all that money?' He told me it's going into the Buffett Foundation, and when he dies, he's going to leave the largest foundation in the world. I suggested that perhaps he ought to give some of it away while he's alive, but I don't think I made a dent."

GLENN H. GREENBERG

"I met him at a Columbia Business School forum in 1986 at a hotel in New York. There were a bunch of . . . [financial speakers] and I went along because he's my hero," said Glenn H. Greenberg, forty-five, managing director of Chieftain Capital Management, Inc. in New York.

"He was surrounded by people and I felt toward him the way some people felt toward my father. There's some human instinct to reach out and make some connection with someone you admire and often it doesn't amount to much," Greenberg said.

"I knew he liked baseball and I asked him if he knew of my father, Hank Greenberg, and he said, '1938—hit fifty-eight home runs, had 183 RBIs in 1937. Heck, I didn't even know them and he repeated three or four statistics. I thought he was trying to show off his memory. As far as I knew, they were correct. He has a photographic memory. He was reeling off the statistics . . . He wasn't telling me [the statistics] because he thought he was coming close.

"My father [Detroit Tigers slugger Hank Greenberg] did hit fifty-eight home runs in 1938, eleven years after Babe Ruth hit sixty. It was not as big a deal as when Roger Maris hit sixty-one, years later . . . and my father was always humble about it and [to fans] would say how much he appreciated that they remembered or that the pitchers were hoping he'd break Ruth's record anyway.

"Meeting him [Buffett] was somewhat disappointing from a personal standpoint. There was a crowd around him . . . but he is without a doubt the best in the investment world. He's done it with no leverage, no cheating . . . He is my hero."

J. RICHARD MUNRO

Buffett, still so much taken with media franchises, bought shares of Time, Inc. in 1982 at a cost of $45 million and by the end of the year the investment was worth $79 million.

Over the next several years, he lowered, then raised, then lowered his investment, and in 1986 he sold out completely. That was the year he also sold a stake in Affiliated Publications, the parent of the Boston *Globe,* for a $51 million profit.

J. Richard Munro, the former chairman of Time, who spearheaded Time's merger in 1989 with Warner Communications, Inc., says he believes Buffett sold out to help finance his stake in the Capital Cities acquisition of American Broadcasting Cos., which occurred in early 1986.

"I can tell you I have respect for him far beyond the business aspect. It's as a human being. He's one of the more interesting people of our time. It's his no-nonsense, Midwestern thing. There are just no affectations. He is a legendary figure . . . What you see is what you get," Munro said.

"When he became a shareholder of Time, the company did not know it . . . His timing of buying and selling the stock was perfect," he said.

When Buffett owned Time, Inc. shares, he would drop by Munro's office at the Time-Life Building in New York about once a year for a chat. "We'd talk about everything. He wanted to know what we knew, and, of course, we wanted to know what he knew. We'd talk about the world and exchange views. He was an admirer of Time," Munro said.

A couple of years after Buffett sold his Time shares, he approached the board wanting permission to make a major investment in the company, according to Munro. "He came to us wanting to become a big investor on the order of five to ten percent," he added. Buffett's overture was rejected. Munro said he and Nick Nicholas were for it, "but the board rejected it." Said Munro, "As I recall, it was big shareholders who just didn't want it," adding that it was something that was considered very quickly and dismissed as just something Time didn't need.

Laments Munro, "If he had become a major shareholder, we probably would not have gone through what we did." What Time soon went through was a $200 a share unsolicited offer for Time from Paramount Communications. The bid was finally beaten back as Time and Warner agreed to a high debt merger that made the combined Time Warner, Inc., the largest media and entertainment company in the world, with huge stakes in magazine publishing, such as Time and Sports Illustrated and in books, cable television, including HBO, and films such as *Batman.*

But the combined company wound up with a debt of more than $10 billion and Buffett didn't think much of that. "I do not think he [Buffett] approved of the merger, but I will be convinced until I go to my grave that it was right. We would have been acquired or become a second-rate company," Munro said.

Malcolm S. Forbes, Jr.

Malcolm S. Forbes, Jr., who inherited the Forbes publishing empire after his father's death on February 24, 1990, says his father and Buffett were good friends. Indeed, they played bridge together in England the night before the globe-trotting Malcolm Forbes's fatal heart attack. The game took place in Old Battersea House, Forbes' London home, a 17th century mansion said to have been built by sir Christopher Wren.

"They were playing in Britain against British Parliament members," recalled the younger Forbes in an interview with this author.

In one match Forbes was partnered with investor Laurence Tisch and in another he teamed with George Gillespie III, a partner in the law firm of Cravath, Swaine Moore.

"My father came home the next day and died there," said Forbes. "Warren Buffett wrote me a nice letter about how much my father had enjoyed the bridge game and how he seemed to be in such a festive mood.

"My father was not all that great a bridge player but he felt he had played well that night. He [Buffett] is an excellent bridge player. If he had taken up bridge as a career he would have done very well. It's math, a card sense and he just sees some extra dimension . . . He has a superb mind.

"Warren Buffett is one of the few people to make their fortunes through investing," Forbes continued.

"We know Buffett as a value investor but I think he's a market timer, too . . . We interviewed him (for Forbes magazine) in 1969 when he was a virtual unknown and he said the market was too high and that he was selling everything. We said, gosh, he sure called that one right. We interviewed him again in 1974 when the market had declined two-thirds in value in real terms, after inflation. He said it was a time to buy and that he felt like a sex-starved man in a harem."

32 AND A FEW CARPERS

"The best CEOs love operating their companies and don't prefer going to Business Roundtable meetings or playing golf at Augusta National."

Buffett has frequently expressed his opinion of those he calls "elephant bumpers"—bosses blinded by the limelight. "If they're bumping into elephants at industry meetings, they think they're elephants too," he told Fortune in the April 22, 1991 issue.

He has never courted the media, but overall press coverage has been laudatory and usually accurate. Recently, however, some writers have seemed engaged in a quest to spot some flaw in Buffett's character on the order of whether he hobnobs with celebrities, owns some expensive suits or has ever stayed at the Plaza.

For the first couple of decades of his career, there was practically no press coverage about Buffett. People who knew him were well aware of his brilliance, but he operated in such a shun-publicity style, or at least choosing his own publicity style, that the press was late with the story.

Buffett is not an easy subject to cover. He rarely gives interviews, and when he buys or sells, he doesn't run to the top of Kiewit Plaza and yell it out.

In the 1960s and 1970s the Omaha *World-Herald* and the *Wall*

Street Journal began running stories about Buffett as a budding investment wunderkind. The first comprehensive story about him was by Robert Dorr in the Omaha *World-Herald,* May 29, 1966, and Jonathan Laing wrote a long profile piece for the *Wall Street Journal,* March 31, 1977.

Buffett's reputation surged in the 1980s, and authors Adam Smith and John Train described Buffett's endeavors in short compilations.

More recently some reporters have taken the tactic that Buffett is overly famous. In short, a number of press accounts began to pick at him.

Now a number of writers say, well, okay he's an investment genius, but here are some flaws.

One of the first critical pieces was a *Barron's* story that suggested Berkshire's stock price was way overvalued. Berkshire shareholders thought the story was replete with errors and omissions about what Berkshire owned. (See Chapter 35).

Then with the Salomon scandal, the press became aware of Buffett and some wrote stories taking the view that Buffett had little experience in running businesses. That's an odd thing to say about a man who founded his own business, runs Berkshire Hathaway, ran Berkshire's insurance business for years and has tinkered for years with businesses such as the Washington *Post* and the Buffalo *News.* And don't forget, he speaks on a minute-by-minute basis with Berkshire's managers.

In fact, there's nothing Buffett loves *more* than running a business, as he made clear in that April 22, 1991 Fortune interview when he said: "The best CEOs love operating their companies and don't prefer going to Business Roundtable meetings or playing golf at Augusta National."

There was plenty of accurate press coverage. Institutional Investor (September 1991), owned by Capital Cities/ABC, weighed in with a balanced and detailed article on Salomon as did Bernice Kanner in a cover story about Salomon for New York magazine (December 9, 1991).

Other articles (such as the one in *Business Week,* February 17, 1992) said that Buffett did well in stepping in to save Salomon but that in running things he has not set a clear direction on strategy, that employee defections have been rampant, that policy has been inconsistent on bonuses, and that Buffett is wrongly trying to run New York-based Salomon from Omaha.

As for Buffett spending only a day or so a week at Salomon, Berkshire's chief financial officer J. Verne McKenzie says, "We have telephones in Omaha," and that Buffett's thoughts are dominated by Salomon.

But the story that finally got under the skin of Buffett fans was Michael Lewis's cover piece in the February 17, 1992, issue of the New Republic entitled "The Temptation of Saint Warren," depicting Buffett as a "fallen angel."

Lewis, author of *Liar's Poker*, about Salomon's excesses, seemed to take to the theme that, because Buffett is not a saint, he's therefore a sinner.

"Suddenly there was a delicious gap between what the moralist said and what he did," wrote Lewis, saying Buffett—as a longtime critic of Wall Street—had suddenly accepted all its excessive ways, because Salomon dealt in leverage buyouts, junk bonds, and all the rest.

Lewis set Buffett up as on a moral crusade about saving Salomon, when what Buffett has said is that he hopes to put the stigma on the Paul Mozers and get it off the good employees of Salomon.

Buffett has talked about changing the corporate culture at Salomon, but he has not talked about becoming a saint himself, and there seems little un-American in Buffett's efforts to save Salomon and help Berkshire.

Lewis maintained that Buffett, as proof of his new fast-buck Wall Street ways, had recently become an arbitrageur, one who speculates on pending takeovers.

Munger, in an interview with the Omaha *World-Herald* (February 12, 1992), said Berkshire has no rule that restricts its activities solely to long-term investing and that Buffett has practiced arbitrage investing on publicly announced takeovers every year for the past forty years and discussed it in Berkshire annual reports.

Further, Lewis portrayed Buffett's financial success as pure luck, in the same way that some one person can conceivably win forty coin tosses in a row.

Newsday's Allan Sloan says of course Buffett isn't a saint. "He hasn't ever said he didn't want to make money." And at times, particularly with Gutfreund, and rightly so, in Sloan's opinion, Buffett can be very tough on people. He will drop people such as accountants and brokers in an instant if they don't see things his way. "But he is an honorable businessman," Sloan said.

Munger also told the Omaha *World-Herald* (February 12, 1992) that Buffett is not some fallen angel. "I'm sixty-eight years of age, and I've known a lot of people for a long time," Munger said. "I would say that Warren has changed less in many decades than almost anybody else I know. What he [Lewis] says is that Buffett has lost his soul. He thinks there's some huge change in the way Warren's mind works, and of course there isn't any big change in the way Warren's mind works."

Munger went on to cite a number of errors in the Lewis story. Lewis, for example, said Buffett considered backing the Ross Johnson bid for RJR Nabisco. Munger said Berkshire, in fact, turned down a chance to participate in the RJR takeover.

Buffett himself is emphatic on this point, "I neither offered nor gave financial backing to Ross Johnson or anyone else involved in the RJR buyout. Berkshire was invited to participate in an early attempt by Hanson Industries to enter the bidding and declined. Salomon elected to support Johnson and I, as a director, said I believed the transaction would work well at $90 a share. Neither I nor other outside directors were consulted about future escalations in price . . .

"On a Sunday in 1988, I was called in Omaha by Salomon and was asked if Berkshire Hathaway would participate in a small way in a purchase offer that Salomon and Hanson Industries might make for RJR. The reason they needed us (or somebody) in the deal was that each partner wished, for some reason, to keep its interest just below 50 percent. I said I had previously concluded that I did not want Berkshire to own a direct interest in the tobacco business (a decision I made when we were offered a chance to buy Conwood Co., a maker of smokeless tobacco products). But I said I had no problem if Salomon itself wished to proceed and indeed thought it a good economic decision at the price being talked about.

"In the process of this discussion about economics of tobacco, I related a story told years before by Father Reinert, then president of Creighton University, as he introduced me to a Creighton class as someone who was going to tell them a lot about investments. But, he said, the real secret of investing was to buy into a business that had a product that 'cost a penny, sold for a dollar, and was habit-forming.' I have told that story many times in speeches to business schools, and also at the Berkshire annual meeting, to make the point about the economic characteristics of certain companies, among them tobacco companies."

As to Lewis's suggestion that Buffett's success is a coin-flipping matter, Munger fired this cannon: "He's got the idea that Warren's success for forty years is because he flipped coins for forty years and it has come up heads forty times. All I can say is, if he believes that, I've got a bridge I'd like to sell him."

33 THE BERKSHIRE HATHAWAY ANNUAL REPORT

"Neither a short-term borrower nor a long-term lender be."

Buffett gained financial control of Berkshire in 1965, assumed policy control in May 1965, and became chairman of the board and chief executive officer in 1970—the year he began writing his annual letter to shareholders. It has since become must reading for Berkshire aficionados.

Berkshire reports have a tendency to start off like this: "Our gain in net worth during 1991 was $2.1 billion, or 39.6 percent. Over the last twenty-seven years (that is, since present management took over) our per-share book value has grown from $19 to $6,437, or at the rate of 23.7 percent compounded annually."

Through the years, the letters have blossomed markedly in style, substance and originality. The letters are filled with humor, uncommon common sense, candor and clarity. He often quotes other authorities, from John Maynard Keynes ("I'd rather be vaguely right than precisely wrong") to Mae West ("Too much of a good thing can be wonderful").

He seems to love to quote Mae West, saying in the 1987 annual report, "Currently liking neither stocks nor bonds, I find myself the polar opposite of Mae West as she declared: 'I like only two kinds of men—foreign and domestic.'"

In the 1985 report he cited Samuel Johnson's observation that "A horse that can count to ten is a remarkable horse—not a remarkable mathematician," then added, "A textile company that allocates capital brilliantly within its industry is a remarkable textile company—not a remarkable business." Next, he repeated one of his most famous statements: "With few exceptions when a manager with a reputation for brilliance tackles a business with a reputation for poor economics, it is the reputation of the business which remains intact." He then added, "Gin rummy management behavior (discard your least promising business at each turn) is not our investment style. We would rather have overall results penalized a bit than engage in it."

Shareholders receive the annual report every year in late March. It's a plain-looking bound publication. On the cover, it simply says "Berkshire Hathaway, Inc., Annual Report;" no photos of headquarters or board members or outstanding employees. Not even a photo of Buffett.

The only mystery about the report's appearance is what color Berkshire has selected for its cover. Silver was the pick for the 1989 report, teal for 1990, and some miserable, uninviting black cover for 1991.

Come winter each year, Buffett begins scrawling the chairman's letter in longhand on yellow pads, eventually turning it over to his longtime friend, Carol Loomis.

Says Loomis, "I weigh in as editor. He's smart enough to know that everyone needs an editor, though sometimes I could kill him for ignoring my suggestions. Anyway, what I do on the report a lot of people who know something about both business and writing could do, as long as they had Warren's trust. What he does, nobody else could come close to doing." (Fortune, April 11, 1988)

Buffett's first letter, dated March 15, 1971, accompanying the 1970 annual report, is a rather simple, less-than-two-page offering summarizing the year's operations. It is a straightforward letter, but offers none of the brilliance in writing, the wit, or the quotes from such figures as Mae West, Goethe, Samuel Goldwyn and Yogi Berra that would later come along.

Here's how the 1970 report begins: "The past year witnessed dramatically diverse earnings results among our various operating units. The Illinois National Bank & Trust reported record earnings and continued to rank right at the top, nationally, among banks in terms of earnings as a percentage of average resources. Our insurance operations had some deterioration in underwriting results, but increased investment income produced a continued excellent return. The textile business became progressively more difficult throughout the year and the final break-even result is understandable, considering the industry environment."

The following year the letter has grown to almost three pages and begins:

"It is a pleasure to report that operating earnings in 1971, excluding capital gains, amounted to more than 14 percent of beginning shareholders' equity. This result—considerably above the average of American industry—was achieved in the face of inadequate earnings in our textile operation, making clear the benefits of redeployment of capital inaugurated five years ago. It will continue to be the objective of management to improve return on total capitalization (long-term debt plus equity), as well as the return on equity capital. However, it should be realized that merely maintaining the present relatively high rate of return may well prove more difficult than was improvement from the very low levels of return which prevailed throughout most of the 1960s."

From the early days, Buffett was constantly hammering away about getting a good return on capital.

"Buffett's success hinges on his obsession with the concept of return on capital rather than on bigness. This, in a nutshell, is what makes Warren Buffett Warren Buffett," says Berkshire shareholder Michael Assael.

The 1972 letter starts, "Operating earnings of Berkshire Hathaway during 1972 amounted to a highly satisfactory 19.9 percent of beginning shareholders' equity. Significant improvement was recorded in all our major lines of businesses, but the most dramatic gains were in insurance underwriting profit. Due to an unusual convergence of favorable factors—diminishing auto accident frequency, moderating accident severity, and an absence of major catastrophes—underwriting profit margins achieved a level far above averages of the past or expectations of the future."

In the 1973 Berkshire report, which sports a light brown cover, Buffett reports that Berkshire earned almost $12 million and he explains that the company's directors have approved a merger of Diversified Retailing Company, Inc., into Berkshire Hathaway.

"Diversified Retailing Company, Inc., through subsidiaries, operates a chain of popular-priced women's apparel stores and also conducts a reinsurance business. In the opinion of your management, its most important asset is 16 percent of Blue Chip Stamps," Buffett wrote.

In addition, Buffett proudly reported that a minor holding, the since-defunct Sun Newspapers, Inc., a group of weekly newspapers published in the Omaha area, won the Pulitzer Prize for local investigative reporting, the first time that a weekly had won in that category.

"Our congratulations go to Paul Williams, Editor, and Stan Lipsey, Publisher, as well as the entire editorial staff of Sun Newspapers for their achievement, which vividly illustrated that size need not be equated with significance in publishing."

In the following decidedly off-year of 1974, the stock market found its own special brand of torpor, and Buffett was forced to report what every shareholder dreads to hear. Inside that year's royal blue cover, he reported: "Operating results for 1974 were unsatisfactory . . . The outlook for 1975 is not encouraging."

From the beginning of 1973 to the end of 1974, Berkshire's stock price took its worst beating ever, falling from $93 a share in the first quarter of 1973 to $40 in the fourth quarter of 1974. It would touch $38 a share in the first quarter of 1975 before getting back on track.

Things may have been unsatisfactory, and Buffett explained that the insurance and textile businesses had subpar years; nevertheless, the operating business year, comparatively speaking, was just fine. Buffett reported that shareholders' equity was up 10.3 percent, the lowest return on equity realized by the company since 1970. It was a stunning performance in a year in which few companies reported any progress at all.

For 1974, his performance was, comparatively, splendid. Buffett was keeping a string of increases in stockholders' equity alive, going back to his start in 1956. Through 1991, the record was still intact.

Later, in the 1974 report, what would become vintage Buffett came through. "Our stock portfolio declined again in 1974—along with most equity portfolios—to the point that at yearend it was worth approximately $17 million less than its carrying value. Again, we are under no pressure to sell such securities except at times that we deem advantageous and it is our belief that over a period of years the overall portfolio will prove to be worth more than its cost. A net capital loss was realized in 1974, and very likely will again occur in 1975. However, we consider several of our major holdings to have great potential for significantly increased values in future years, and therefore feel quite comfortable with our stock portfolio. At this writing, market depreciation of the portfolio has been reduced by half from yearend figures, reflecting higher general stock market levels."

Buffett was indeed right. Although his holding in the Washington Post Co. sank from about $10 million to about $8 million in the first years after the 1973 purchase, it would one day be worth hundreds of millions of dollars to Berkshire.

For the 1975 year Buffett reported that both the property and casualty and textile businesses were just God-awful. "The property and casualty insurance had its worst year in history during 1975. We did our share—unfortunately, even somewhat more. Really disastrous results were concentrated in auto and long-tail [contracts where settlement of loss usually occurs long after the loss event] lines.

"Economic inflation, with the increase of cost of repairing humans and property far outstripping the general rate of inflation, produced ultimate loss costs which soared beyond premium levels established in a different cost environment. 'Social' inflation caused the liability concept to be expanded continuously, far beyond limits contemplated when rates were established—in effect, adding coverage beyond what was paid for. Such social inflation increased significantly both the propensity to sue and the possibility of collecting mammoth jury awards for events not previously considered statistically significant in the establishment of rates."

Of Berkshire's textile interests, Buffett wrote, "During the first half of 1975 sales of textile products were extremely depressed, resulting in major production curtailments. Operations ran at a significant loss, with employment down as much as 53 percent from a year earlier." There was a rebound in textiles in the second half of the year.

During the year Buffett bought more textile operations— Waumbec Mills, Inc. and Waumbec Dyeing and Finishing Co., Inc., of Manchester, New Hampshire—only to report the following year that they had not performed well.

"Our textile division was a significant disappointment during 1976," he wrote. In the pea-green-covered 1976 report, his five-page letter listed each stockholding of Berkshire with a market value of more than $3 million on December 31, 1976:

141,987 shares of California Water Service Co. . . . Cost $3,608,711

1,986,953 shares of Government Employees Insurance Company Convertible Preferred . . . Cost $19,416,635

1,294,308 Government Employees Insurance Company Common Stock . . . Cost $4,115,670

395,100 shares Interpublic Group of Companies . . . Cost $4,530,615

562,900 shares Kaiser Industries, Inc. . . . Cost $8,270,871

188,900 shares of Munsingwear, Inc. . . . Cost $3,398,404

83,400 shares of National Presto Industries, Inc. . . . Cost $1,689,896

170,800 shares of Ogilvy & Mather International . . . Cost $2,762,433

934,300 shares of The Washington Post Co. Class B . . . Cost $10,627,604

Total $58,420,839

All other holdings $16,974,375

Total equities: $75,395,214

He praised Eugene Abegg, chief executive of Illinois National Bank Trust Co. of Rockford, Illinois, who in 1931 opened the doors of the bank Berkshire later bought.

Buffett wrote: "Recently, National City Corp. of Cleveland, truly an outstandingly well-managed bank, ran an ad stating 'the ratio of earnings to average assets was 1.34 percent in 1976 which we believe to be the best percentage of any major banking company.' Among the really large banks this was the best earnings achievement but, at the Illinois National Bank earnings were close to 50 percent better than those of National City, or approximately two percent of assets."

By statute, the bank was divested in 1980, the same year Abegg died. Buffett described him as a man who, during Buffett's purchase of the bank, put all the negative factors face up on the table, but said as years went by undiscussed items of value popped up. That's the reverse of many business transactions, where the good points are touted up front and negatives pop up after the check changes hands.

Toward the end of the 1976 letter, Buffett reported that Berkshire had increased its stake in Blue Chip Stamps to 33 percent of the company's stock.

He also devoted two sentences to K&W Products, an automotive products company. He noted that in its first year with Berkshire, the unit had performed well, with sales and earnings up moderately.

In 1976 there were 2,000 Berkshire annual reports printed. By 1985 there were 15,500 and there was a second printing of 2,500 more.

By 1977 Buffett was copyrighting the annual reports and eventually, in response to an increasing demand for back Berkshire reports, the company compiled Buffett's letters into bound volumes.

The company has compilations of letters for the 1977–1983, the 1979–1985 and the 1984–1988 years.

In the 1977 report a small position in Capital Cities Communications, Inc. popped up.

The following year that position was gone, but there was a holding of American Broadcasting Companies, Inc., and GEICO and Washington Post remained mainstays, as they always would.

Buffett continued to educate his shareholders about Berkshire's holdings, and about the intricacies of subjects such as accounting or insurance. But it was not until the middle of the 1979 report that he delivered his first real effort at humor: "Overall, we opt for Polonius (slightly restated): 'Neither a short-term borrower nor a long-term lender be.'"

From that point forward he never looked back. In subsequent years he got funnier and funnier (and richer and richer), always with the purpose of helping shareholders better understand their investment.

The letters accompanying the annual reports have turned into twenty-page documents with magnificent, profound and witty dissertations on subjects such as the intricacies of accounting, insurance and the stock market and the fear and greed of human nature itself. The reports have become a kind of *Prairie Home Companion*, in which Wall Street is Lake Woebegon and Buffett gets out to tell what awful truths are really going on there.

The 1987 report was in full bloom with the introduction of "Mr. Market," a mythical character he picked up from Ben Graham, his teacher at Columbia Business School. Buffett says anyone in the stock market should imagine the daily stock quotations coming from a remarkably accommodating fellow named Mr. Market, who is your partner in business. Mr. Market flashes you stock quotes on business constantly, but there is one thing you need to know about him: Mr. Market has emotional disorders.

At times Mr. Market feels good and offers high buy-sell prices. At other times he is depressed and offers only low buy-sell prices.

Of course, you are free to ignore (and often should) Mr. Market and his prices. He will be back tomorrow with another price that may interest you. The trick is to know the difference in Mr. Market's emotional offerings—to buy when he is sad and sell when he is happy—and operate on your own and not under the influence of Mr. Market's manic-depressive personality.

Buffett counsels that Mr. Market is there to serve you, not guide you. It is Mr. Market's pocketbook, not his wisdom, that the true investor is interested in.

People, including Adam Smith, have said that a reading of the Berkshire annual reports is possibly a better education than business school itself. Says former Younker department store chairman Joseph Rosenfield: "He [Buffett] sends me some annual reports every year and I give them to my friends. Everything's in there."

34

THE AIRPLANE

"It's shameful how much I love it."

In Berkshire's 1986 annual report the following message appears in diminutive type: "We bought a corporate jet last year." The jet has been the butt of jokes, mostly from Buffett himself, ever since.

"It's shameful how much I love it . . . I can't explain it. It's a total blank in my mind. I've given speeches against them for years," he says.

The first airplane was a twenty-year-old Falcon jet Buffett picked up for just $850,000. It cost about $200,000 a year to operate. In 1989 he turned it in for a really first class jet, although once again a used one, he bought for $6.7 million.

"The old plane had lots of problems," said one source at Omaha's Eppley Airport. The new one—a Canadair Challenger—is a sleek, white jet seating about ten people. It is housed at the Sky Harbor facilities at Eppley Air Field across the runway from the main airport building. It has no insignia at all—nothing that would suggest it belongs to Berkshire.

The pilots for the plane are from the Peter Kiewit firm in Omaha.

Buffett uses the plane often because he travels about sixty days a year, mainly tending to the boards on which he sits. (Business Week, August 19, 1991) He's glad to share it with people who have Berkshire business.

"He'll let us piggyback in the plane," says a Borsheim's employee. "He usually reads."

The plane is the one toy of the rich that Buffett has accepted for the convenience it provides.

But Munger himself has never traveled in the jet, refusing to get in it and kidding Buffett that the thing is a monstrosity against shareholder interests and he refuses to recognize its existence.

Munger himself travels on commercial coach flights and carries his own bags. He showed up at Borsheim's once carrying his own luggage, one suitcase in each hand.

Privately Munger has said if any CEO deserves a jet it is Buffett and that for his needs it makes sense, but Munger's public stance is that the purchase of the airplane is total extravagance and something about which he is not familiar. With that much needling from Munger, Buffett has threatened to name the aircraft "The Charles T. Munger," but instead it has been dubbed "The Indefensible."

In a Fortune story of November 5, 1990, when Berkshire's stock price had fallen to $5,550 a share from the beginning of the year price of about $8,675, Buffett was asked about The Indefensible and quipped, "That'll be the last thing to go."

When the Salomon crisis was at its height and Buffett was constantly using the plane to take him from New York to Omaha, he re-dubbed the aircraft "Somewhat Indefensible."

When Berkshire billed Salomon for $168,688 for the cost of using The Indefensible for Salomon business, a Salomon shareholder questioned whether Buffett could have flown more cheaply by using commercial airlines. Buffett cited his $1 a year salary from Salomon, adding: "I work cheap, but I travel expensive." (Wall Street Journal, May 7, 1992).

Of course, nothing could beat the punchline in the 1990 annual report, where Buffett said if he left the scene Munger immediately would sell the corporate jet, "ignoring my wish that it be buried with me."

35 WHAT'S BERKSHIRE REALLY WORTH?

"Well, add it all up and then subtract something because I'm running it."

So-o-o, what's Berkshire really worth?

Well, that's a tricky one because Berkshire isn't the easiest company in the world to evaluate.

Shareholders and Wall Streeters sometimes try to take a stab at it, and, although the question is posed to Buffett almost every year at the annual meeting (after all, father should know best), he usually says he doesn't want to "spoil the fun" for shareholders by figuring it out for them. Sometimes he'll say: "Well, add it all up and then subtract something because I'm running it."

Buyers and sellers generally have a pretty fair value price on Berkshire stock, possibly taking their cue from Buffett, who has repeatedly said he wants Berkshire to trade near its intrinsic value, or real value, rather than at some inflated or depressed level.

And he notes that reasonable businessmen might value Berkshire 10 percent higher or lower than its intrinsic worth, that even he and Munger might differ by 10 percent about Berkshire's intrinsic value.

It is doubtful that even Buffett carries around in his head a precise figure for Berkshire's worth, although everyone would like to know what he's thinking.

Occasionally Buffett offers little nudges when the price gets out of whack. After the stock soared over $3,000 a share following Berkshire's acquisition of a stake in Capital Cities/ABC, he indicated the stock price was too high.

And there were signs he thought it too high when it soared to $8,900 in late 1989 when he sold the zero-coupon convertible bonds tied to Berkshire's stock price. The convertibles have a right to convert into Berkshire stock. Because Buffett does not easily issue new stock, he probably thought the stock would go nowhere for a few years. In the past two and a half years the stock has gone nowhere. The stock apparently was overpriced. In fact he has responded to a February 12, 1990 article in Barron's, which argued that Berkshire's price was too high, by saying that he did not disagree with the overall conclusion, only with some of the calculations used in reaching the conclusion.

In addition to telling shareholders, Buffett also told *USA Today* that the Barron's piece undervalued some of Berkshire's holdings. "There's a mathematical error in their numbers," he said. "The figures are wrong." But privately he implied he could accept Barron's conclusion that Berkshire's stock price was too high.

Still Barron's did miss the mark in its story of February 12, 1990. Respectful of Buffett's abilities, the story said Berkshire itself was greatly overvalued.

Berkshire was trading at about $7,900 a share at the time and the story sent the stock down $700 the following day. The story had a point in that Berkshire was overvalued, but not nearly by the amount the story suggested.

The writer, Thomas N. Cochran, concluded Berkshire was worth only about $4,695 a share and that the $7,900 share price was a 68 percent premium to that.

Berkshire shareholders and others fired off angry letters to Barron's, which ran selections from them.

One Berkshire shareholder, Dr. Wallace Gaye, wrote: "Poor Thomas N. Cochran. He apparently wouldn't be able to tell the difference in value between a lump of coal and a diamond because they share a similar structure."

The most serious problem with the Barron's article was that it assigned the stock market value to Berkshire's preferred stock holdings as if they were common stocks. It is true that the stock prices of three of the four preferred stock investments were down sharply. But the point is, Berkshire doesn't own the common stock. It owns the preferred. And since it earns about nine percent, tax-advantaged at that, on these preferred stock investments, there's no way the preferred could drop in value like the common. They can be redeemed for the original amount of the investment.

So there is no loss, only potential gain, plus a nine percent dividend a year.

The press has time and again talked about "losses" Berkshire has suffered on its convertibles, when Berkshire has yet to lose a penny on any of them. With the safety and conversion privileges these investments offer, not to mention the long periods they have to become more profitable, Berkshire is sitting on some extraordinary investments worth considerably more than their original cost. These investments are not available on the market and the only way to own them is through Berkshire. Figuring the worth of these is not easy.

Buffett said at the 1991 annual meeting, "The hardest value to figure by far is the worth of our insurance business. That doesn't mean it isn't valuable. It just means that it's hard to assess—although it might have a bigger effect on the valuation of Berkshire than See's Candy or World Book."

He went on to say, "How the insurance table in our [1990] annual report develops over the next twenty years will be a major factor in what the intrinsic value of Berkshire is today . . . The source of intrinsic value of the insurance business is the ability to generate funds at a low cost. That's what creates value . . . If you can figure out how that table will look in the next twenty years, you'll have a good handle on our future. We think there is significant potential in it. In terms of dollars, we think that it's bigger than that of our other directly owned businesses."

Cochrane assigned a P/E of just 12 to Berkshire's operating businesses at a time when the market P/E was 14. Ring up Buffett and ask him if he'll sell See's or the Buffalo *News* or World Book for twelve times earnings and see how long he stays on the phone.

Cochran used an old earnings figure, but even if it were the latest, Berkshire's earnings had already ploughed ahead. If you're talking about Berkshire from its latest report, you're probably millions of dollars behind the times. For one thing, Buffett reports as late as possible, about forty-five days after the quarter has ended. You're even farther behind if you're citing figures from the annual report, which comes out in late March and reflects the status as of the prior December 31. Berkshire's earnings already have increased by about another $100 million by the time you get the report.

Also, during the period Cochran in which was writing, the market was declining, so Berkshire's tab for deferred capital gains taxes should have been lower than the figure Cochrane used. And are deferred capital gains taxes really a 100 percent liability, as Cochrane implies? It's true that if Buffett sold everything today, he would have to pay Uncle Sam a very large tax bill. But Buffett tells us he's not selling everything today. In fact, he may hold some investments forever; hence, there's a less than 100 percent capital gains tax liability. Besides, the deferred tax liability is non-interest-bearing and has no redemption date. If it were a bond, it might be redeemed at twenty cents on the dollar.

Cochran made no mention of Berkshire's enormous "look-through earnings," which you can think of as Berkshire's share of the earnings of corporations in which Berkshire invests but which are not included in Berkshire's income statement.

Look-through earnings are not unique to Berkshire, of course, and it can be argued such earnings are already reflected in the stock prices of the corporations in which Berkshire has an investment.

Also, there is an extra worth that should be attributed to Berkshire's commanding stock positions. Some even suggest attaching a 20 percent premium, for example, for the huge stock positions such as GEICO.

There are other beauties at Berkshire. Consider how Buffett has structured Berkshire's debt. He is paying less than five percent on all of the debt, largely because of the zero-coupon financing. That is even less than the so-called "risk-free" rate for the U.S. government to borrow money.

Berkshire has very little debt compared to equity and is also paying very little for that debt. "His debt is triple-A rated. There are not many companies in the country that can say that," notes one Berkshire shareholder.

And also consider what he is paying for other people's money. At year-end 1990, Berkshire had a float from its insurance operations of about $1.6 billion, more than $2 billion by late 1991. Buffett notes that the cost of those funds to Berkshire for the year was 1.65 percent, perhaps a percent higher, really, when other tax considerations are included.

Still, wouldn't you like a huge loan, for, say, under three percent? In fact, in some years when Berkshire has had an underwriting gain, Berkshire's cost for that float is nothing.

Buffett points out that in twenty of the twenty-five years the Berkshire insurance firms have been in operation Berkshire received money at a cost below that paid by the government.

There have been a few years when Berkshire has had a high cost of funds, but overall, since the insurance companies began providing him a float of $17.3 million in 1967, the cost of the funds has been low.

The insurance operations have mainly given Berkshire large interest-free loans over the years.

"If the float is $1.6 billion, and he's paying two percent for the money, then there's a built-in six percent profit, and if you put a multiple of ten on that, then the insurance business is worth $1 billion—and that's based on a 1990 figure and doesn't account for possible growth. $1.25 billion for the insurance business would be a conservative figure," a Berkshire shareholder said in the summer of 1991. (By the end of the third quarter the "float" was more than $2 billion, although the cost of funds in 1991 rose above six percent.)

And because of the extraordinarily high capital of the insurance businesses, Berkshire possesses an enormous capacity to write business in the future at a time most propitious to itself. "There is a hidden potential to write huge business in the future. And that fact that insurance business has grown over the years—the fact that he can get to this position is indicative of the strength of the insurance business."

Finally, there is one other item of value to which it is difficult to assign a dollar figure. Warren Buffett is running this operation, not Saddam Hussein.

In any case then, what is Berkshire really worth?

Adding the worth of the stocks and bonds is easy enough. It's easy —even fun—to figure that the Coca-Cola investment, say, is worth about $4 billion, and we won't even get into whether it is worth more, which it surely would be, were it sold as a block.

It is also comforting that, with Buffett on the boards of many of the companies in which he has investments, he has some say over how their cash flows are invested. But there is the argument that some of the companies have higher P/Es than they might were Buffett's magical name not associated with the company.

But in any case, go ahead and take whatever the stock market says its shares are worth.

And you should be able to put at least fifteen times earnings on the operating businesses in Berkshire's portfolio and come up with some sort of reasonable number.

After all, this group of businesses has among the highest return on equity of any group of businesses in the country. Very high return on equity with practically no debt. You can loosen up a little and put a healthy P/E on things.

Earnings reported by Berkshire are understated.

Not only are there earnings reported by Berkshire, but also the earnings of Berkshire's investees. The percentage of those so-called look-through earnings are not reported by Berkshire, but in a real sense they still belong to Berkshire. The interests are not big enough to allow Berkshire to report pro rata shares of the investee's income, but they do, however indirectly, belong to Berkshire.

True, they should be reflected in the stock price of the investee, but they are not always reflected in a depressed market.

Berkshire has millions of dollars in "look-through earnings" of such companies as GEICO, Capital Cities/ABC and Coca-Cola, earnings that go unrecorded on Berkshire's income statement but add value to Berkshire nevertheless. As stated previously, look-through earnings are not unique to Berkshire, but because Berkshire holds large common stock positions as compared to other companies, Berkshire's look-through earnings are a huge proportion of its total earnings.

In addition to Berkshire's $370 million in operating earnings in 1990, Buffett said there were also about $220 million in operating earnings retained by investees so that, in a sense, total earnings were about $590 million. That was about 14 percent more than in 1991.

Then you've got the question of what the insurance companies are worth and that's a tricky one. Are they worth zero, as some say? Absolutely not. Are they worth perhaps $2 billion, as some say? No. But they definitely have a worth somewhere in between—perhaps to $1.5 billion dollars—perhaps more, even though the business is cyclical and Buffett's companies only write business when things are good for them, which does not lead to steady, longtime customers.

The insurance companies provide Buffett with a great investment vehicle and a huge amount of float, always important cash for his investing needs. The insurance companies provide huge earnings, though, essentially, they are coming from the dividends from such investments as Coca-Cola and the preferred stock stakes.

There's always the matter of subtracting debt and subtracting something for deferred capital gains taxes—taxes Berkshire would pay if and when it sold stock or bonds at a gain.

Another way to value Berkshire, perhaps, is to take Berkshire's book value figure and assign a value at, say, 1.5 times book. That times 1991 yearend book value of $6,437 would give a stock price of about $9,650 when it was trading at $9,050.

Another estimate comes from a savvy investor and longtime Berkshire shareholder, Yves Mojonnet of San Francisco, who estimates that at a time in October 1990, when Berkshire was trading at $5,550, it was really worth a lot more, perhaps $2,400 for the operating businesses and $9,000 to $10,000 overall. "It trades at a discount to net asset value," he said.

And that was in one of the most panicked moments the stock

market has had. Obviously, Berkshire is priced higher when the stock market is on a bull run. But it is also true that Buffett is at his best when stocks are selling at half their intrinsic value.

A more expansive appraisal of Berkshire's worth was offered by Berkshire shareholder Dr. Wallace Gaye in an interview appearing in the Outstanding Investor Digest issue of February 11, 1991. The interview was conducted prior to that time, when Berkshire was trading at about $6,700, and Gaye said he thought the worth was between $9,000 and $9,500 a share. "If you take the book value of Berkshire and assign all of it to the insurance company—which is fudging a little—and estimate its value, you get an idea," Gaye told OID editor Henry Emerson.

"For example, Fund America was taken out at 1.4 times book value. And Fund America has nowhere near the record Buffett has in growing book value 23 percent a year for twenty-three years. So 1.4 times book is probably conservative. And then you have to value the operating companies—the newspaper, See's Candies and all that stuff.

"Berkshire's book value is around $4,800 per share. That could indicate a value of about $7,500 per share for the insurance company. You're left with $1,500 to $2,000 a share for the operating companies. That's a total valuation of $9,000 to $9,500 a share, and it's trading around $6,700."

In an interview several months later, on March 10, 1991, after a big war victory rally, Gaye was even more expansive, assigning a worth of better than $14,000 a share to Berkshire when it was trading at $7,900.

"If the book value is about $6,000, do two times book—GEICO sells for three times book—and you get $12,000. Add $2,500 for the businesses. That's $14,500," Gaye said. "The price is high, but it's not an expensive stock . . . It's cheap," he said.

Noted money manager Mario Gabelli, value investor and longtime Berkshire follower, said in the July 1, 1991, issue of *Outstanding Investor Digest*, "Today, it's $8,500 a share. And it's probably worth $12,000 to $13,000 a share."

Various Berkshire shareholders, in 1991, offered valuations for

Berkshire's shares that ranged between about $9,000 and $14,000. The Gabelli estimate seemed about the most representative.

But, finally, how do you really value Berkshire's commanding stock stakes? Not just by the numbers alone. Most of the positions are so large, they are therefore more valuable because of their semi-controlling nature.

Some say the large stock positions may be worth a 20 percent premium to their trading price. For getting at the worth of Berkshire, you probably want to be conservative and use the stated stock price. But in the real world these large chunks of Capital Cities and Gillette, for example, carry a premium.

Probably Berkshire's 48 percent ownership of GEICO is worth more than stated market value because, if Buffett sold the whole stake, the new owner would essentially control the company. A huge acquirer would no doubt offer more than the market price of Berkshire's stake in Coca-Cola to control what is perhaps the best bullet-proof franchise in the world.

All of Buffett's preferred stock stakes represent large positions in the companies, not to mention the extra value of the investments themselves—that they are redeemable at par, that they provide excellent dividends, and they offer the possibility of really huge pots of gold if things go well.

The conversion privileges of the preferred stock investments alone, although volatile, are worth millions.

Oh, and taxes. Buffett is a keen reader of the tax code. Insurance operations get tax breaks. The dividends on the preferred stock investments are largely tax exempt and the investment in low income housing is another tax break of which Buffett takes advantage.

Many of Buffett's investments, such as stocks purchased by Berkshire's non-insurance subsidiaries, are carried at cost. Many of the businesses that were purchased a long time ago are also carried at historical cost. Is See's, bought in 1972 for $25 million, worth more than that today? Of course. Is the Buffalo *News*, for example, really worth the $33 million Buffett paid for it in 1977?

Better to try about $500 million, although, admittedly, huge taxes would be owed if the newspaper were sold. But then Buffett isn't likely to sell See's or the Buffalo *News*.

You can also be sure that Buffett's accounting is as conservative as it comes.

"And there are no hidden liabilities," says one Berkshire shareholder. "So many companies have large pension and health liabilities but Berkshire's pension plan is overfunded."

Isn't Buffett himself valuable far beyond his stock picking and management abilities? With huge financial resources and longtime relationships with such people as Tom Murphy, Laurence Tisch, and Katharine Graham, can't something valuable happen for Berkshire in the future if those sorts of people and Buffett come up with an investment or business combination idea?

Buffett's elite circle of friends meets every two years for a retreat at places like Lyford Cay in the Bahamas, Williamsburg, Virginia, the *Queen Elizabeth II*, Santa Fe, New Mexico, and Victoria, British Columbia. What Buffett calls "the Graham Group," and what everyone else calls "the Buffett Group" began in 1968 with thirteen people and now has sixty, including Mrs. Graham, Murphy, Tisch, Keough and Johnson & Johnson chairman James Burke and his brother, John J. Byrne, who heads Fund American Companies.

Buffett is also friends with people like Walter Annenberg, and in fact advised him to go ahead with the $3 billion sale of his Triangle Publications, which included TV Guide, to Rupert Murdoch. Nancy Reagan once sent her son, Ron, to Buffett for a little career counseling.

Many top people run attractive business ideas by Buffett. He can take the best one or two every year.

Berkshire has more diversity and more flexibility than most companies.

Its diversity—stocks, bonds, cash, newspapers, television stations, razor blades, soft drinks, uniforms, candy, brokerage and financial services, oil, paper, steel, jewelry, furniture, encyclopedias, air compressors, vacuum cleaners, automotive compounds and liquor, etc.—is obvious.

And its flexibility comes in a number of forms.

With Buffett owning such a large block of the stock, he can be on the spot with cash in hand on a moment's notice, as he was with the purchase of Scott & Fetzer when other bidders were in the wings.

He has no limits on geography or even type of business. He could buy anything, whether it be in California or England, and never leave his office. He can decide quickly that Berkshire could gain from more media or soft drink properties, or a shoe or a food company, should something attractive be offered.

Isn't there extra value because Berkshire's managers pay themselves so little and Buffett and Munger serve on the boards of some of the investees? Their talent and time, for a tiny shareholder fee, is most valuable. After all, Munger outperformed the S&P by a factor of about four over a period of about a dozen years, ringing up a 19.8 percent average annual return from 1962–1975 for his own partnership while the S&P gained only 5.2 percent annually. For that, let's assign some value. How much, no one knows, but do you want chances of making 19.8 percent or 5.2 percent on your portfolio?

There are some technical things that add to Berkshire's worth— Berkshire's corporate structure's using the insurance vehicle to make investments brings Berkshire some tax breaks. Also, Buffett operates with such size and efficiency that it's difficult to imagine that even his commissions, say, on buying a billion dollars worth of Coca-Cola aren't lower than any other fund manager's would have been.

Berkshire's consistency, because of Buffett's money managing abilities, is certainly worth a premium.

If you could find someone who could bring you a 30 percent annual return for years to come, would that not be close to a priceless find?

Berkshire might one day sell for $100,000 a share. Of course, Berkshire cannot deliver anywhere near an average increase of 25 percent a year in stock price, but a common sense view might suggest Berkshire will continue to outperform the market by a wide margin.

Berkshire is a world-beater investment vehicle. And there is a sort of X factor with Berkshire—some proprietary things that Buffett hasn't explained to shareholders. He has said, "There's not much of that sort of stuff." But there is some and it is unlikely that the worth of it is zero.

Finally, does it really make much difference what Berkshire is worth now if it can keep outperforming 90 percent of the world?

Would it have made much difference whether it was slightly un-dervalued or overvalued in 1965 when it traded at $12 a share? Wouldn't it have been nice to buy Berkshire at $20 or $200 or $2,000 a share, regardless of whether it was a bargain that day or not?

Berkshire clearly is unique, and if Buffett can keep working his magic at anything approaching his past rate of return, Berkshire will continue to make a lot of people rich.

36 BUFFETT'S PERSONAL WEALTH

"My personal portfolio is Berkshire."

In addition to Buffett's 42 percent ownership in Berkshire, which makes him a billionaire more than four times, Buffett also has a substantial personal portfolio.

Lord only knows what the best investor of our time has tucked away in there. Information about it is skimpy.

In his Buffett Partnership letter of January 25, 1967, Buffett said his investment in the partnership represented more than 90 percent of his family's worth, so that, clearly, all along his major personal investment has been his stake in the partnership and, later, in Berkshire stock.

In 1967 he said he had most of his money in the partnership, excluding an investment in Data Documents stock. In 1977 Buffett told Dow Jones reporter Jonathan Laing his personal portfolio of stockholdings was worth $30 million.

If those holdings have increased twenty-five times since then—substantially less than the rate of Berkshire's growth—today they would be worth $750 million. And that's if Buffett has made no new investments.

In late 1986 Buffett invested about $38 million in the stock of Illinois's Servicemaster for his personal portfolio. Servicemaster cleans hospitals and provides contract services such as laundry, food preparation and maid services for hospitals, colleges and some factories. The company operates on Christian principles. The name means Service to the Master. There were subsequent reports that Buffett was selling the stake, and Servicemaster officials have said he is out of the stock.

That investment came to light because Buffett bought slightly more than five percent of Servicemaster stock, making it a public transaction, and when confusion arose as to whether Berkshire bought the stock, Buffett told shareholders the purchase had been made for his personal portfolio, not for Berkshire. When some shareholders said they wished he had bought Servicemaster for Berkshire, he explained that the investment, because of tax reasons, was better suited for personal accounts.

Over the years, reports of small personal investments have come to light: one in FirstTier Bank in Omaha; an early one in Nebraska's small and only minority-owned bank, Community Bank of Nebraska; and a small investment in the Omaha Royals. It's safe to say Buffett is not standing idly by as his own investor, although by all accounts the huge majority of his investment thinking is devoted to Berkshire.

Just what is to become of Buffett's personal portfolio, which, just guessing, could be worth a billion dollars, is an intriguing question. Something good will come of it. Asked about the fate of his personal portfolio at the annual meeting in 1991, Buffett that said almost all his money will ultimately be returned to society, and in any case, "My personal portfolio is Berkshire."

37 CHARLES MUNGER

"In bad years, he's my senior partner."

Berkshire's vice chairman Charles Munger is Buffett's friend, soulmate, sidekick and "interchangeable" partner. Munger has about half his net worth in Berkshire. It's a good thing, because he has eight children.

Together, Buffett and Munger are the Bartles and Jaymes of corporate America: two oldtimers sitting on the porch taking a shrewd, realistic look at an imperfect world and having a ball trying to figure out how to make the most of it.

In many ways Munger is a great foil for Buffett, especially when the two are at the dais conducting the April annual meeting. Once Buffett was talking about trying to keep Berkshire's investments quiet. Buffett: "Unfortunately, we have to file certain reports. And it has lately been our policy to list our year-end holdings which total $100 million or more in our annual reports. But in between, we don't say much. Charlie?"

Munger: "No comment."

Quick with colorful language, Munger once said of the less rosy prospects for media companies, "We used to think they had a first lien on the advance of time."

When reporters can't get Buffett, which is most of the time, they'll sometimes call Munger for an observation of Buffett and he'll say something such as, "He takes his work seriously, but he doesn't take himself seriously."

Munger, who has an eye problem and lost an eye in the early 1980s, wears uncommonly thick glasses, concedes that Buffett is somewhat more talented than he is.

But that does not leave Munger in the dummy department.

Munger's career is distinguished in his own right, as a lawyer, businessman and investor.

Munger, who grew up in Omaha, has said that his family and Buffett's knew one another, but that he and Buffett did not actually meet until 1959 when they were introduced by mutual friends, Dr. and Mrs. Edwin Davis.

Dr. Davis, now deceased, set up the meeting. After Buffett made a call on Davis one night, as he did to many doctors in Omaha in the early days seeking money for their partnership, Buffett asked Davis why he so quickly decided to invest with him, and Davis told him it was because Buffett reminded him so much of Munger.

"I knew everyone in the family except Warren," Munger has said of meeting Buffett. Munger once worked in the grocery store belonging to Buffett's grandfather, Buffett & Son, which did not survive the arrival of supermarkets.

Buffett and Munger had dinner—at Johnny's Café in Omaha—and spent it talking about the securities markets. But Munger has said that on meeting Buffett he was instantly impressed, recognizing Buffett's sensational abilities on the spot.

"I wasn't just slightly impressed, I was very impressed," Munger has said. (Linda Grant in the Los Angeles *Times*, April 7, 1991)

The two became fast friends and Buffett kept telling Munger that investing was a quicker way to riches than the law. Munger became convinced and established a long, successful investment record himself, even while keeping one foot in his law practice.

In 1959, Buffett and Munger, who founded the Los Angeles law firm of Munger, Tolles & Olson, became "mental partners" and hooked up officially after the Berkshire-Diversified Retailing merger of 1978. Munger continued to live in Los Angeles, where he is also chairman of the Los Angeles Daily Journal Corp., publisher of the Los Angeles *Daily Journal* for lawyers and eleven small newspapers in California.

The *Daily Journal*, which has about 320 employees, did not have a stellar year in 1991. On revenues of $29 million, it came up with profits of just $1,000.

In his annual letter to Daily Journal shareholders, Munger puts things in his usual succinct way in describing a pre-tax loss of $300,000 at the company's California Lawyer, a monthly magazine published in cooperation with the State Bar of California.

"The venture plainly (1) is a contribution to the social order, (2) creates the best style of communications between the State Bar and its members, and (3) works well for its advertisers. But its economic effects continue to be unsatisfactory to our company as owner."

Munger has 34.5 percent of the shares of the over-the-counter company, which he holds through his 16.7 percent ownership of Munger, Marshall & Co., a California limited partnership, according to the 1991 Daily Journal Corp.'s notice of annual meeting. It also says that Munger's close friend, J.P. Guerin, owns 22 percent of the shares through Guerin's 80-percent-owned Pacific Partners.

Neither Munger nor Guerin takes any compensation for work on the company and Munger admits they underpay company president Gerald Salzman.

From the early 1970s to the late 1980s, Munger and Rick Guerin ran the New America Fund, which had a terrific record before it was liquidated.

Munger became a director of Berkshire on December 30, 1978, with the merger of Diversified Retailing into Berkshire, and he has served as vice chairman of Berkshire. He has long been Buffett's "interchangeable" partner.

Munger himself is quick with the quips and often comes up with important common sense lessons of his own: "The first chance you have to avoid a loss from a foolish loan is by refusing to make it. There is no second chance."

Munger is a staunch Republican and Buffett is a Democrat.

Munger likes to fish in lakes and particularly for big salmon in

Alaska rivers, and Buffett cares little about fishing. Aside from politics, fishing and "The Indefensible", however, the men have few disagreements.

The two see eye-to-eye about investing, particularly when it comes to doing things as conservatively as possible and keeping the balance sheet clear of debt. In the early days Buffett was obsessed with buying assets as cheaply as possible. He has said it was Munger who stressed to him over the years the importance of buying quality businesses for the long run, even if you have to pay a little more.

Munger has addressed the question of strict value investing versus paying up a little for a quality business. At the 1991 Wesco annual meeting, Munger observed that "both Warren and I sometimes wonder what would have happened if we'd started out in better businesses instead of trading stamps, aluminum, textile companies—we even had a windmill company at one time. It took us a long time to wise up." (Outstanding Investor Digest, May 24, 1991)

Munger and Buffett work quickly and efficiently and have worked together so long each knows how the other will view something.

"Charlie Munger and I can handle a four-page memo over the phone with three grunts," Buffett has said. (John Train, *The Midas Touch*) "Charlie and I are interchangeable on business decisions. Distance impedes us not at all; we've always found a telephone to be more productive than a half-day meeting," Buffett told Train.

Buffett also has said, "My idea of a group decision is to look in the mirror."

But if Buffett gets beyond making the decision himself, Munger is the first person to whom he turns.

38

"SIR, WHAT IF YOU DIE?"

"The exact location of my body shouldn't matter."

"Sir, what if you die?"

What Buffett calls the "if I get hit by a truck question" is posed almost every year.

"Nothing will be forced by estate taxes if I should step in an elevator shaft absent-mindedly," Buffett said at the Berkshire 1986 annual meeting.

Asked at the 1991 meeting what would happen to Berkshire should he die, Buffett deadpanned, "Our businesses are run as if I am not there. So the exact location of my body shouldn't matter."

Buffett has assured shareholders that "not a single share of my stock will be sold." His entire block of Berkshire stock is going to the Buffett Foundation to be used to reduce the threat of nuclear war and curb world population growth.

"It's a marvelous society that lets me do what I do. I wouldn't be worth a damn in Bangladesh or Peru or some place. The fact that I have a lot of fun with it and can consume some of it, I think I should give it back to society. I see no reason why I should create some dynasty of wealth that can go around fanning themselves," he said on Adam Smith's "Money World" show.

Should Mrs. Buffett outlive her husband, she would inherit his 42 percent stake and with her resulting 45 percent of the company, would effectively control Berkshire, making her one of the richest people in the country, possibly the richest. After her death, her Berkshire stock is slated to go to the Buffett Foundation, of which she is president.

Buffett has said leaving his Berkshire stock to the foundation "preserves the most flexibility in terms of any future changes in the laws." (Forbes, October 21, 1991)

Here's how he put things in the 1990 annual report: "I feel strongly that the fate of our businesses and their managers should not depend on my health, which, it should be added, is excellent— and I have planned accordingly. Neither my estate plan nor that of my wife is designed to preserve the family fortune; instead, both are aimed at preserving the character of Berkshire and returning the fortune to society."

Berkshire shareholders should not lie awake at night and worry that Berkshire is going back to $13 a share the day Buffett goes.

"I don't do the normal exercise and I don't eat a normal diet. But we do have someone in mind who would be our successor if Charlie and I were to die at once. And on my death, not a share of stock has to be sold. I have promised people that my affairs will not cause people any surprises," Buffett said at the 1988 annual meeting.

At the meeting in 1991, he said, "You have two questions as shareholders that you have to think about: Will the owners behave any different as owners? And will the managers behave any different as managers?"

He made it clear the answer to both questions is no.

Added Munger, "I think it's obvious that if Warren died tomorrow the prospects of our company would be somewhat reduced. Certainly the capital allocation process couldn't be made better under any foreseeable scenario. However, I do think a company like Berkshire would have a lot of time to find a successor. And you only need one." Buffett: "Maybe less."

Munger: "And I don't think that you should assume that the personality who put the whole thing together would be incapable of finding a successor."

Buffett: "It's an easy company to run. And the capital allocation process may be self-defeating anyway over time. And there's nothing that says we can forever allocate the capital better than you. So as the years go by, it's not inconceivable that we could have a policy on dividends that would be dramatically different than the present one because we believed you could do a better job of allocating the capital than we could—partly because the sums would be so large. And Charlie says we're looking forward to that day."

At the annual meeting in 1987, Buffett made a remarkable comment after an explanation about how, if he should go, then Munger would run things "and we have a provision beyond that." Adding that he almost never gave a stock tip, he advised: "When I die, buy the stock." He suggested the stock price might drop, making Berkshire a real buy. He repeated that none of his stock will be sold.

At the annual meeting in 1986, Buffett had said, "Charlie will be running it. No Berkshire holding will be sold. It will be kept intact. Capital Cities/ABC and GEICO will continue. There will be no surprises for management . . . Nothing will be forced by estate taxes. I owe that to people in case I step in an elevator shaft absent-mindedly."

He said that when he goes the stock shouldn't change price much, wisecracking, "I'll be disappointed if it goes up a lot," a reference to some stocks rising in relief when certain CEOs go. "No you won't," Munger quipped.

Replied Buffett of Munger, "He'll be flattered," by Berkshire rising in anticipation of Munger's reign.

For years Munger has been in the capital asset allocation process with Buffett and is brilliant in his own right.

Would things be as good as under Buffett, the true glue that keeps the disparate parts of Berkshire together? No. They would not. Buffett is an original, one of a kind. Would they be bad? Not at all.

As Munger has put it, "Capital allocation would not be as good as under him. But it would not be bad, either."

Says one Berkshire shareholder, "Munger can do everything Buffett does except be funny at the annual meeting."

Buffett has said that if both he and Munger were to leave the scene, they have someone else in mind to run things, but they have not named that person.

Buffett's successor could be Bill Ruane, Buffett's friend since Columbia days, who runs the Sequoia Fund. Mike Goldberg, who runs Berkshire's insurance operations, is a possibility. Rick Guerin seems to be a close, respected friend of Buffett's. Of course, there may be someone else, but you have to believe it is someone whose asset allocation abilities Buffett thinks the world of.

Buffett always means what he says and says what he means.

"When I die, buy the stock." What does he mean? No one knows for sure. But, with Buffett saying it, it means what it says.

One shareholder says, "He probably means that if Berkshire took a big dip upon his death, the stock would be undervalued and be a buy."

Buffett never makes idle comments and his comment about buying the stock means something, but it's unclear just what.

Buffett's comment certainly seems to suggest some final offering, a gift, from Buffett to the world—perhaps both to Berkshire shareholders and, more broadly, to society when his estate passes to the Buffett Foundation.

Buffett's net worth of more than $4 billion would make the Buffett Foundation the second largest charitable organization in the nation, second only to the Ford Foundation, with about $6.1 billion. Buffett's children are each to receive roughly $5 million. (*Wall Street Journal,* November 8, 1991)

When the day is done, Buffett is a giver, not a taker.

"The other significant question about Berkshire is to figure out how to recognize the next Warren Buffett," said a Berkshire shareholder, adding that he has often tried to convince others of the appeal of Berkshire, with almost no results.

"I have seen so many people pass it up," said one Berkshire shareholder. "I would like for my children to be able to recognize the next Berkshire that comes along."

Of course, one answer is to recognize this one and not worry too much about searching out another.

It's the same proposition for those investors who try to figure out where Buffett is investing or to copycat his investments.

The way to be sure you are doing what Buffett is doing when he is doing it is simply to be a Berkshire shareholder, that is just sit back and leave the driving, the investing, to him. Why try to second-guess Buffett? Why not just enjoy what he's doing?

Occasionally, there are rumors that Buffett is up for a government job or is under consideration to head the New York Stock Exchange, but he has sidestepped all this with the assurance, "I'll be doing this as long as I live." (Linda Grant, Los Angeles *Times,* April 7, 1991)

"I think he's an American genius . . . He has a sterling reputation," said Irving Kahn of Kahn Brothers, who adds his only bone to pick with Buffett is why, as he's gotten older, Buffett has continued to concentrate on amassing wealth rather than giving more consideration to what that wealth can do for society.

"After all, it's money he's made from other people. He didn't create the telephone or invent something . . . Sooner or later some of that money should go back to society," Kahn said. "Warren Buffett looks good versus the other nefarious collectors of corporate shares. Yet his gains equal the losses of all who sold to him . . . Maybe after so many brilliant achievements, Warren Buffett will use his energy and brains for broader and deeper national problems."

Buffett may believe that the more wealth he can accumulate, the more he can help the world. And of course Buffett has offered a lot in human terms already, setting examples in human and financial behavior for all. And the Buffett and Berkshire story is unfinished.

It may well be that Buffett plans on surprising people by doing what he's doing until a very late age.

Perhaps a good response to the "what if he dies" question is, "What if he lives?"

From all that I can see of him, he seems to be a healthy, happy and energetic man and he just may live beyond the next quarter's earnings statement.

Once at Harvard Business School he was asked when he planned to retire. "About five to ten years after I die," he replied.

POSTSCRIPT

(The following material was prepared at the request of the Publisher by Stanley H. Brown, formerly a senior editor of Forbes magazine and an associate editor for Fortune magazine. He is also the author of H.L. Hunt *and* Ling: The Rise, Fall, and Return of a Texas Titan.*)*

Since the hard-cover edition of this book appeared in 1992 the Buffett legend has grown to the point where this almost magically effective investor has become a virtual metaphor for financial performance, as in Tiffany or Rolls Royce. Buffett, who is world-renowned for his modesty, is often cited by other financial people as a shining goal like the emerald city.

"I would like to think we can be the Warren Buffett of biotech," said the head of a recently formed investment fund that specializes in fledgling drug research companies. And when Leon Black, who did mergers and acquisitions at Drexel Burnham Lambert and then at his own firm, Apollo Investment Fund, talks about his plans for his young firm, he says, "We want to be like Warren Buffett."

Neither start-up biotech nor aggressive mergers-and-acquisitions business is much like Warren Buffett or Berkshire Hathaway, with its history of making long-term unusually profitable investments that are rarely sold. But even this master of finance has altered his view of the world of investments. In the annual letter he wrote to shareholders of Berkshire Hathaway in the spring of 1993 he did something he has generally disparaged in the past; he made a stock-market forecast.

"We've long felt," he wrote, "that the only value of stock forecasters is to make fortunetellers look good." But, he added, "we are virtually certain the return on the Standard and Poor's 500-stock index over the next ten years will be far less than that of the past ten years."

The reason he gave is forthright and simple: "stocks cannot forever overperform their underlying businesses, as they have so dramatically done for some time."

Buffett, however, had little reason to be gloomy at that point. In the previous year the firm's investment in the insurer Geico Corporation, which the firm had begun making in the 1970s, rose 63 percent to $2.23 billion. Regarding the performance of Berkshire's holding of General Dynamics Corp., the giant defense contractor: "We were lucky," he wrote. The GDC shares had been bought for a small profit in a short time. But the military supplier's plans to unload many of its businesses apparently caused Buffett to change his mind. "In short order I dumped my arbitrage thoughts and decided that Berkshire should become a long-term investor."

Berkshire had acquired 15 percent of the company's stock in the summer of 1992 for $312.4 million, and by the end of that year the holding was worth $450.8 million.

Buffett did cite disappointment with the performance of the firm's investments in Salomon, Inc., Champion International Corporation, and USAir Group, Inc., in which Berkshire lost some $90 million during the year.

The year 1993 marked another new direction for Berkshire. Its executives began looking into the prospects for investing in the depressed real-estate market as banks and other lenders stuck with bad loans were seeking to bail out. Sophisticated investors willing to wait long-term for the market to rise again were buying choice real estate at what they hoped would one day prove to be bargain prices. Executives at Berkshire were looking into this market, figuring that real estate values were lower than they should be simply because of the recent bad outlook.

Considering Buffett's view that the stock market was not likely to do as well in coming years as it had been doing, Berkshire had ready cash to invest in real estate. The word on Wall Street was that he was looking to invest $200 million to $300 million in existing or new loans. But in 1993 the company made no big news in the real-estate market, reflecting Buffett's innate caution. Which did not foreclose significant moves in that direction in the future.

Meanwhile, Berkshire's interests in Salomon Brothers remained strong, even though Buffett replaced himself as chairman and stepped down to a lesser position as chairman of the executive committee. In August, Berkshire filed with the SEC for permission to increase its stock holdings in the investment-banking firm from just under 15 percent to just under 25 percent. The news of Buffett's apparently increased confidence in the worth of the trouble-ridden securities firm caused others on Wall Street to follow his lead, and the stock began to move up. Few, if any, in the financial community can move a stock the way Warren Buffett often can.

In the fall, Berkshire traded $420 million of its stock to acquire Dexter Shoe Co., one of the largest independent shoe makers in the country. Berkshire already had a substantial position in the industry with its 1991 purchase of H.H. Brown Shoe Co. Buffett called the Dexter company "exactly the type of business Berkshire Hathaway admires." He cited its "long profitable history, enduring franchises and superb management." There may be no glamor in shoes, but there are profits to be made in the domestic part of an industry that, like so many others, has moved abroad.

Late in 1993, when Capital Cities/ABC announced it was "buying in" shares, Berkshire said it would tender a million of its CapCities shares. It was unusual for Buffett to sell anything, especially that stock. The announcements led to much speculation on Wall Street regarding an acquisition or a divestiture, especially in a world where media deals had become breakfast-table talk all over America. But no big deal took place, either by CapCities or by Buffett using the money he had gotten for selling those Berkshire shares back to CapCities.

For some years Buffett had been telling shareholders he was looking for an investment that Berkshire Hathaway could make for $2 billion to $3 billion, but nothing appropriate had turned up by the time he wrote his 1994 letter to shareholders. Among reflections on the state of various investments—the shoe business was up, the insurance business was damaged by claims arising from such disasters as the January 1994 Los Angeles earthquake—the master investor invited shareholders to an Omaha Royals minor league baseball game on April 23, two nights before Berkshire's annual meeting. Buffett, who owns 25 percent of the team, indicated that it was not exactly a sellout event and offered tickets at $5 apiece, writing that "I regret to report that you won't have to buy them from scalpers."

In the Berkshire Hathaway annual report two years earlier, Buffett wrote about his renowned reluctance to sell any holdings: "We like to buy. Selling, however, is a different story. There, our pace of activity resembles that forced upon a traveler who found himself stuck in tiny Podunk's only hotel. With no TV in his room, he faced an evening of boredom. But his spirits soared when he spied a book on the night table entitled: *Things to do in Podunk.* Opening it, he found just a single sentence: 'You're doing it.' "

A FEW LAST WORDS
FROM WARREN BUFFETT

"It's just not necessary to do extraordinary things to produce extraordinary results."—widely quoted.

"We like to buy businesses, but we don't like to sell them."—Berkshire annual meeting in 1987.

"Anything that can't go on forever, will end."—Berkshire annual meeting in 1987.

"Someone's sitting in the shade today because someone planted a tree a long time ago."—NewsInc. January 1991.

"Anything that can happen will happen."—widely quoted.

BERKSHIRE STOCK PRICES

1965	High	Low
First Quarter	16;	13
Second Quarter	21;	16
Third Quarter	19;	17
Fourth Quarter	22;	18

1969	High	Low
First Quarter	40;	34
Second Quarter	45;	35
Third Quarter	39;	31
Fourth Quarter	44;	34

1966	High	Low
First Quarter	27;	30
Second Quarter	27;	21
Third Quarter	23;	18
Fourth Quarter	18;	17

1970	High	Low
First Quarter	47;	40
Second Quarter	47;	32
Third Quarter	43;	35
Fourth Quarter	43;	39

1967	High	Low
First Quarter	20;	17
Second Quarter	19;	17
Third Quarter	21;	18
Fourth Quarter	21;	19

1971	High	Low
First Quarter	51;	40
Second Quarter	55;	48
Third Quarter	53;	51*
Fourth Quarter	74;	70*

1968	High	Low
First Quarter	24;	20
Second Quarter	31;	23
Third Quarter	33;	26
Fourth Quarter	39;	32

1972	High	Low
First Quarter	76;	73*
Second Quarter	78;	78*
Third Quarter	84;	80*
Fourth Quarter	80;	80*

1973	High	Low
First Quarter	93;	80
Second Quarter	87;	85
Third Quarter	88;	83
Fourth Quarter	87;	71

1974	High	Low
First Quarter	76;	72
Second Quarter	76;	64
Third Quarter	64;	49
Fourth Quarter	49;	40

1975	High	Low
First Quarter	51;	38
Second Quarter	51;	45
Third Quarter	60;	41
Fourth Quarter	43;	38

1976	High	Low
First Quarter	56;	38
Second Quarter	60;	55
Third Quarter	73;	61
Fourth Quarter	95;	66

1977	High	Low
First Quarter	97;	85
Second Quarter	100;	95
Third Quarter	107;	100
Fourth Quarter	139;	107

1978	High	Low
First Quarter	142;	134
Second Quarter	180;	142
Third Quarter	180;	165
Fourth Quarter	189;	152

1979	High	Low
First Quarter	185;	154
Second Quarter	215;	185
Third Quarter	350;	215
Fourth Quarter	335;	240

1980	High	Low
First Quarter	360;	260
Second Quarter	340;	250
Third Quarter	415;	305
Fourth Quarter	490;	385

1981	High	Low
First Quarter	505;	425
Second Quarter	525;	485
Third Quarter	520;	460
Fourth Quarter	590;	460

1982	High	Low
First Quarter	560;	465
Second Quarter	520;	470
Third Quarter	550;	430
Fourth Quarter	775;	540

1983	High	Low
First Quarter	965;	775
Second Quarter	985;	890
Third Quarter	1,245;	905
Fourth Quarter	1,385;	1,240

1984	High	Low
First Quarter	1,360;	1,240
Second Quarter	1,345;	1,220
Third Quarter	1,305;	1,230
Fourth Quarter	1,305;	1,265

1985	High	Low
First Quarter	1,930;	1,275
Second Quarter	2,160;	1,725
Third Quarter	2,235;	2,005
Fourth Quarter	2,730;	2,075

1986	High	Low
First Quarter	3,250;	2,220
Second Quarter	3,160;	2,640
Third Quarter	3,100;	2,525
Fourth Quarter	2,925;	2,620

1987	High	Low
First Quarter	3,630;	2,800
Second Quarter	3,530;	3,330
Third Quarter	4,220;	3,420
Fourth Quarter	4,270;	2,550

1988	High	Low
First Quarter	3,500;	3,000
Second Quarter	4,150;	3,400
Third Quarter	5,000;	4,040
Fourth Quarter	5,050;	4,600

1989	High	Low
First Quarter	5,025;	4,625
Second Quarter	7,000;	4,950
Third Quarter	8,750;	6,600
Fourth Quarter	8,900;	7,950

1990	High	Low
First Quarter	8,725;	6,675
Second Quarter	7,675;	6,600
Third Quarter	7,325;	5,500
Fourth Quarter	6,900;	5,500

1991	High	Low
First Quarter	8,275;	6,550
Second Quarter	8,750;	7,760
Third Quarter	9,000;	8,325
Fourth Quarter	9,125;	8,150

| Year-end 1991: | 9,050 | |

1992	High	Low
First Quarter	9,125;	8,675
Second Quarter	9,275;	8,850

* These figures were provided by the National Quotation Bureau but they only show the price on the last day of the quarter at a time when Berkshire was not listed in the National Association of Securi-

ties Dealers Automated Quotation (NASDAQ) system. Instead, Berkshire was listed in the "pink sheets" because it was not a marginable secruity. The National Quotation Bureau has only end-of-the-month listings from that time.

INDEX